Black Savannah
1788–1864

Black Community Studies

WILLARD B. GATEWOOD
General Editor

Black Savannah

1788–1864

Whittington B. Johnson

❦

THE UNIVERSITY OF ARKANSAS PRESS

FAYETTEVILLE   1996

02   01   00   99   98   5   4   3   2   1
First paperback printing 1998

Designed by Gail Carter

☻ The paper used in this publication meets the minimum
requirements of the American National Standard for Perma-
nence of Paper for Printed Library Materials Z39.48-1984.

Library of Congress Cataloging-in-Publication Data
Johnson, Whittington Bernard, 1931–
    Black Savannah, 1788–1864 / Whittington B. Johnson.
        p.   cm. — (Black community studies)
    Includes bibliographical references (p.   ) and index.
    ISBN 1-55728-406-7 (cloth : alk. paper)
    ISBN 1-55728-546-2 (paper : alk. paper)
    1. Afro-Americans—Georgia—Savannah—History.
2. Afro-Americans—Georgia—Savannah—Social
conditions. 3. Afro-Americans—Georgia—
Savannah—Economic conditions. 4. Savannah
(Ga.)—History.
    I. Title. II. Series.
    F294.S2J64   1996
    975.8'72400496073—dc20   95-47299
                                                CIP

TO

Westley W. Law

A legend in his own time

Acknowledgments

In writing this work, I have joined the legion of other persons who are indebted to the staffs of the archives, libraries, and research centers in Georgia, Miami, and Washington, D.C. They serve the needs of a diverse group of researchers politely, professionally, and promptly. I wish the names of each of those persons could be listed here. In doing so, however, I might overlook someone. Words cannot express my sense of gratitude to the fine persons at the Georgia State Department of Archives and History, the Atlanta University Library, the Woodruff Library at Emory University, the University of Georgia Libraries, the Georgia Historical Society, the Central Records Office of the Chatham County Courthouse, the Savannah Public Library, and Savannah State College Library. I am equally grateful to the staffs of the National Archives and the University of Miami Richter Library.

My thanks to Agnes Scott College, the University of Georgia, Savannah State College, and Mount Vernon College, for allowing me to live on their campuses while I used nearby research facilities.

The University of Miami demonstrated its commitment to encouraging faculty research by granting me a sabbatical leave the fall semester of the 1988–89 school year as well as back-to-back Orovitz Fellowships during the summers of 1987 and 1988. The Southern Regional Education Board awarded me a stipend the summer of 1988 which helped defray copying expenditures. I am grateful to both institutions for their financial support.

A number of persons were very generous with their help. The Reverend Dr. Charles L. Hoskins, rector of Saint Matthew's Episcopal Church in Savannah, directed me to little-known local history sources and allowed me to copy Saint Stephen's Parish Records. Reverend Perry Quarterman, of Second African Baptist Church, provided information about the early history of that church. Responsible persons at First African Baptist Church authorized the use of microfilm copies of conference minutes housed at the Georgia Historical Society. W. W. Law, perhaps the most knowledgeable person on the history of black Savannah, allowed me to pick his brain and took me on a tour of the recently opened (at the time) black archives and museum. He was also

instrumental in getting the city of Savannah to clean up and reno-
vate Laurel Grove Cemetery South, the black cemetery, which
facilitated my effort to locate graves that, in some instances, were
over a hundred years old.

Donald Spivey, Timothy Huebner, Janet Martin, Kathy
Gordon, Randall Miller, Phinizy Spalding, and Edward Dreyer read
the manuscript, in spite of the pressing demands of their teaching,
research, and other professional and personal responsibilities. The
insights and suggestions of these persons have led to a significant
improvement in the style and substance of this work. I thank them
for doing what they did as thoroughly as they did it. I assume
responsibility, however, for all shortcomings of the work.

Maria Reynardus of the College of Arts and Sciences Word
Processing Center typed the manuscript. Judy Thompson operated
behind the scenes, but her cooperation expedited matters. Lenny
del Granado, history department secretary; Ada Orlando, the
department's former staff coordinator; and Faye Sylvester-
Benjamin all catered to my many requests.

Finally, I thank the Johnson household. Gene excused my
absences, even on our anniversary. Toni, Traci-Liegh, and Todd
did not give me demerits when my research necessitated that I be
away from home and miss Father's Day two consecutive years.
They understood why I spent more hours in my study than with
them, and they showered me with love. I am honored to be the
husband and father of such caring individuals whose support and
encouragement have made this a labor of love.

Contents

Introduction

PARTICULARS RESPECTING WARDS
AND DISTRICTS IN SAVANNAH

*Franklin Ward (new) . . . Population 406 whites,
201 colored. In this ward is situated the Second
African Baptist Church. . . .
Greene Ward . . . population 252 whites, 250 colored.
In this ward is situated the First African Baptist
Church . . .
Oglethorpe Ward . . . Population 999 whites, 1327
colored. In this ward are situated . . . the Third
African Meeting House, the Methodist Meeting
House for colored people . . .*
—JOSEPH BANCROFT, CENSUS
OF THE CITY OF SAVANNAH

Traditionally, studies of the African-American experience have segregated the slave experience from that of free African Americans. This study breaks with tradition and presents a holistic interpretation of African Americans in a major southern city, Savannah, Georgia. This approach has been embraced because although slaves and free African Americans had separate legal statuses, their religious, economic, and social activities normally were integrated. Since black Savannahians generally did not subscribe to the legal distinctions between groups of African Americans that whites etched into the laws, free African Americans had no qualms about selecting slaves as their religious leaders, business associates, and mates. This is a different kind of study, therefore—one that focuses on efforts of African Americans, free and enslaved, working together to create and maintain an independent black church, to work for and make a niche for themselves in the economy, and to form black families, all of which resulted in the growth and development of an autonomous black community in the Old South, in spite of legal, economic, and social impediments imposed by whites.

This study also departs from the traditional chronological framework, 1790–1860, that is generally used in works on the African-American experience in the Old South. Accordingly, the scope of the study begins and ends with two very important historical events in Savannah: the founding of the independent black church (1788) and the abolition of slavery (1864).

The black community of Savannah is the subject of this study because it is one of the few in the Old South that has not been studied. The history of black Savannah challenges the prevailing view of the Old South as a monolithic entity and raises anew questions of regionalism and black community development. This study addresses what kind of African-American community emerged along the shores of the Savannah River during the years from 1788 to 1864 and how that development differed from that of other black communities in the Old South.

The African-American experience in the antebellum South has been well chronicled. Thanks to recent studies, we have a more accurate picture of the region, one that does not reject the traditional perception, but modifies the old notion of a totally homogeneous region. For instance, when the subregions—the Upper and Lower South—have been studied as distinct entities, intraregional differences among African Americans have surfaced. Accordingly, the black experience in Charleston, New Orleans, and Savannah were similar, while those in Baltimore, Richmond, and Washington, D.C., were similar. This is the generalized picture that emerges from the existing literature.

Charleston and New Orleans, both with a high percentage of free African-American artisans and a significantly larger number of property owners than other cities, had the most prosperous free

African Americans in the Lower South. According to Michael P. Johnson and James L. Roark, the "freedom to choose an occupation and own property" was treasured by free African Americans in Charleston,[1] who were not prohibited from owning real estate. These authors further state that "Color made a difference in the economic welfare of free Afro-Americans. On the average, mulattoes were better off than blacks."[2] Black Charleston's efforts to establish an independent church were thwarted by state statute, but in 1818, African Americans eventually left their biracial church and formed the African Church of Charleston. The church enjoyed a short existence before the authorities closed all black churches in the city after the Denmark Vesey conspiracy. African Americans were allowed to operate schools until an 1834 law prohibited them from doing so, but this law was ignored, and several schools quietly continued to operate. The self-hire of slaves was also banned, first by a city ordinance in 1796 that applied only to slave mechanics, and later by state statutes; the one in 1822 applied to males only, but the one in 1849 included all slaves, males and females.[3]

The New Orleans experience of African Americans was similar to Charleston's in some ways and different in others. H. E. Sterkx maintains that mulattoes in New Orleans fared better than blacks. Moreover, free African Americans comprised about one-half of the skilled workers by 1850. That same year, free African Americans in the Crescent City, who were not prohibited from owning real estate, owned property worth $2,214,020. An 1850 statute, which prohibited the establishment of black churches, lodges, and clubs, mortally wounded the already weak black church. Most free African Americans attended biracial churches, mainly the Catholic church. Unlike in Charleston, however, African Americans in New Orleans were allowed to testify in court against whites, and their schools were not banned.[4]

The picture of Charleston and New Orleans that emerges from monographs on African Americans in South Carolina and Louisiana is consistent with the one in regional studies on the South. The portrait of black Savannah that emerges from that literature, on the other hand, does not delineate the ways in which Savannah deviated from the regional picture. For instance, in describing the living arrangements of self-hired slaves, Richard C. Wade made the following observation: "No doubt occasionally some bettered themselves . . . But most took what they could find—a room above a stable, a little space in an unused shed, a shanty converted for sleeping."[5] In his study of black slaveholders in South Carolina, Larry Koger discovered that they permitted their slaves to hire their time. Those slaves only paid a portion of their earnings to their masters and kept the remainder, frequently paid the capitation tax assessed free African Americans, and were often listed erroneously in the census and other public documents as free persons of color.[6] "Nominal slaves" in black Savannah had white masters who allowed them to hire their own time and experience other privileges, but they were less extensive than those allowed their counterparts in South Carolina.

Similarly, social stratification among African Americans in Savannah did not conform to the three-caste system Ira Berlin describes in his study of free African Americans: "the elevated status of the free people of color and the lowly condition of slaves in the Lower South allowed a three-caste system much like that of the West Indies to develop wherever free Negroes were numerous."[7] Later in his discussion of this practice, Berlin identifies Savannah as a community that practiced this system, "The three-caste system . . . introduced into South Atlantic cities like Charleston and Savannah by West Indian émigrés flourished," he writes.[8] Although a color bias existed in Savannah that favored mulattoes, the social line between free African Americans and slaves was blurred.

The free African-American population was smaller in Savannah and its percentage of the total African-American population (free and slave) was significantly less than in any other major southern city. In 1860, free African Americans comprised only 8.3 percent of the total African-American population; they composed 44 percent in New Orleans, 18.8 percent in Charleston, and 9.7 percent in Mobile. Conversely, in Chatham County (Savannah) nonmulattoes comprised a higher percentage of the free African-American population than in any other county with a major southern city. Nonmulattoes constituted 31.1 percent of the free African-American population there, whereas they constituted 25 percent in Charleston

County (Charleston), 24 percent in Orleans Parish (New Orleans), and only 9.3 percent in Mobile County (Mobile).[9]

The most glaring example of the existing literature's failure to take into account the distinctive feature of the black community of Savannah is found in Leonard P. Curry's study of urban free African Americans. Curry discusses the organization and development of black churches in many cities throughout the nation, but he fails to mention the largest independent black church in the South, the one in Savannah.[10] No other community in the region could boast of a black church as large as Savannah's.

Unlike Charleston, which experienced a slave conspiracy, and New Orleans, which was threatened with a slave attack by bondsmen from the nearby countryside, Savannah experienced neither. The reasons for this are probably consistent with those Eugene D. Genovese gives in his study of slave revolts.[11] The cautious, but influential, black clergy inadvertently may have played a role in reinforcing the obvious—revolt was fruitless. In spite of the absence of a conspiracy and slave revolt, slavery in Savannah was just as oppressive as it was in other major cities in the region. There were other experiences in Savannah that were similar to those in the other major southern cities. Curry identifies a number of restrictive laws which regulated the social behavior of African Americans. In South Carolina, for instance, African Americans were "forbidden to smoke a pipe" or "segar" in "any street, lane, alley, or open place," or to walk with a cane or stick unless "blind or infirm."[12] The Georgia legislature passed laws with a similar purpose, although their language was different. Furthermore, Loren Schweninger's study of black property owners reveals that free African-American women property owners in the South outnumbered men;[13] the same situation existed in black Savannah. Similarly, free African-American women constituted a majority of the free black population throughout the region.

In broad scope, this study examines what kind of black community emerged along the shores of the Savannah River from 1788 to 1864 and in what ways it differed from other black communities in the region. Moreover, this work attempts to answer a number of more specific questions in the process of answering the major ones.

What was the origin of the independent black church? Why did whites allow it to exist? What roles did it perform in the black community? Did the makeup of the religious community change over time? Which legal privileges were allowed and which were denied? What economic endeavors did free African Americans pursue, and what was the extent of their property holdings? Did the dynamics of the job market change over time? Were the experiences of city slaves significantly different from those of their country cousins? Did allowing slaves to hire their own time make a difference? Did the cultural diversity of the earlier years disappear over time? What was the basis of social relationships among African Americans? Did a social class system exist in the conventional meaning of the term? What was the status of race relations? Did a pattern of residential racial segregation develop? And finally, how did the black community fare during the Civil War?

The answers to these questions will leave us with a portrait of the black community during its formative years. Amid the adversity occasioned by slavery and racism, black Savannah developed into an autonomous community for which the ethos and leadership came from an independent black church. This institution provided black Savannah with a degree of autonomy unlike that enjoyed in any other black community in the Lower South. Free African Americans, moreover, evinced a camaraderie toward slaves that was the antithesis of the three-caste system which flourished in Charleston and New Orleans. Black Savannah was not a replica, therefore, of other communities in the Lower South.

hallelujah!
Praise the Lord

*Sunday an agreeable day . . . The Negroes go to their
place of worship. They all assemble by themselves,
have a Negro to preach to them, and really there was
more appearance of devotion in them than in whites.*
—MRS. ———SMITH'S JOURNAL, MARCH 17, 1793

Savannah was the principal city and capital of the last colony established in British North America (1732). Early on, rice and indigo
became the leading export crops and slave labor became popular
even though this violated a provision upon which the colony was
established. On the eve of the American Revolution, the whole
colony contained considerably less than fifty thousand inhabitants,
approximately 40 percent of whom were black. Savannah was
captured early in the war (1779) and spent most of it watching from
the sidelines. After the Revolution, the town buzzed once again with
activity. This vibrant town on the bank of the Savannah River, with
its picturesque bluff and excellent harbor would subsequently
nurture one of the most progressive black communities in the South.

The black church was the cornerstone upon which black community development rested. It, furthermore, was the oldest and
largest black public institution in Savannah, as well as its most
influential, pervasive, and visible black organization. Unlike most
black churches in the United States, the black church in Savannah
did not result from a schism within a biracial church over the desire
of disgruntled black worshipers for their own church. Rather, it was

begun by African Americans, mainly slaves, who did not have a church home. The black church in Savannah, moreover, was the most dynamic black religious institution in the South. This did not happen by chance. In its early years, the black church came under heavy criticism from whites, but it survived this attack, unlike black churches in other major southern cities. It survived primarily because William Bryan, the influential owner of Brampton Plantation, allowed his slave preacher, Andrew Bryan, to hold services in a barn on that plantation and protected the fledgling black church from white critics who wanted to destroy it. Once the initial threat to the church's existence disappeared, Andrew Bryan won the confidence of other whites and trained a cadre of younger black men who carried the torch after his death. Two additional factors figured prominently in the black church's survival and phenomenal growth: (1) the staunch support which it received from African Americans (free and slave) who attended it and (2) the approval of whites who created a friendly environment for it. As a consequence, the number of black congregations and Protestant denominations represented in the black church increased over time.

The prospect of Savannah getting a black church dimmed near the end of the American Revolution when George Liele, a black who had been preaching to slaves on Savannah River plantations and who might have eventually organized a church, left with the British when they evacuated Savannah in 1782. Just before he left, however, Liele baptized Andrew Bryan on Brampton Plantation.[1] Bryan filled the void created by Liele's departure. He gathered a few supporters around him each morning to pray and sing before beginning their chores and again at night after the chores had been completed.[2] This was not an invisible church[3] because there was no need to steal away, hide, and muzzle the sounds out of fear that the worshipers would be punished. Instead, the slaves scheduled their worship early and late to avoid conflicts with working hours.

These small informal gatherings developed into something that became formal and, later on, permanent when on January 19, 1788, Andrew Bryan was called to the ministry and subsequently examined and found acceptable "to preach the Gospel and to administer the ordinances, as God in his providence may call." The day following his ordination, forty-five slaves were baptized, and the church was organized. That church, which has been operating ever since, has been known by several names: Abraham Marshall called it the Ethiopian Church of Jesus Christ at Savannah in 1788.[4] The Sunbury Association called it the "colored" Baptist Church, until 1822.[5] It has generally been called First African Baptist Church since the 1820s; and descendants of Third African Baptist Church call it First Bryan Church.

If Andrew Bryan and his followers expected a warm greeting from whites for casting their lot with God and forsaking the devil, they were sadly mistaken. In 1788, angry whites succeeded in achieving the following grand jury presentment:

> I) We present as a grievance Negroes in different parts of this country being permitted to assemble in large bodies under pretence [sic] of religion, by which that holy institution is not only become a mere mockery, but a cloak for every species of blasphemy, theft, and debauchery . . .

> IV) We present William Bryan, Esquire for permitting Negroes to assemble, in large bodies, at the plantation called Brampton, within this county, in violation of the patrol law.[6]

William Bryan, whose father (Jonathan Bryan) had been a strong supporter of George Whitefield during the Great Awakening and promoted evangelization efforts of black preachers among slaves, allowed blacks to worship in his barn on Brampton Plantation. The intercession of Bryan on behalf of those worshipers was an early turning point in the development of an independent black church in Savannah as the movement avoided strangulation during its infancy. The harassment of black worshipers stopped when the whites came to the same conclusion that William Bryan had and realized that Andrew Bryan and his congregation facilitated peace and concord between the races by encouraging morality and sobriety, accepting the status quo in social convention, and focusing attention on otherworldiness. Before reaching this point of enlightenment and issuing a decree that allowed blacks to worship between sunrise and sunset, however, the city fathers subjected Andrew Bryan and other leaders of the black congregation to the ultimate form of humiliation, a public whipping.[7]

After the black church survived this early attempt to destroy it, the movement to create an independent black church gathered momentum, and over the course of the next eight decades, Savannah's black church became the strongest institution of its kind in the South. A key component of its success and longevity was a succession of able and effective leaders, beginning with Andrew Bryan. Andrew Bryan, who filled the vacuum created by the departure of Liele, was the only black preacher in the area during the years immediately following ratification of the Federal Constitution. He was born in 1716 to slave parents, (his father, Caesar, being an African) at Goose Creek, South Carolina, about sixteen miles from Charleston. Since most of the early plantation owners at Goose Creek had emigrated from Barbados one or both of Bryan's parents may have lived there before coming to South Carolina. It is not known when he was brought across the Savannah River into Georgia, but it occurred before the American Revolution. About eight or nine months after Liele left for Jamaica in 1782, Bryan began exhorting on Brampton Plantation and learning to read.[8] In May 1789, about sixteen months after he had been ordained and the church had been established, Bryan was allowed to purchase his freedom for fifty pounds sterling.[9] The next year, he purchased a lot on Mill Street in Oglethorpe Ward, on which a church was built for twenty-seven pounds sterling.[10] Bryan, who did not start his ministry until he was well into his sixties and did not organize a church until he was two years beyond the biblical life span of threescore and ten, led First African Baptist Church for nearly a quarter of a century before he died on October 12, 1812, at the age of ninety-six.[11] This man of God with the white "fleecy" well-set locks of hair, who "dressed like a bishop of London," had jet black skin, "and a pair of fine black eyes sparkling with intelligence, benevolence, and joy,"[12] was an impressive role model for the younger black men in the community.

One of those younger black men was Henry Cunningham, formerly of McIntosh County, where he was born a slave in 1759, but he was manumitted prior to moving to Savannah. Cunningham was among the overflow crowd of worshipers at First African Church, but he apparently stood out from the crowd and so must have impressed Bryan, who subsequently selected him as one of the two young men who should be ordained and appointed to head other African churches that would be established because First African Church was too crowded. Shortly after Cunningham was "dismissed" to join Savannah Baptist Church, he was among the African Americans who were dismissed from Savannah Baptist to organize Second African Baptist Church, which they did on December 16, 1802. The following January 1, Cunningham was ordained and called to lead the church, which he did for forty years until his death on March 29, 1842, at the age of eighty-three.[13] Cunningham could read and write, unlike Bryan, and he held an equal position of leadership and trust on the east side of the city to the one held by pastors of First African Baptist Church on the west. He was a charter member of both the Savannah River Association and the Sunbury Association, but probably an illness during the late 1830s prevented him from attending the conventions. Henry Holcombe, former pastor of Savannah Baptist and a highly respected minister nationally, admired Cunningham, and white Savannahians perceived him as an able minister and a stabilizing force in the black community;[14] nevertheless, his greatest contribution to the community was the seven or eight black preachers who received their start under him and went on to have successful careers in the ministry.

Andrew Marshall credited his uncle, Andrew Bryan, with serving as a role model for him, but Marshall was a member of Cunningham's church, where he was baptized. Marshall, who was born a slave in South Carolina and was slightly older than Cunningham, came to the Savannah area before the American Revolution, purchased his freedom early in the nineteenth century, and was called to be the pastor of First African Baptist Church in the 1820s when he was over seventy years old. He remained in the ministry longer than his uncle, serving as pastor of First African Baptist Church for thirty years, 1826–56, during which he started a Sunday school, preached to the Georgia State Legislature and to the Sunbury Association—the only black preacher to be accorded these honors. He baptized about thirty-eight hundred, converted over four thousand, married two thousand, and was generally regarded as the most outstanding black Savannahian of his day. Andrew Marshall died on December 7, 1856 at the age of one hundred.[15] The memorial read at the Sunbury Association's convention the next November is a fitting tribute to this venerable black preacher:

> The Committee on Deceased ministers beg leave to report: that five of its ministers have been called from their labors on earth. The first in order of time is our aged and venerable "Father In Israel" Andrew C. Marshall . . . For many years he was the leading religious spirit among our colored brethren and maintained . . . the respect and confidence of the white community.[16]

Andrew Bryan, Henry Cunningham, and Andrew C. Marshall were the ablest black preachers in a community that produced many able preachers, and this triumvirate was instrumental in training others who made their mark in the church.

William C. Campbell, a Marshall protégé, may have been the ablest of the next generation of black preachers. He was born a slave in Savannah on January 1, 1812, joined First African Church, and sang in the choir. He was ordained a deacon, later ordained to the ministry, subsequently appointed assistant pastor by Marshall, and upon Marshall's death, called to become the pastor of the church in 1857, at which time he was still a slave. [17] Campbell accomplished what Marshall had hoped to accomplish before he died: he built an impressive new seven-hundred-seat stone church with a gallery and a basement in 1859 and had it consecrated in 1861.[18]

John Benjamin Deveaux, whom Cunningham mentored, was also born a slave in Savannah but years before Campbell, on October 5, 1774. His wife, Catherine Deveaux from Antigua, was free. In her home, she and her daughter, Jane, secretly taught black children to read the Scriptures. Deveaux directed the choir of his church, Second African Baptist Church, and from there moved up the ladder first to deacon, then to ordained preacher in his church before receiving a call to become pastor of Third African Church in 1841.[19]

The first deacon of First African Baptist Church, Sampson Bryan, younger brother of its founder, served in that capacity from the early years of the church's history until his death at the age of fifty-three on January 23, 1799.[20] Other deacons of note in that church were Adam Johnson, a Bahamian who led the unsuccessful fight to oust Andrew Marshall in 1832–33; Stephen McQueen; Sampson Whitefield, grandson of the founder; Josiah Lloyd; Robert McNish; and James M. Simms. Deacons of note in Second African Baptist Church were Evans Grate, Thomas Anderson, Isaac Roberts, John Cox, William Rose, and William Ferguson.[21] Most of these deacons were either free or later gained their freedom, became ordained ministers of the Gospel, and subsequently were called to head congregations either in Savannah or in outlying settlements.

The mother church of black religious institutions, First African Baptist Church, evolved from plantation services. On the plantation, prayers were spoken extemporaneously, and songs were often spirituals. When a hymn was sung, it was "lined" without benefit of a musical instrument, with the worshipers swaying their bodies, clapping their hands, and stomping their feet to maintain the tempo.[22] (For those in the congregation who could not read, hymns were "lined"; that is, a deacon, or someone who could, read the words to the hymns line by line, and after each line was read, the congregation sang that line.) Doubtless, in some of the songs the verses were composed spontaneously by the person who led them, and the other worshipers joined in singing the chorus. The prayers were probably very emotional and other world oriented. These songs and prayers that were a part of the plantation worship were probably the same ones Bryan used in the barn that was their first church.

At the time of Bryan's death in 1812, First African Church had 1,498 members, or nearly 28 percent of membership of the Savannah River Association, of which the church was a charter member.[23] Because of this growth, the congregation left the barn and moved into a wooden structure in Yamacraw Village that was built upon a lot which Bryan had purchased.[24] This became the church's second home. In 1832, the congregation purchased a large frame building that had formerly housed Savannah Baptist, located in Old Franklin Square, and services were held[25] there until a fourth church home was constructed, this one of stone, in 1859 under the leadership of William Campbell, Andrew Marshall's successor.[26]

Stable leadership was a hallmark of First African Church. During the years from 1788–1864, the church only had three preachers, none of whom resigned from office after being called to minister to the church; both Andrew Bryan and Andrew Marshall remained faithful to their ministry of First African Church until death removed them from the pulpit. Bryan, moreover, encouraged the establishment of other black congregations. Within a matter of two weeks in the early 1800s, two new black Baptist churches were established in the Chatham-Savannah area: Second African, founded by Henry Cunningham in December 1802 and located on the east side; and Ogeechee African, founded in January 1803 and located about fourteen miles south of Savannah in the country.[27]

Some of the more financially able free African Americans of that day composed the pioneer members of Second African Church, including Evans Grate, Richard Houstoun, Susan Jackson, Leah Simpson, Charlotte Walls, and Elizabeth (Betsy) Cunningham, the pastor's wife.[28] Second African Church, which quickly became the second largest Baptist church in the city, attracted most of the well-to-do free African Americans and worshiped in a "comfortable building 67 feet by 30 feet."[29] Nevertheless, this church lived in the shadow of the much larger First African Church throughout the period. Second African Baptist Church trained more black preachers than any other Baptist church (white or black) in the county. Andrew Marshall, who later became pastor of First African Baptist Church, as well as the first four pastors of Third African Church, Thomas Anderson (1833–35), Stephen McQueen (1835–41), John Deveaux (1842–45), and Isaac Roberts (1845–48), had been members of Second African Church. Anderson returned to Second African in 1841 to replace Cunningham who had become incapacitated; Deveaux left Third African in 1845 and returned to Second African to replace Anderson, who had died; similarly Roberts returned in 1849 to succeed Deveaux. Furthermore, John Cox, Roberts' successor in 1850, was baptized and ordained in Second African, and Evans Grate, a former deacon of that church, later became pastor of nearby White Bluff African. While First African had the numbers, Second African apparently had the talent.[30]

Third African Baptist Church was the youngest, smallest, and the most unstable of the three sister churches. Established in 1833 after the senior deacons and nearly 150 members left First African Baptist Church over a dispute, Third African Baptist Church had seven pastors between 1833–64. In addition to the four from Second African Church mentioned above, the remaining pastors were Bristol Lawton (1849–50) from Beaufort, South Carolina; Garrison Frazer (1850–61) from Virginia; and Ulysses L. Houston (beginning 1861), a slave member of the church.

The Methodists, the other major evangelical denomination to attract blacks, did not establish a conference in Georgia until 1835, and another decade passed before a black church was built. Unlike the black Baptist churches, however, whites built Andrew Chapel, its pastor was a white missionary, and whites staffed its Sunday school. The blacks whom the Methodists licensed to preach assisted the white missionary,[31] an arrangement that probably discouraged blacks from joining that church in numbers approximating those in the black Baptist churches. As a result, Andrew Chapel had fewer members than Third African.

Christ Episcopal Church had black communicants who were baptized, confirmed, and buried in that church long before the Diocese of Georgia decided to build a parish within the city limits of Savannah solely for African Americans. Priscilla Moody, a free African-American shopkeeper, Robert and Mary Woodhouse, William Garey, Mary Ann Sabatte, Jane Hume, and Mary Gordon were among the free African Americans who stood as sponsors at the baptisms of relatives and friends (baptisms were held after services). Priscilla Moody was confirmed there on April 26, 1826, and buried there at the age of seventy on June 17, 1840.[32] Hannah Cohen, whose mother Maria migrated from Saint Augustine, Florida, and was a favorite of her guardian, Richard D. Arnold, a prominent physician and community leader to whom Maria bequeathed one of her slaves,[33] married James Gibbs there on May 22, 1844.[34] Although an accurate number of the African Americans who worshiped in Christ Episcopal Church in 1856 is unavailable, the number exceeded five, the often quoted figure.[35]

The Episcopal Church earlier had established a mission for slaves who lived on the plantations along the Savannah River, but no special effort had been made to attract African Americans within the city limits of Savannah until Bishop Stephen Elliot Jr. appointed Sherod W. Kennerly, priest of the Savannah River Mission, to establish the chapel, at the urging of William Claghorn, a free African-American owner of a large bakery in the city. The first services were held in January 1856 in a large workshop above Claghorn's bakery.[36] This commenced efforts of the Episcopal Church to establish black parishes in Georgia, and it was only the second black Episcopal parish established in the South.[37] The parish, named Saint Stephen's Chapel in honor of the bishop, had twenty-five communicants in 1856, for whom services were held in the evenings, thus allowing the Reverend Kennerly to minister to his mission in the mornings and supervise the Sunday school at Saint Stephen's in the afternoons.[38] The Reverend Kennerly reported in 1858 that "The regular congregation now will number from 150–200, and often filling the house, which can seat some 300 . . ." In the same report, however, he said the parish had sixty-one communicants.[39] Apparently many slaves attended services but were not placed on the register.

The physical demands of the ministry took its toll on the priest, who resigned his charge in 1859 and accepted a less demanding one in a North Carolina parish. He was succeeded by Thomas J. Staley, a candidate for the priesthood in the diocese, who conducted services twice a day and under whose leadership a lot was purchased for six hundred dollars—the seller contributing two hundred dollars toward its purchase—and a building was acquired in 1860 from the Unitarians and moved on rollers to the lot bounded by Harris, Habersham, Macon, and Lincoln Streets. The Reverend Staley, who also became ill, left the parish in 1863 shortly before Bishop Elliot consecrated the church.[40] The young priest's inexperience in working with African Americans probably is partially responsible for the parish's slow growth, the same number of communicants being reported 1858–61, although the bishop reported that seven persons had been confirmed in both 1859 and 1860.[41] In the meantime, a few free African Americans and some slaves of prominent white parishioners continued to worship at Christ Episcopal Church.[42]

The Catholic and Presbyterian churches in Savannah maintained biracial churches. Most of the black Catholics were immigrants from Saint Domingue, but their American-born children may have had a "culture gap" with their parents because many of the second generation from this group joined other churches, especially the Episcopal church. They probably joined other denominations because Protestant churches were more popular in the United States than the Catholic church, and they felt more comfortable in them. Joseph Dubergier was perhaps the most active Catholic among the free black French émigrés. Some of the other free blacks who, along with Dubergier, appeared as sponsors at baptisms and marriages in Saint John the Baptist Catholic Church were Francis Jalineau, Louis Mirault, Sophia Mirault, Julien Fromantin, and Lewis Levesque.[43] Similarly, the Independent Presbyterian Church was the religious home of prominent free blacks in the community: Nancy Golding and her family from Liberty County; Clement Sabatte Sr. from St. Domingue, whose wife, Mary Ann, was an Episcopalian; and Georgiana Guard. Moreover, seventy-five other free African Americans were on its communion rolls, 1829–66.[44]

The black evangelical churches had an overwhelming majority of slaves on their membership rolls. A major problem with this was that slaveholders had the final say in whether slaves would be allowed to attend church and get baptized. Andrew Bryan learned early in his ministry that slaveholders could decide the fate of his ministry. He had converted about 350 slaves in 1788, but could not baptize them because the owners had not given their permission.[45] Frances Kemble recalled that a young slave on her husband's plantation wanted to be baptized and came to her for permission, without which he could not experience "this ceremony of acceptance into the bosom of the Christian Church."[46]

Charles C. Jones, one of the most highly respected religious leaders in the state, believed blacks, especially slaves, did not respond positively to sermons of white preachers. These sermons were intended for whites and were too difficult, he opined, for blacks to comprehend. This missed the mark. Blacks in Savannah did not warm to sermons of white preachers because they did not address their needs, which were almost wholly different from those of white churchgoers. Blacks needed sermons that spoke to the heart; that provided them with a frame of reference to endure the constant degradation and hardships; that restored their image as human beings; that assured them that God, impartial, caring, and loving, would not desert them; that assured them of redemption; and that promised punishment for the wicked, whether black or white. Those who saw blacks in the same negative light that a slave-holder would were incapable of preaching such sermons. "Their stupid looks, their indifferent staring, their profound sleeps and their thin attendance," as Jones depicted black churchgoers,[47] constituted their most effective and innocuous means of conveying their contempt for sermons that condoned and provided scriptural justification for the peculiar institution and racism.

Some of the same blacks who slept in white churches or during sermons of white preachers came alive in black evangelical churches. They held services three times a day on Sundays, and these services had spirited extemporaneous preaching, animated praying, good singing, shouting, talking back, and testifying.[48] According to a visitor who attended First African Church in the 1790s, "The performances were far beyond expectations . . . The preacher['s] . . . delivery was good and [he was] quite the orator . . ."[49] Another white who heard Bryan preach spoke less glowingly but still approvingly: "I . . . have heard him preach; his gifts are small but he is clear in the grand doctrines of the Gospel."[50] Good preaching continued to flow from the pulpit of First African Church after Bryan's death, if we are to believe persons who heard his successors preach. One who heard Andrew Marshall said he was "scarcely, if at all, below the average stand of the composition of white ministers."[51] Furthermore, Joshua Hale, who probably heard William Campbell preach in 1858, although he wrote in his letter that it was Marshall, said "I heard him preach yesterday an excellent sermon—better than the one I heard in the forenoon at the Independent Presbyterian Church."[52]

Sermons were delivered with great animation but without notes because the preachers could not write (most of them could read), but what did they say? Sir Charles Lyell worshiped at First African Church one Sunday morning in January 1846, and he and about six hundred other worshipers heard Marshall preach the sermon, "An

Eagle Feathereth Its Nest," which along with "Dry Bones" has become two of the classic black sermons. In the sermon, Marshall compared the probationary state of the pious to that of "an eagle teaching her newly fledged offspring to fly by carrying it up high into the air then dropping it, and if she sees it falling to the earth, darting with the speed of lightning to save it before it reaches the ground." Marshall told the worshipers that similarly the pious is left for a while to guide himself, but whenever danger appeared in his life and he is unable to handle it, God would rescue him; thus he would be "saved by the grace of God." Marshall admonished worshipers "to look to a future state of rewards and punishments in which God would deal impartially with the poor and the rich, the black man and the white."[53]

In another sermon, Marshall spoke on the subject of how the Savior acted when he was on earth and why he came to earth. First he described a visit of a president of the United States to Savannah and how during the visit a cord was placed around the house where he stayed to keep blacks and other poor people from approaching him. They could only observe the president from a distance through a window which he sat near, while on the other hand "the great gentlemen and the rich folks" were welcomed inside the house to shake the president's hand. Then Marshall asked, rhetorically, "Now did Christ come in this way? Did he come only to the rich? Did he shake hands only with them? No! Blessed be the Lord! He came to the poor! He came to us, and for our sakes, my brothers and sisters." Hallelujahs and amens resounded throughout the church as the congregation shouted, clapped their hands, stomped their feet, laughed and cried, joy beaming upon countenance after countenance.[54] Albert Raboteau devotes considerable attention to this type of behavior, as well as to the baptismal practice of immersion, while addressing the issue of whether they are manifestations of Africanisms as some scholars believe. He seems to believe they probably are, which is a plausible conclusion given their close similarity to cultural practices of areas of Africa hit hardest by the diaspora.[55]

The sermons alluded to above dwelled upon a popular theme in the black evangelical church: God is just and will deal impartially with everyone. Marshall and the other black preachers assured their worshipers that the distinctions of the world are man made, and they will vanish when humankind stands before the Creator. Instead of rhapsodizing upon theological doctrines, or drawing upon hard-to-discern analogies, those preachers depicted experiences to which their members could relate and alluded to scriptural passages that were relevant to the downtrodden. At no time, however, did black preachers praise slavery or glorify slaveholders. The sermons provided blacks with the inner strength to persevere until their change came. Being a product of the same environment as their members, black preachers shared their degradation, despair, disfranchisement, and disillusionment. Their sermons thus contained tonic for themselves as well as for their worshipers because they were a part of the crowd on the outside looking in.

Unlike contemporary Baptist churches, which usually have a baptismal pool, the black churches in Savannah did not have such a facility on their premises; hence members were baptized in the Savannah River as the statement below indicates:

> After morning services they [blacks] went to the River to dip. Several numbers of white people had assembled to see them. After that ceremony was performed they returned in procession to their place of worship singing psalms, their deacon reading every line, all the men with their hats in hand. Then the sacrament was administered . . .[56]

The Lord's Supper was administered quarterly;[57] the business conferences were held monthly.

Singing was a distinctive and important part of the service. In most churches, good singing was given high priority, and church leaders went to great lengths to encourage it. Some of the preachers started in the church as choir members; Thomas Anderson, John Benjamin Deveaux, and William Rose of Second African Church, as well as James Porter of Saint Stephen's are but a few of the religious leaders whose careers took this route. The "peculiar songs," as Fredericka Bremer called the spirituals and gospel songs, "are as soft, sweet, and joyous as our people's songs are melancholy."[58] Joseph Burke of First African Church and William Rose and Frank Keating of Second African Church were the premier black singers in the city. Keating, a slave until 1864, also became a preacher, but he is remembered most by Savannahians for his moving rendition of a hymn at the funeral of Mayor James Moore Wayne, at the request of the bereaved family.[59]

The premier black instrumentalist was James Porter of Saint Stephen's Chapel. Born in Charleston, South Carolina, of free parents in 1826, Porter received the best education offered African Americans of his day, which included training in ancient and modern languages. He studied music (instrumental and vocal) under George O. Robinson, who subsequently moved to Savannah to become organist of Savannah Baptist Church and manage August Music Store. Bishop Elliot, a native South Carolinian, obtained the services of Porter to train the Saint Stephen's choir which he developed into a competent group that efficiently handled the music of the Anglican Communion.[60] This marked a major departure for black church choirs that commonly had been identified with the "peculiar songs" of the plantations, where the traditional hymns were lined. The choir which Porter trained sang the hymns and anthems as they were composed, without lining and improvising.

As one walked, or rode, through black Savannah on Sunday mornings and evenings, a strange mixture of music pierced the air. From the evangelical churches came the "peculiar songs" as one white described them, those songs to which African Americans had applied "a new and refreshing originality,"[61] while from the black Episcopal chapel came the standard anthems and hymns. This music and the parishioners' enthusiastic participation in the prayers and responses provided irrefutable proof that the services of the Episcopal church were indeed suited for African Americans; conversely, the "peculiar songs" that came from the evangelical churches demonstrated that African Americans retained some of their African forefathers' culture(s). Among those songs, none was sung with more emotion than "The Year of Jubilee," which blacks felt comfortable singing now that they had their own church.

In 1860, Christian worshipers in Savannah were divided by race in all the churches, except the Catholic and Presbyterian churches, but it was not always that way. In its early years, Savannah Baptist

Church accepted African Americans, but by the 1830s, the open door policy had been discarded. In 1836, when John Simpson, Arthur Stevens, and Martha Munger of Third African Church tried to join Savannah Baptist Church, their applications were rejected by a slim majority, in spite of an endorsement from a committee of whites and a letter from Third African which said they were in good standing and only desired to leave "to obtain greater edification."[62]

At its 1839 convention, the Sunbury Association requested membership reports the following year which distinguished between whites and blacks.[63] Accordingly, at the 1840 convention, the churches listed their members by race, with the Savannah churches giving the following reports: Savannah Baptist 279 whites and no blacks; First African Church 2,012 blacks and no whites; Second African Church 1,307 blacks and no whites; Third African Church 234 blacks and no whites.[64]

Biracial churches were the exception, not the rule, in Savannah. White Baptists were in a distinct minority in Savannah, and this probably figured in the decision to exclude blacks from membership in the white church. At the monthly business meetings blacks could dictate policy by outvoting whites. The Methodists did not allow blacks to join Trinity Methodist Church in Savannah[65] for racist reasons since blacks in that church did not constitute a majority. The Episcopal church built a church "for the exclusive benefit of the Colored people"[66] which suggests that it preferred to have the blacks segregated, but Christ Church did not turn blacks out.[67] The Catholic and Presbyterian churches sent a different message to African Americans in that they did not invest in separate black churches. Did this mean those churches were less prejudiced than the others? Hardly. They simply followed a common practice of other communities; in Charleston, for instance, the races worshiped together, even in the evangelical churches, with blacks sitting in a special segregated section of the biracial churches.

Although white Baptists did not worship with African Americans after the 1830s, this did not constitute a religious caste system because blacks and whites did belong to the same religious association.[68] First African and Second African Churches were charter members of the Savannah River Baptist Association and of the Sunbury Baptist Association that evolved from it in 1818. The black delegations and reports from their churches were included in the minutes of the annual meetings. Much that is known about the pre–Civil War black churches in the Chatham-Savannah area is contained in those minutes. Therefore, while black Baptist churches in Savannah were allowed to develop a religious style and organization to meet the particular, and in some instances peculiar, needs of African Americans, those churches were also allowed to maintain contact with the mainstream of their denomination.

Because it was the only black public institution in a city where blacks were disfranchised, denied access to schools, prohibited from attending cultural events, barred from joining fraternal orders, and usually characterized as having low morals, the black church extended its ministry outside the walls of its edifice to encompass areas in the black community that in the white community normally were covered by secular agencies. For example, the black church was the primary institution for enforcing the morals of blacks.[69] Members of their church feared Andrew Bryan and Andrew Marshall, and slaveholders often called upon them to chastise wayward slaves, who "quaked" in their presence.[70] The reprimand was intended to remind those members that fighting, lying, stealing, drunkenness, and adultery did not comport with conduct expected of Christians. Slaveholders may have exploited this, but Bryan and Marshall were not dupes. Scholars who depict them (and other preachers) as such misunderstand that black preachers perceived themselves as shepherds and viewed church members as their flock. Those black preachers therefore acted to spare slave members from the wrath of God, not from the whip of slaveholders.

The monthly business conference in the Baptist church and the quarterly conference in the Methodist church were used to monitor the behavior of their members who were expelled if found guilty of fighting, dancing, using profanity, having illegitimate children, committing adultery, engaging in fornication, getting drunk, or beating their wives.[71] For instance, at the Third Quarterly Conference of Andrew Chapel in July 1851, Clara B. Bacote, who had been expelled for immoral conduct, appealed to the conference for a new trial and had one granted.[72] George Young, who was expelled from First African Church Baptist in 1859, was not allowed to restore his membership until twelve years later.[73] During those years Young was not allowed to join another Baptist church because an expelled member was not accepted by another church as long as the offender's former church remained open.[74]

The black church was vigilant in monitoring its members to ascertain whether they imbibed alcoholic drinks. This type of behavior was disdained; hence the churches fought alcoholism in the community, with church-sponsored temperance societies having large memberships. Second African Church had 667 members in its society in 1832.[75]

At the same time it punished wrongdoers, the black church showed a deep humanitarian stewardship, by visiting, praying, and contributing financially to the care of the aged, lame, sick, orphaned, and the poor[76] in the absence of support from governmental and white philanthropic agencies. In 1859, First African Church contributed more to the Widows' Fund than any other church in the Association and ranked fourth in contributing to home missions. Second African Church ranked fifth in contributing to home missions. Third African Church also contributed to this effort, although the amount was less than the sums of the two larger black churches.[77] Women auxiliaries also contributed to churches' benevolent societies and missions; they were reported to have given more than the white females' missionary societies to those endeavors.[78]

The black church often provided its worshipers with an outlet for self-expression and spiritual reinforcement to help sustain them when storms raged in their lives.[79] The "shouting," fervent prayers, singing, and emotion-filled services were often therapeutic stress relievers for those who needed such relief. Black worshipers were reminded that this world was not their home; that cross bearing was the price one paid for crown wearing; that they could take their burdens to the Lord and leave them there; that man looks at the outside but God looks at the heart; and that "when we all get to heaven what a day of rejoicing that will be."

As the foremost public institution in the community, the black church was a major source for settling individual disputes and disseminating information. When William Boufeuilet and a fellow church member had a dispute over a mule, he suggested that they allow the church to settle it, but the second party refused to cooperate.[80] When Anna Grant, a "freedwoman," sought to establish contact with her sisters from whom she had been separated fourteen years, the Freedmen Bureau agent in Savannah asked black churches to announce that Anna resided in Galveston, Texas, and that she wished to come to Savannah to visit her sisters. The sisters were located.[81]

In the absence of legally sanctioned schools, the black church became the chief educational institution in the community. As early as 1800, the union of church and education was realized when Andrew Bryan expressed a desire to have Henry Francis, a free black Baptist exhorter in Augusta, Georgia, move to Savannah "to exercise the handsome ministerial gifts he possesses amongst us, and teach our youth to read and write."[82] Francis made the move, but whether he established the Sunday school is unknown. If he did, the school may have collapsed after Francis left the area to assume leadership of the Ogeechee African Church.

The white churches also realized the importance of operating Sunday schools for African Americans. Accordingly, in either 1826 or 1827, the Independent Presbyterian Church started a Sunday school solely for African Americans (free and slave) which was generally well attended during its early years; in the 1830s, however, attendance began to fluctuate, a low point coming on Christmas Eve 1837 when only 30 pupils attended. Just a few years earlier, on December 7, 1834, the Sunday school introduced a new catechism written by Charles C. Jones,[83] who recommended "Let the teacher ask the question and repeat the answer, and explain it; and then continue the question until the answer is committed to memory, the scholars answering all together or one after another . . ."[84] Christ Episcopal Church had 185 pupils in its Sunday school in 1854, 100 of whom were black.[85] This Sunday school probably also used the catechetical approach with no effort made to teach the pupils to read since the intent of Jones in developing the catechism was to avoid teaching black pupils to read.

The Sunday schools run by the black churches, on the other hand, did attempt to teach pupils reading skills, although this was done discreetly since it was unlawful to teach reading and writing to African Americans. In spite of the dangers that loomed in the background if they were caught teaching the children, all three black churches operated Sunday schools.[86] Saint Stephen's did not enjoy the autonomy which the Baptist churches did, but it probably had similar goals to those churches and was just as indifferent to the laws proscribing teaching educational skills to its 125 pupils,[87] especially since at least two of its parishioners—James Porter and Mary Woodhouse—operated schools clandestinely in the black community.

Since African Americans were proscribed from participating in politics and they were restricted by convention and resources in what kinds of economic activities they could pursue, the black church provided African Americans with the surest avenue of advancement and the most reliable opportunity to acquire leadership skills.[88] Religious leaders were the pillars of the black community, having gained the respect of their followers and the confidence of whites, who normally allowed them full sway in running churches as long as the congregations maintained order and did not flaunt social conventions. The black church in Savannah capitalized upon this opportunity by providing the community with strong religious leadership, producing a number of able preachers, and developing a strong cadre of able deacons and choir leaders. Most of this happened in the Baptist church because in that denomination being called to preach and having a certain degree of piety were the prerequisites for entering the ministry,[89] unlike in the Catholic, Congregational, Episcopal, Lutheran, and Presbyterian churches where extensive formal education was required and emphasized over being "called to preach."

The leadership training which blacks received in their churches proved invaluable when opportunities opened in other fields. The first African-American public-office holders were all former leaders in their churches. Ulysses L. Houston, pastor of Third African Baptist Church, James M. Simms, ordained minister and pastor of Third African Baptist Church for a short while, and James Porter, organist and warden at Saint Stephen's, were all members of the Georgia Legislature in the 1860s. Porter was also a school principal.[90] There is little questioning, therefore, the importance of the black church during the years 1788 to 1864. The black church was a leadership institute; community center where gatherings for funerals, weddings, suppers, bazaars, and religious revivals were held; meeting hall for youth groups, missionary societies, deacons, and benevolent societies; and home of the only institutionalized education for blacks. Primarily, however, it was a house of worship.

As important as the black church was, however, it was still a man-managed institution and as such reflected the failings that are a part of human nature. Relations within some churches and between some churches were stormy at times. The black Baptist church was the most democratic institution in Savannah because nowhere else were African Americans—male and female, free and slave—allowed to vote, and the majority rule principle scrupulously observed. In the business meetings, laity and clergy lost those distinctions, and all became sisters and brothers. There was no earthly authority in the Baptist church higher than each congregation. Church polity was circular in the Baptist church; whereas it was triangular in the Catholic, Episcopal, and other churches with bishops and a hierarchy. As Sylvanus Landrum, a pastor of Savannah Baptist Church, stated, "Each Church is a sovereignty by itself. The majority that controls is a majority of those present at conference . . . The pastor has no power of government . . ."[91] Ulysses L. Houston, highly regarded pastor of First Bryan Baptist (formerly Third African Baptist Church), voicing a similar view of church polity, said: "Each body establishes its own rules, and can violate its rules. A majority of the church are a majority who are present at a regular conference."[92]

The obvious conclusion to reach from these statements is that black women had voice and vote in the business meetings. Women doubtless outnumbered men in the black church and, thus, played an influential role, even though they did not hold major offices. By force of their numbers, their position as church mother (the female counterpart of deacon), and their role as Sunday school teachers and by virtue of their financial support of the church, black women exercised influence in the Baptist church. They were not allowed to preach and be ordained as deacons, the formal positions of power in the Baptist church, and as Evelyn Brooks Higginbotham laments: "Male-biased tradition and rules sought to mute women's voices and accentuate their subordinate status vis-a-vis men."[93] Black women nevertheless ingeniously circumvented these obstructions and made their presence known. Drawing conclusions about the status of women in the black Baptist church on the basis of the gender of its officeholders is therefore as ill advisable as reaching conclusions about the practice of slavery in the Old South on the basis of the black codes.

Membership in an association did not adversely affect a church's autonomy.[94] When churches had conflicts, they could ask the association to help resolve them,[95] as First African and Second African Churches did in 1823 when there was trouble between them, and the association appointed a committee to look into the matter.[96] The following year, the committee reported to the association that it "had happily succeeded in restoring harmony to those churches."[97] The association did not threaten to suspend the charters of the churches if they did not behave, neither did it threaten to remove the black preachers who headed them. The association could not have done this even if it wished to do so, because only the voting majorities of those churches could have removed the pastors from their pulpits.

It is important to understand the great value Baptists attached to the principles of congregationalism and majority rule when one views the schism within First African Baptist Church in 1833. This event was discussed at length by several well-informed persons who were all members of First African Church at one time, though not at the same time. All three agreed on the sequence of events that led to the schism, but one of them disagreed with the others on the legitimacy of First African Church's claim to be the oldest black church in North America.[98]

Just before the confrontation unfolded, First African Church voted to build a new church, and on August 25, 1831, the city fathers granted permission for the church to erect a building on lot 71 in Yamacraw, provided property owners in the immediate vicinity did not object.[99] Shortly after this decision had been reached, Savannah Baptist Church decided, at a special meeting held on April 4, 1832, to sell its property in Franklin Square, including its old church.[100] Two weeks later at a discipline meeting on April 23, the deacons reported they had agreed to sell the old church and the sixty-by-seventy-foot lot on which it stood to First African Baptist Church for fifteen hundred dollars, with a down payment of eight hundred dollars, and the remainder due by November 1832.[101]

Meanwhile, Marshall had incurred the wrath of the Sunbury Association for having allowed Alexander Campbell, a white minister and leader of a small dissident group of Baptists in western Pennsylvania, to preach at First African Church. Campbell disagreed strongly with fundamentalist Baptists over what they considered key issues and subsequently disassociated himself from the Baptist church.[102]

At the convention in November 1832, the Sunbury Association approved a resolution dissolving its relationship with First African Church "on account of its corrupt state." The association, further, advised blacks in the outlying areas of Savannah to secure letters of dismission from First African Church and unite themselves with other Baptist churches or form new churches. In what must have been a violation of the spirit of the First Amendment, the association sent a copy of its resolution to the city council implicitly inviting that body to intervene in the affairs of First African Church.[103]

Upon returning home after the convention, Marshall soon became the center of a dispute as supporters and detractors took sides. The situation grew ugly, as religious confrontations sometimes do, with worshipers carrying clubs, brickbats, and other potentially lethal objects to church. On one occasion the situation became so disorderly the mayor went to the church and chased everyone out.[104] While the doctrinal dispute between Marshall and the Sunbury Association was at the heart of the controversy, it developed into a power struggle between Marshall and the deacons who had filled the void in the church's leadership after the death of its founder. Adam Johnson, Adam Sheftall, Jack Simpson, and Josiah Lloyd had represented First African Church at the conventions from the formation of the Sunbury Association in 1818 through

1825,[105] those years when the church did not have a permanent pastor. The "old guard" deacons sided with the association in the dispute and tried to force Marshall from his pulpit.

The dispute was finally resolved at a church conference in which, by a consensus vote, the congregation approved a motion to retain Marshall as its pastor and to transfer ownership of the old dilapidated church building in Yamacraw (the place where they had worshiped after they left the barn) to the Deacon Johnson–led minority of the church. Consequently, Marshall and 2,640 members, including his aunt Dolly Bryan, continued worshiping in the recently acquired building, while deacons Adam A. Johnson and Sampson Whitefield, the grandson of the founder, and about 155 other members returned to their former place of worship.[106]

We are not privy to the reason why Marshall allowed Campbell to preach in First African Church, whether because he shared Campbell's theological point of view, was curious to hear what it was, could not bring himself to deny a white preacher access to his pulpit, or was not aware of how white preachers in the association felt about Campbell. His action was costly because it led to a split in his congregation, near violence in the church, the breakup of a long friendship between him and his longtime friend deacon Adam Johnson, expulsion from the Sunbury Association, and a public admission that he had erred. Marshall obviously did not use good judgment in the Campbell affair. His accomplishments in the later years, his long and distinguished ministry, and the honor that he subsequently brought to his church, however, show conclusively that the majority in First African Baptist Church demonstrated excellent judgment in voting to retain him. Furthermore, Marshall's church retained charter rights to the name "First African Baptist Church."

This was obvious to the Sunbury Association, at any rate, which in a resolution the preceding year (1832) had invited members of the First African Church to separate themselves from that church and form "new churches." This is what the Deacon Johnson–led minority did. Accordingly, at its November 1833 convention, the association approved "the conduct of S. Whitfield, J. Clay and others who [had] separated from First African Church" and recommended "them to full fellowship with all the churches."[107] Third African Church is the name the new church assumed and retained until after the Civil War. Inscribed upon the tomb of Adam A. Johnson, who died on March 18, 1853, is the epitaph: "Sacred to the memory of Adam A. Johnson, late deacon of Third African Church."[108] In principle, formation of Third African Baptist Church in 1833 was analogous to that of Second African Baptist Church three decades earlier, although the conditions surrounding the exodus of Deacon Johnson and his followers from the mother church were far less sanguine than those of the Cunningham group in 1802. Hence, Second and Third African Baptist churches both were legitimate offsprings of First African Baptist Church.

First African Church was re-admitted into the association in 1837,[109] but in the ensuing years friction erupted between it and Third African Baptist Church. In 1837, the issue was the "proprietary of one church receiving excommunicated members of another."[110] Allowing an expelled member to join another congregation undermined the intent of the punishment. As was mentioned earlier in this chapter, the association did not allow expelled members to join other churches as long as their churches remained open. In 1844, trouble surfaced once again between First African Church and Third African Church, but no cause of the problem was given other than noting there was "disaffection" between the two churches and animosity between their pastors—Andrew C. Marshall and Stephen McQueen.[111]

The rivalry among the three black Baptist churches degenerated into a condition that poisoned their relations, adversely affected their ministries in the community and nearby plantations, and prevented them from making a concerted effort to ameliorate the condition of slaves in the Chatham-Savannah area. But those three churches did not have a patent on turmoil within their Christian family, because the Methodists in June 1861 reported internal strife in Andrew Chapel, the nature and cause of which were not stated.[112]

Did the stormy relations reflect poorly upon those black congregations? The 1832–33 dispute did, but the other disagreements did not leave enough information to judge. Does this mean those black congregations were not ready for democracy? No! The majority can be wrong, or so thinks the minority when it loses a hotly debated issue. Some accept losing gracefully and remain in their church; some accept it gracefully, but leave their church. On the other hand, some refuse to accept defeat, sometimes turning a war of words into a war of fists and weapons, as almost happened in the First African Church schism. This congregation was not the first one to experience a schism, nor was it the last. The democratic process can survive schisms, which some people view as natural, but it cannot survive settling differences violently. First African Church obviously learned this lesson well because it recently celebrated its bicentennial, making it the oldest Baptist church in Savannah.

In spite of the occasional stormy relations that existed among the churches, going to church became the popular thing to do in black Savannah. From the 1780s until the early 1840s, church memberships grew steadily, and at times spectacularly, with the number of black churchgoers peaking in 1841 when the three black churches recorded a total membership of 4,021—First African (2,296), Second African (1,454), and Third African (271)—which meant nearly 21 percent of the community was churched.[113] This placed the percentage of the churched in black Savannah above that in any other major southern city, and well above the national average, which was an estimated 15 percent.[114] In 1844, Second African Church's membership dropped precipitously from 1,510 the previous year to 460; two years later, First African Church experienced a similar decline, from 2,052 the previous year to 1,200 in 1846. On the other hand, Third African Church did not suffer membership losses, but neither did it have a significant membership increase. The churches never reached those membership levels again.

Why did church attendance decline among blacks? Was it a result of a population decrease? Was it the result of expulsions, dismissals, or deaths? Was it because black churchgoers stopped going to church? The black population increased between 1830 and 1840.[115] Moreover, the expulsions, dismissals, and deaths did not increase during the 1840s. First African Church did remove five hundred names from its roll in 1854 for lack of attendance,[116] but that was after the huge decline in 1846. The other churches in the Sunbury Association maintained stable memberships, experiencing neither huge losses nor huge gains; similarly, Andrew Chapel did not benefit from the decreases. The two black churches that experienced the losses had able ministers in their pulpits, with Marshall at First African Church and Thomas Anderson at Second African Church. No probable political reasons existed for the decline. The most serious slave uprising in United States history, Nat Turner's Revolt, had occurred over a decade earlier, and its impact upon the black churches was negligible. The city fathers' refusal to remove Marshall from his pulpit during the schism, as the association hoped they would, is illustrative of this. Moreover, the African Colonization Movement did not draw huge numbers from Savannah; the peak year of the exodus occurred after 1846.

Since the decline did not result from any formal action of the two black churches that were most seriously affected by it, from actions of white public officials, or from the African Colonization Movement, the reasons must lie with the slaveholders and their slaves. The owners may have stopped allowing their slaves to attend services because they (1) became disenchanted with those churches; (2) moved to another area and took their slaves with them; or (3) commenced sponsoring services on their plantations or because of some other unknown reason, or a combination of the ones stated above. On the other hand, a large number of slaves may have lost interest in church, or they may have become disenchanted with the pastors of the affected churches. One suspects, however, that the Sunbury Association would have complained to the slaveholders, if black members had stopped attending church of their own volition. The white leadership of Savannah was apparently not displeased with the black church, if the absence of negative remarks in the city council, grand jury, and local newspaper can be construed as reflecting the attitude of the group. Hence the decline in attendance among slaves was not indicative of the imminent collapse of the independent church. The subsequent upswing in attendance supports this assessment.

The decline had run its course by the late 1840s. In 1850, both churches enjoyed increases in membership and their numbers continued to grow during the decade, with membership in First

African Baptist Church reaching 1,500 and in Second African Baptist 1,146 in 1860.[117] Even though the numbers never reached the levels of 1841, Savannah's black Baptists remained the largest independent group of black Baptists in the South.

An independent black church was the first public institution established in the black community, and that institution conducted a comprehensive ministry that went beyond meeting only the spiritual needs of its worshipers. The number of black congregations increased from one in 1788 to five by the end of the 1850s. The strength, stability, and durability of the black church resulted from (1) the perseverance of the pioneer members who failed to succumb to severe religious persecution and physical punishment; (2) its ability in the early years to attract charismatic black leaders; (3) the support of William Bryan during those trying times in the late eighteenth century; (4) its ability to attract many of the economically advantaged free African Americans; (5) its ability to produce able replacements for deceased leaders; (6) its success in winning whites' acceptance; and (7) above all, its multifaceted ministry in the black community.

The black church facilitated the development of black Savannah. The future leaders of the community were trained in the black church; the poor, infirm, aged, and needy were provided succor by it; the inner strength and values needed to sustain black Savannahians during the awful ordeal of slavery were nurtured in the black church; and the musical and oratorical talents, sense of civic responsibility, and distinctive fatalistic way of viewing life (i.e., "if God is willing, I am going to the market tomorrow") were perpetuated by the black church. The black church, moreover, provided a visible physical landmark that attracted admiring white visitors and created a sense of pride among African Americans. It was the foremost and first major collective manifestation of self-help in the black community. The black church brought African Americans together—slaves and free persons of color, blacks and mulattoes—in a positive meaningful way; there could have been no viable black community without it. The black church contributed to community development also by being an agency of inclusion, rather than of exclusion. Consequently, within the walls of the black church, Savannah's sizable slave population shed their status as property and assumed human qualities. They sang in the choir, served on auxiliaries, held offices, and exercised other responsibilities. Finally, the black church fostered black families, an essential feature of community development, with the faithful often marrying within the faith.

CHAPTER II

Citizenship Denied; Justice Compromised

There was no real freedom until Sherman's Army came; when did we ever walk in the city without a ticket? —GEORGIA KELLY

The Savannah City Council and the Georgia Legislature did not pass ordinances and statutes that encumbered efforts of African Americans to establish churches, but those governmental bodies did legislate in most other areas affecting life in black Savannah. Consequently, in order to get an accurate picture of the mechanism of social control whites employed against African Americans to encumber their efforts to earn a living, entertain themselves, and commingle with whites, it is essential to peruse the plethora of laws and ordinances and study the criminal justice system.

In the late 1850s, free African Americans in South Carolina came under intense pressure, and their freedom was threatened. One threat came from the legislature in the form of bills to enslave free African Americans, but all those bills were tabled and never saw the light of day. The other threat, which was more serious, "the enslavement crisis," came from legislation that was already on the books: an 1820 law banning manumissions. The law, which previously had not been enforced, was suddenly given new life and strictly enforced. Persons caught without proper documents attesting to their free status prior to 1820 were enslaved.[1] Free African Americans in Savannah also had their freedom threatened, but it occurred much earlier in the century, and once the legislation was repealed, they did not walk that road again.

African Americans who appeared before the Southern Claims Commissioners after the Civil War echoed the above statement of Georgia Kelly. One witness lamented "I was born free but was most as much a slave as any other colored person till the Union Army came."[2] In other words, the person assumed slavery was the normal condition of blacks in the community. Another witness observed, "I bought myself and family free but you know what that freedom was, I suppose I really wasn't free until the Army came here."[3] And a third witness, who was not manumitted until Savannah was captured, described the situation of a friend thusly, "He was a free man only in name though that's all; he was not free until General Sherman."[4] These three persons quoted above took different routes to freedom. One acquired it through birth, another through purchase, and the third through a general emancipation, but they all seemed to have agreed on the true status of free African Americans, a view which other blacks also shared.[5]

African Americans were well aware also of a message that came through quite clearly in the city council ordinances, state statutes, and opinions from the state supreme court: blacks were not citizens. Apparently this was so well established by 1789 that a provision in the 1777 state constitution denying the franchise to blacks was not included in the state constitution of 1789 which had a provision granting the franchise to "citizens and inhabitants."[6] Since they were not citizens, the state tried hard to discourage free African Americans from settling in Georgia. A major effort in this regard was an 1810 statute which required free African Americans to have guardians.[7] Almost a decade later, the state sought to make life within its boundaries even more unattractive for free African Americans when it passed a law in 1818, section five of which required free African Americans to "make application [register] to the clerk of the Inferior Court" each year on or before March 1; and section eight forbade them from purchasing or acquiring real estate (this only applied to Savannah and several other municipalities).[8] The prohibition on black ownership of real estate was unique to Georgia and underscored its position that African Americans were not citizens. Throughout the South, African Americans were denied citizenship, but no other southern state denied them the privilege of owning real estate. A section of the 1818 law also authorized the sale of free African-American lawbreakers into slavery, but it was repealed in 1825.[9] In 1842 the General Assembly of Georgia approved a joint resolution which proclaimed African Americans were not citizens of the United States, and Georgia would never recognize them as such.[10]

White Savannahians treasured and enjoyed the right to vote and the privilege of owning property, but voting was beyond the reach of the residents of black Savannah. No amount of public posturing and protesting, rioting, and petition writing would have changed that; so blacks did not pursue those avenues. Disfranchised free blacks in Savannah, therefore, stood outside voting places and looked in.

If the list of proscriptive legislation had stopped with disfranchisement, black Savannahians may have breathed a sigh of relief, but denial of the franchise was among the least of their worries. Throughout the period, a plethora of more inhibiting ordinances and statutes poured from local and state governments which, had they been enforced rigidly, would have made life even more difficult for free African Americans and slaves. Some laws made a distinction between free African Americans and slaves, while some did not. The laws which curtailed or prohibited economic activities were especially ominous. A case in point was an 1834 ordinance which prohibited granting licenses to free African Americans to "retail spirituous liquors, cordials, or other articles containing spirits." Four years later, the city council forbade free African Americans from piloting vessels on the bar of Tybee and the Savannah River.[11]

The latter prohibition was in stark contrast to a state law in the 1780s that allowed slaves to own vessels, creating a situation in which slaves were allowed to pursue occupations denied to free African Americans. Slaves who hired their own time piloted vessels on the Savannah River, and owners employed other slaves to pilot vessels. Merchants, ship owners, and plantation owners who depended on the labor of slave pilots would not have tolerated any legislation that tampered with this practice. Free African Americans did not have a group of white sponsors to speak for them, which made them vulnerable to pleas of white pilots for the council to reduce the number of black pilots.

The same year it passed the piloting ordinance, the council tightened the language of an earlier ordinance dealing with spirituous liquors. Although the new legislation did not prohibit slaves and free blacks from selling those drinks, it required the presence, at the time of the sale, of the establishment's owner, a white clerk, apprentice, or some other white person whom the owner authorized.[12] In 1854, the state passed similar legislation, but that statute was more restrictive since it prohibited the sale of any spirituous liquors, cordials, wines, ale, beer, porter, or any other intoxicating liquors by a free African American.[13] This act was intended to retaliate against whites and free blacks who had collaborated to circumvent an earlier state law.

Perhaps one of the most obvious examples of legislative badgering of blacks were the laws that required free blacks to perform public work without receiving compensation. When feudalism was practiced in Europe, serfs were required to give their lords a fixed number of days of uncompensated labor each year, but once the practice was abolished, freemen paid taxes—quitrents (quitted meaning they were free)—which relieved them of the labor obligation. All efforts to establish feudalism in North America failed, but the idea that freemen would pay taxes instead of perform public work was adopted. Forcing free blacks to perform public work, therefore, reinforced the perception which many free blacks had of themselves: They were not free in every sense of the word. In 1818, the state mandated that all registered free African Americans between the ages of fifteen and sixty could be required to give a maximum of twenty days in any calendar year working on public projects in their county or town. Those who failed to comply with this law could be fined or subjected to whatever punishment local officials deemed appropriate.[14]

The next year city officials approved an ordinance which required free African Americans to work in the hospital instead of on the streets.[15] There was probably an epidemic in 1819, and the city needed help with victims of the disease. It apparently did not matter to those officials that some free blacks had not been adequately immunized and may have become victims themselves if exposed to the disease. According to conventional wisdom, blacks were not susceptible to yellow fever. This was probably what influenced the legislation, this and the helpless condition of free blacks who did not have economic interests which coincided with those of influential whites.

Slaveholders were not inclined to donate the free labor of their slaves to the city, except in emergencies, so they probably used their influence to prevent the ordinance from applying to slaves. This ordinance thus created another situation where nominal slaves had the best of both worlds. They were free from their masters' supervision, and they were free from legislation that applied to free blacks, and so benefited from the lag that developed between the creation of this anomaly in the peculiar institution and the creation of laws to regulate it.

In 1820, all male free African Americans were required to level a part of the line of forts on Farm Street and to do whatever other work the Street and Lane Committee ordered;[16] this marked the third consecutive year city officials passed an ordinance requiring free blacks to perform public work. Henry Cunningham, Simon Jackson, and a few other free blacks may have escaped this, and other public work, by sending their slaves as substitutes. Those who controlled the city may have been amenable to this arrangement because it obligated those black leaders to them. Even if the handful of free blacks gained exemption from this work, however, it did not affect the mass of free blacks, nor did it diminish the power which whites exercised over blacks.

Since most whites favored bans on blacks (slave and free) acquiring reading and writing skills, antiteaching and school attendance ordinances applied to slaves and free African Americans. An 1839 ordinance prohibited anyone (black or white) from either teaching free African Americans and slaves to read and write or to operate a school which allowed them to attend.[17] Blacks' and whites' violation of the ordinance,[18] should have been known to those who passed it since Savannah was small enough, and blacks and whites lived close enough to each other to render keeping secrets in the black community very difficult. The pervasiveness of the violations suggests that a combination of factors worked against the ordinance, not the least of which was the "thine and mine syndrome"—the ordinance was intended for thine, not for mine. The ordinance, moreover, did not expressly forbid African Americans from learning how to read and write; it merely forbade teaching them those skills in any setting, thus creating a readily exploited loophole.

Half-hearted enforcement of the prohibitive education ordinance was the rule. Whites failed to do so collectively as a community, as well as separately as individuals, which suggests that whatever fears and apprehensions whites harbored toward blacks acquiring an education were manifested mainly in preventive legislation. Although enforcement efforts went beyond benign neglect— some energy was expended enforcing the ordinance, albeit sporadically and ineffectively—white Savannahians were too busy taking care of more important mundane concerns, that is, keeping their business books, to devote serious attention to enforcing the ban on blacks attending school. The ordinance, therefore, was a statement of whites' concern about blacks learning how to read; casual enforcement of the ordinance was a statement of their lack of commitment to doing much about it beyond legislating.

Throughout the period, the city fathers also circumscribed social privileges of African Americans. They were not allowed, for instance, to gamble or play "any game for other purposes"; their dances were monitored closely and had to end at 10:00 P.M.;[19] and on Sundays, they were not allowed to congregate on West Broad Street and Augusta Road, where apparently African Americans gathered to the annoyance of whites. Two constables were placed at that location to discourage blacks from gathering there.[20] African Americans were also prohibited from riding through Savannah and neighboring hamlets on Sundays.[21] Finally, in 1860, the council considered passing an ordinance prohibiting African Americans from loitering near stores, bars, and shops in Savannah,[22] but the council may not have passed the bill because more pressing matters—namely, the Civil War—caught its attention.

Judging from the nature and number of ordinances dealing with social gatherings outside normal family settings, the city fathers were acutely aware of the social habits of African Americans. Those ordinances stemmed less from fears of conspiracies and revolts than from irritation with the noisy behavior of blacks, who were rowdy on occasions, but not riotous. Since blacks were not citizens, they could not demand the First Amendment right to assemble peacefully. Robbed of their humanity for the most part, and denied participation in the political process, blacks had cause to be riotous, even if they did not show a propensity to do so. The intent of the ordinances was to impress upon African Americans that they were the subordinate group and enjoyed privileges at the pleasure of whites, who could even forbid them from creating enjoyment to mitigate their misery if they wished. Further, as the dominant group, whites would determine the time and place for blacks to congregate. While Sundays may have been the right time, street corners were not the place; dancing and "frolicing" were permissible, as long as they ended two hours before midnight; but there was never a right time to frequent bars. The night watch, city marshal, and constables were the major enforcement brigade to ensure the ordinances restricting the social privileges of African Americans were obeyed.

In order to do an adequate job of policing blacks, it was important to ascertain how many free African Americans were in town, who they were, where they lived, and how they earned a living. The information on slaves, although important, was left to slaveholders to provide since slaves were their responsibility. Accordingly, in February 1814, the city marshal was directed to take a census of all free African Americans in the city and report this information to the council at its next meeting the following month. In addition to the normal concerns about the presence of free blacks roaming through the city, whites were concerned about the security of the city during the War of 1812.[23] The British were in position to operate sabotage activities from Spanish-owned East Florida and stir up trouble among free blacks. A more comprehensive census including blacks and whites was conducted in 1848, and according to that one, Savannah had 637 free African Americans and 5,686 slaves, giving the city a total black population that was over 46 percent of the city's total of 13,573.[24]

The taxing of African Americans had its genesis in the colonial period when the first legislation of this kind was enacted in 1768.[25] Similar legislation was passed during the Confederation period (1781–88) and again after the adoption of the Federal Constitution, although the rates were reduced gradually for a while; in 1799, they were $.31¼ for free African Americans between the ages of fourteen and sixty.[26] In 1857, however, free black carters, draymen, hucksters, and artisans were assessed a $10.00 poll tax; all other free blacks between the ages of sixteen and forty-five, except firemen, were assessed a poll tax of $6.25.[27]

Black real estate owners were also taxed, and some of them had the same difficulty some whites had in scraping together money to pay them. In 1799, Andrew Bryan and three other free blacks were among the legion of persons who did not pay their taxes.[28] Bryan's name appeared on at least one other list of tax defaulters in subsequent years.[29] In an effort to discourage free African Americans from settling in Savannah, some of whom may have joined the ranks of property owners, in 1857 the council placed a one-hundred-dollar tax on each free African American between the ages of fourteen and sixty who moved to Savannah from another location for the purpose of residing there. The levy was payable within thirty days.[30] There seemed to have been no limit to the kinds of taxes municipal public officials were prepared to levy upon African Americans, especially upon the free ones.

An 1839 ordinance associated free African Americans with skin color, but the provisions were applicable to all three groups. In addition to the "Negro and mulatto" classification, the ordinance introduced a third group, mestizo, but the black (Negro) and mulatto classifications remained the most commonly used. That ordinance also divided African Americans by gender, but it required all sellers of small wares in Savannah, whether Negro, mulatto, or mestizo and whether male or female, to purchase an eight-dollar badge.[31] To reiterate, light-skinned African Americans did not receive any special legal consideration in Savannah.

From an 1853 listing of vocations that required badges to pursue them, practically all occupations in which blacks normally worked required badges. The practice of using badges was a common means of regulating black labor throughout the South. In Savannah, the rates were based upon occupations rather than upon legal status (whether free or slave), and in those small minority of instances where males and females pursued similar occupations, badges for males cost more than for females. Women laborers and porters paid less for their badges than males in those jobs, $3.06¼ and $4.56½, respectively; these were the lowest priced badges. Cabinetmakers, house or ship carpenters, caulkers, bricklayers, blacksmiths, tailors, barbers, bakers, and butchers were charged $10.00 for their badges, the highest rate set in the ordinance.[32] One major difference between the ordinances in 1839 and 1853 was that the earlier one was specifically directed toward free African Americans, whereas the latter was not restricted to that group.

Tax collection was inefficient. In 1860, only 126 free African Americans between the ages of fourteen and forty-five, firemen excepted, paid their $6.25 poll tax.[33] There were slightly over seven hundred free blacks in the city at the time, maybe as many as 65 percent of whom were in their prime years.[34] Even with the large number of free black firemen, the 126 who paid seem like a minority of those who were eligible to pay the tax. Just as revealing, only two of the skilled free blacks purchased ten-dollar badges as required by city ordinance. Free African Americans may have been good citizens, behaving in socially acceptable ways, but they were probably no different than their white counterparts when it came to paying taxes. Their poor track record for paying the taxes reduced the burden somewhat.

The answer to the question why only a minority of the free blacks paid their taxes is not readily discernible. The unfairness of taxes initially may have generated little enthusiasm among African Americans to pay them, and when the authorities did not take forceful action against those who were not in compliance, a signal may have been sent to African Americans that they would not be punished for the offense; or African Americans may have been influenced by the long list of whites who did not pay their taxes. There were instances when blacks were financially unable to pay their taxes, and the treasurer did not push the issue. For some, this even may have been a means of protesting the subordinate status of African Americans. These are all plausible reasons, but what actually caused the low percentage is unknown. The taxes were still unjust and constituted taxation without representation, even though they went unpaid. One could wink at some of the discriminatory laws, such as one which did not allow free blacks to testify against whites, but forcing them to support oppression was the worst form of insensitivity. Frederick Douglass was right when he said, "No man has a right to make any concession to tyranny, which he would refuse to make if he were the victim."[35] Unfortunately, white leaders in Savannah did not subscribe to this position.

The criminal justice system appears to have been sensitive to African Americans in some areas and insensitive in others. African Americans received the most compassionate treatment in civil proceedings. In 1837, when Paul Dupon applied to the Court of the Ordinary for permission to sell a female slave which belonged to the heirs of one J. Langevin, he said proper notification had been published in the *Gazette of the State of Georgia,* as required by law, and no objections had been raised. Whereupon, the judge approved the sale, provided proper public notice of the time and place of the sale was given.[36] If the race of the deceased and her heirs had not been given, the careful attention to the law and apparent genuine efforts to protect the interest of the heirs would have led one to believe they were white instead of black. Judges of the Court of the Ordinary consistently required scrupulous subscription to the law when matters concerning the estates of deceased African Americans appeared before them. This was inconsistent with the way whites in Savannah usually treated African Americans.

When Andrew Marshall wished to transfer title of real estate in Yamacraw to his son Joseph, their trustees handled the transactions. The names of the trustees are prominent on the indentures; nevertheless, it is quite obvious they were acting for the two Marshall men. A provision in one of the indentures stated the Marshalls had used the property to keep their horses and drays, and the property also contained houses, outhouses, stable, and gardens.[37] The Marshalls were successful small businessmen, and the elder Marshall, well into his nineties at the time, desired to transfer the business to his younger son. If they had been white, the transactions would not have required middlemen. In spite of the circuitous legal maneuvers required to transfer ownership of the properties from father to son, the system, in a backhanded way, recognized the privilege of African Americans to own and dispose of real estate and other property.

The estate transaction and the Marshalls' property transfers are representative of the way African Americans were treated in property sales. It appears the court cared how the property of the deceased free black female was administered and required of the estate's executor the same integrity and adherence to the law it required of those handling estates of whites. In abiding by the law, the lawyers who handled the Marshalls' transactions acted in the best interests of their clients and were careful to avoid losing the property through some undetected legal loophole. If those lawyers had really wanted to render the Marshalls propertyless, they would have used their knowledge of the law, which African Americans in Savannah were not allowed to practice, to exploit them.

Requiring free African Americans to have guardians was not intended to be beneficial to them, but it inadvertently reduced the probability of black property owners being exploited by greedy unscrupulous lawyers. In making the property ownership laws, lawmakers probably did not take into account the sense of fairness of the men who were sworn to uphold the law and the persons who agreed to become trustees of estates. Apparently, they were generally honorable men who rose above their racial prejudices when they were required to represent African Americans in civil proceedings. If they had been dishonest, and if the judges in civil proceedings had looked the other way during those transactions, the history of the residents of black Savannah would have been even more distressful than it was.

During the 1830s, the Court of the Ordinary handled very few matters concerning free blacks registering or applying for guardians,[38] an indication that Nat Turner's Revolt did not lead to a major white backlash in Savannah. Had whites become nervous about a ripple effect from the revolt surfacing in their city, blacks would have come under closer scrutiny, and compliance with the registration statute would have been monitored more closely. This low turnout to register continued unabated into the early 1860s when no free blacks applied for registration or to have guardians appointed in 1862 and in the January term of 1863.[39]

The greatest distinction between slaves and free blacks occurred in civil proceedings in the Court of the Ordinary. Slaves were property in civil proceedings, hence could not use that court in the same manner as free blacks. Slaves' legal identity in civil proceedings was similar to horses and other personal property of their masters. In criminal matters, however, a world of difference existed between the slaves and horses. Both slaves and horses were capable of killing human beings, but only slaves, of the two, could be charged with murder. In criminal cases, therefore, slaves were transformed from property to human beings who could be held responsible for their misdeeds. No other group in Savannah had this dual legal identity. Whites in Savannah failed to explain the logic behind this.

Slaves were reunited with their other black brothers in criminal cases, when they were tried under the same laws, which often differed significantly from those which regulated the behavior of whites. Since a double standard of justice, which favored whites, pervaded the criminal justice system, justice was compromised. Prior to 1811, free blacks and slaves were tried before a justice of the peace and a jury of no fewer than seven freeholders, but that year a separate tribunal for slave criminal offenders was created under the jurisdiction of the inferior court. Any justice of the peace could issue an arrest warrant for an accused free African American, and the trial was conducted by three, or more, justices who were empowered to issue corporal punishment sentences in noncapital cases.[40] According to a December 24, 1821, statute, the following were capital offenses when committed by slaves and free blacks: insurrection, or attempt to incite; rape, or attempted rape of a white female; murder of a white; murder of a slave or free African American; and poisoning a human being.[41] Rape of a black female did not constitute a capital offense, but both attempted rape and rape of a white female were capital offenses. Since the law did not make a distinction between the two categories of sexual assault, a fearful perpetrator of an attempted rape might murder the only witness to the alleged crime and hope the prosecutor would not find sufficient evidence to convict him.

Savannah had more brothels (nine of which were large and well known and many others which were less visible) than it had churches, and the number of liquor shops greatly outnumbered cotton exporting establishments, the city's leading commercial enterprise. Such a situation was bound to create crimes. African Americans were among the lawless element, as they were constantly arrested for drunkenness, fighting, and disorderly conduct, their major offenses. Only rarely did a black commit murder, and it was usually against another black.[42] Between 1830 and 1864, the board of health recorded four killings by blacks, and one of them was ruled as self-defense.[43] After the Civil War, it was common to find the proportion of black jail inmates exceeding the proportion of blacks in the general population, but in the 1850s (and probably earlier), whites in the Savannah jail outnumbered blacks two to one.[44] Whites also owned the shops which provided the liquor that led to the drunkenness, fighting, and disorderly conduct in the black community.

The judicial procedures used to handle cases concerning African American criminal offenders differed from those for whites. Disorderly conduct cases involving African Americans were heard before the mayor. For a short while, 1816–17, the state authorized the governor to grant pardons and commute sentences of free African Americans, upon written request from their guardians, but the policy was discontinued after operating for that year.[45] Capital cases were tried in the inferior court until 1850 when they were switched to the superior court. After the state supreme court was established in 1846, the superior court retained some of its former duties and assumed some of the duties of the inferior court (each county had an inferior and superior court). In Savannah, a five man jury was required when the offense was committed within the city limits, and the clerk prosecuted the case as a part of his dual responsibilities. Slaves and free blacks were allowed to testify against each other (neither could testify against whites), and the verdict could be appealed, in which case the verdict was suspended for forty days.

In criminal cases involving African Americans, the courtroom scene and practices reflected Savannah's blatant racism. Whereas the defendants and witnesses were black, the judges, prosecutors, and jurors were white. The latter group was from the same element of society which had made the laws and did not express concern about whether they were fair to African Americans. This situation was mitigated, somewhat, by state laws which required legal counsel for slave defendants and forbade their spouses from appearing as prosecution witnesses, a practice (in the latter case) that was unique to Georgia among southern states. Free blacks (and whites) did not have a right to legal counsel.[46] In criminal cases, therefore, free African Americans were subjected to an indignity which no other free persons endured—slaves testified against them—but they had to fend for themselves, as other free persons, in securing legal counsel. This seemed to have been a contradiction, especially since free African Americans, normally wards of the court, were required to have white guardians. Nevertheless, conventional wisdom did not mandate otherwise.

Whereas generally African Americans (free and slave) were equally unequal in the opinion of whites, a close look at the laws reveals slaves were given due process denied free African Americans. Confinement in jail was a different story. The city jail rivaled the city market for attracting a heterogeneous gathering of persons in Savannah. The jail housed blacks and whites, females and males, the sane and the insane, slaves and free persons, residents and nonresidents, and civilians and sailors all under the same roof, but in separate cells. The jail was the place where criminals were incarcerated for breaking laws ranging from felonies and misdemeanors to nonpayment of debt and where persons who had not committed crimes were placed for safekeeping, such as black seamen on ships anchored in the harbor and slaves whose masters went away on business and left them with the jailer.[47]

Jail was deplorably hot in the summer, wretchedly cold in the winter, poorly ventilated, and unsanitary.[48] The food, moreover, was awful. One prisoner who had been taken to jail with his hands tied behind him for an eight-week stint in the facility complained afterwards of a diet which consisted of "one quart of corn ground then boiled," after the husk had been removed. Salt was available at times, but he was never fed any meat.[49] The number of blacks incarcerated for long periods of time was probably very low since slaveholders preferred to have slaves whipped and returned to their control where they could be put to work rather than languish in jail, and the city preferred to have free blacks whipped, fined, or both, rather than incarcerated. The decision in each instance was based upon economic considerations, not upon humanitarian concerns.

Slaves and free African Americans were incarcerated in the same cell and fed the same food. They both suffered from the summer heat and winter cold, and in the eyes of the jailer, they both belonged to an inferior race. Once they entered jail, whatever slight advantages slaves enjoyed over free African Americans in criminal proceedings and whatever advantages free African Americans enjoyed over slaves in civil proceedings disappeared. Their common African ancestry emerged as the factor that brought them to the same level. Since blackness carried negative connotations in the eyes of the jailer, whatever advantages each group enjoyed prior to its incarceration were negated by it.

In 1848, a number of free blacks who normally would have faced incarceration were spared the ordeal when the state supreme court overturned a Savannah ordinance mandating incarceration for failure to pay a one-hundred-dollar fee required of all free blacks who moved to Savannah from other parts of the state; the fee was payable within thirty days after their arrival. Although the court subscribed to the position blacks were not citizens and did not have any political rights, the judges declared blacks had personal rights, "one of which is personal liberty." Then, the court invalidated the one-hundred-dollar fee, ruling it was nothing but a tax and as such could not be enforced by imprisoning defaulters. Consequently, the portion of the ordinance which mandated imprisonment for nonpayment of the fee was ruled to be "repugnant to the laws of the State and void."[50] This ruling was an aberration; nonetheless, it was welcome news in the black community.

In a few rare instances, blacks and whites suffered similar punishment for breaking the law, but one senses the crimes were ones associated with the lower classes of whites. An example was an 1810 ordinance which mandated a five-dollar fine for anyone caught nude in the streets, lanes, and squares of the city. Free African Americans and whites who could not pay the fine were jailed until they did, and slaves were also jailed until their owners paid the fine.[51] The ordinance held free blacks, slaves, and whites to the same standard of conduct and subjected them to the same punishment when they faltered, but slaveholders were required to pay for their slaves' misdeeds, while free blacks were held to the same responsibility as whites. A person was likely to be nude in public either because he did not have clothes, a home, the proper "social graces," or all three, and such a person probably would not have the funds to pay the fine. Normally, blacks were held to a higher standard of conduct than whites, but not in this instance.[52]

As mentioned above, fines were preferable to incarceration. Andrew Marshall was fined one dollar in 1842 for driving his dray on the sidewalk,[53] and blacks who did not purchase occupational badges were fined from twenty to fifty dollars depending upon how they earned a livelihood. Although whipping was an option in some instances where fines were not paid, it was not included in the 1842 ordinance. Whipping was included as an optional punishment for blacks who sold small wares without purchasing a badge. Offenders were either fined twenty dollars or less or whipped. The decision was left to city officials.[54]

Public work was another weapon available in the arsenal whites assembled to punish black lawbreakers. Under an 1857 ordinance, all free African Americans between the ages of fourteen and sixty who moved to Savannah and did not pay a one-hundred-dollar fee within thirty days of their arrival could be put to work on the public streets until the fee had been paid. Males were credited with one dollar toward the payment of the fee for each day of work on the streets, and women were credited with seventy-five cents.[55] This punishment was obviously intended to meet the objections which the state's highest court had raised in invalidating a similar act in 1848. The drafters of the new ordinance were oblivious to the inequity of the punishment prescribed for free female offenders, who were required to work 125 days to pay the fee; whereas black males worked 100 days, yet the fee was the same for both sexes. The council was authorized to assess the fee since the state court did not rule otherwise in its 1848 decision, but females were punished more severely for violating the ordinance than males. The council could have achieved the purpose of its ordinance, which was to discourage free blacks from moving into Savannah, by charging females a seventy-five-dollar fee, which for most females was just as prohibitive as the one-hundred-dollar fee.

Whipping was by far the most common form of punishment, and it also may have been the most demeaning, especially since it was often administered publicly. The prescribed number of lashes, thirty-nine, was administered with a cowhide whip, although paddles with holes bored in them were used sometimes. Slaveholders called this form of punishment "Moses law."[56] Andrew Bryan and many of his followers were whipped early in Bryan's career for holding worship services,[57] and Andrew Marshall was whipped for allegedly buying stolen materials from slaves to build his two-story home.[58] By the late 1830s, whipping whites had fallen into disfavor, but it remained a form of punishment for African Americans. This was apparent in an 1839 ordinance which fined white offenders of a proscriptive education ordinance one hundred dollars, while it mandated a whipping, not to exceed thirty-nine lashes, for slave and free African-American offenders.[59] James M. Simms was whipped publicly for getting caught violating this ordinance. He thus followed in the footsteps of his illustrious predecessors and role models at First African Baptist Church.

The denial of citizenship to African Americans and the disparity in administering justice would have created greater unhappiness, want, and despair in black Savannah if the ordinances and statutes had not been enforced rigidly and the civil procedures had not shown some sensitivity to African Americans. In fact, slaves, who probably committed a higher percentage of the crimes than free African Americans, received due process to a greater degree than free persons of color. On the other hand, free African Americans, the property owners in the black community, could expect a fair airing of their civil cases, the same body of law where slaves did not have a standing as a person. Furthermore, fortunately for those who lived in black Savannah, the fervor generated for enactment of some ordinances was often absent from their enforcement. Although statutes and ordinances affecting black life were passed throughout the period, their scope and severity did not increase with the passing years. In fact, the nature of those laws had been established by 1830.

Savannah's judicial system and the laws enacted to control the behavior of African Americans generally did not differ from those in the rest of the South. Savannah had less of a white backlash, however, after the Nat Turner Revolt and during the 1850s when, as a rule, tension throughout the South increased over the slavery issue. A case in point was Charleston where, as Johnson and Roark have argued, free African Americans experienced an "enslavement crisis." The major reason why whites in Savannah did not overreact to these crises is perhaps the presence of the independent black church and the history of responsible leadership associated with it. Whites were accustomed to African Americans assembling to worship, so they did not overreact when African Americans gathered indoors in large numbers. Loitering in the streets, on the other hand, constituted a different matter, and the white power structure moved to discourage it. Moreover, white mechanics and other workers did not carry much weight; therefore, rivalries between them and black artisans were not translated into oppressive legislation further limiting opportunities of African Americans. Finally, white Savannahians doubtless believed they had an effective system of social control which did not require additional safeguards. The popular contemporary statement, "if it is not broken, do not fix it," probably was the operating principle of that day as well.

CHAPTER III

Affluence and Autonomy amid Adversity

For Sale
*A house suitable for a small family, with two rooms
on the floor, with out-buildings all in good repair . . .
For particulars, inquire of Andrew Morel opposite
The Planters Bank.*
—Daily Georgian, December 4, 1819

Denied citizenship and with the scales of justice heavily weighted against them, African Americans had tremendous obstacles to overcome. The encumbrances barring free access to business, labor, and the professions were even more ominous because they had the potential to reduce free African Americans to a state of destitution. Instead of succumbing to adversity, however, African Americans parlayed the restricted economic opportunities into profitable ventures which created affluence in the black community and resulted in blacks gaining a measure of economic autonomy. This was achieved mainly through working in a number of skilled and unskilled jobs—mostly in the building trades, transportation, and personal service among black males and as seamstresses, washerwomen, and domestic servants among African-American females.

Before discussing how free African Americans succeeded in these endeavors, an overview of Savannah's economy should be helpful. The chief commercial center in Georgia, Savannah was one of the nation's leading exporters of lumber, and it ranked fourth in the South behind New Orleans, Mobile, and Charleston in the export of cotton. Savannah merchants also exported rice, wheat, copper ore, flour, wool, hides, peltry, fallow, beeswax, and drugs. In 1855–56, the total value of Savannah's exports was $22,027,500, with the vast majority of it, $19,100,000, being for cotton.[1] Furthermore, Georgia was the largest manufacturer of cotton goods in the South and had the second largest woolen industry in the region.[2] Some of the lumber produced in Savannah was used by local saw mills, some was shipped coastwise, but by far the largest portion of it was exported to foreign countries, mainly to Great Britain. Prior to the 1830s, a large part of Savannah's lumber was shipped to the West Indies—to Kingston, Barbados, St. Thomas, Nassau, and Havana. In the 1840s, Canada and Great Britain replaced those markets as destinations, and by the 1850s, Great Britain had become the main destination of Savannah's lumber.[3]

Savannah did not have enough white laborers to perform the skilled, semiskilled, and unskilled jobs created by its economy nor enough farmers to grow sufficient food for its inhabitants, which opened opportunities in these areas to African Americans, both free and slave. Positions were not available, however, in the medical and legal professions, or as owners of banks, mills, railroads, factories, and mercantile enterprises. As a result of this situation, African Americans were confined to jobs in a clearly defined sector of the economy, with little distinction made between free African Americans and slaves, except in the ownership of property and perhaps the operation of certain kinds of businesses, such as shop-keeping. The term "blue collar workers" most accurately describes free African Americans' status in Savannah. Even small business-men usually worked at the same jobs as other black workers, but they were self-employed. In the black community, moreover, females predominated in the work force. The development of the community depended in large part on the ability of African Americans to make the most of this unenviable situation. Free African Americans who worked in the numerous mills throughout Savannah usually did so upon receiving authorization from their white guardians. These workers, some of whom were carpenters, engineers, and sawyers earned an average of approximately twenty dollars a month, which was comparable to wages paid unskilled white mill workers.

A large part of the lumber sawed by the mills along the Savannah River and its tributaries was rafted to Savannah.[4]

In addition to the sawmills, Savannah also had rice and cotton mills, according to an 1848 census of Joseph Bancroft. Most of the eighteen mills he found operating in Savannah were medium sized, but among the larger ones was the Upper Steam Rice Mill which employed a regular work force of forty-eight persons that was increased by an additional fifty persons—all black females—from four to six months each year. In only three instances did Bancroft indicate that workers in a particular mill were mainly white, which suggests that workers in the other mills were either all or mostly black.[5] Furthermore, since only four of those eighteen mills owned slaves outright, the others probably hired slaves and free African Americans.[6] In 1859, Upper Steam Rice Mill advertised for "Negro men, women, boys and girls . . . immediately for whom liberal wages will be paid."[7] Normally in such an advertisement, the company was interested primarily in hiring slaves, but free African Americans were also acceptable.

The number of free African Americans who worked on industrial jobs, such as the mills mentioned above and some who worked on common labor jobs, such as John F. Freeman, a janitor at Oglethorpe Medical College,[8] was not reflected in the occupations given by free African Americans when they registered with the county in 1823, as required by law. That year drayman (8), tailor (7), carpenter (6), butcher (5), cooper (5), and barber (3) were listed as the leading occupations of free African-Americans males,[9] and if related occupations are grouped, personal service, building trades, and the transportation industry were the most popular. In 1848, Bancroft's survey revealed that building trades (34), personal service (5), and the ministry (3) were the leaders.[10] In 1860, the leading industries were the building trades, transportation, and personal service. In those industries, mariner (21), carpenter (19), bricklayer (18), laborer (14), porter (12), and cooper (11) were the most common.[11]

Free African-American males therefore had mixed fortunes in the job market. On the upside, the number of different jobs, as well as the number of persons employed in these, increased over time, an indication that the influx of immigrants did not impact negatively upon black labor in Savannah as it did in northern cities such as Boston and New York where Irish immigrants accepted employment in domestic service jobs that traditionally were regarded as colored jobs. On the downside, the nature of the jobs did not change over time.[12] Free African-American males were engaged in the same kinds of work in 1860 that they pursued at the turn of the century. There were several reasons for the mixed fortunes: (1) the huge pool of slave labor dampened the enthusiasm of many immigrants who might have settled in Savannah; (2) whites did not show a preference for employing immigrants over African Americans; and (3) free African Americans developed a reputation for their reliability and competence.

Transportation jobs—both those on land and sea—fitted neatly into Savannah's exporting activities. Bay Street was the main thoroughfare used to transport merchandise from place to place in the city, and the inefficient processing of some items increased busness for draymen and wagon drivers as the following description of how cotton was processed indicates:

> It [cotton] was first hauled from a railroad depot, or from a wharf on the river, to a warehouse for storage until sold, and when sold it was hauled to the compress, and from the compress to the side of the ship. It will be seen by this that the same bale of cotton was handled not less than three times.[13]

This inefficient handling of cotton created more jobs for its land-based transporters than the volume justified, thus swelling the income of black draymen, who normally received eight cents for each bale of cotton they transported.[14] Andrew Marshall, Evans Grate, Jack Simpson, James Oliver, Joseph Marshall, and William Pollard were among the draymen who were able to live comfortably from income earned in that occupation.

The shipping industry was another area where employment opportunities were very good for free African-American males, but usually as workers rather than as small businessmen; draymen and wagoners were usually independent operators. The local newspaper often advertised for black deckhands, stewards, engineers, firemen, and stearnmen.[15] Advertisements for ocean-going ships were primarily intended for free African Americans because it is highly improbable that a slaveholder would chance hiring his slave(s) to a captain of a vessel that might have anchored in a free state, or what is worse, in a foreign country, such as Great Britain, where Lord Mansfield, in *Somerset v. Stewart* (1772), ruled that slave laws were unenforceable in English courts. The Iron Steamboat Company and the Georgia Company were two of the main shipping companies home based in Savannah,[16] and they probably hired free African Americans who listed mariner as their occupation. Some blacks were also pilots, serving as the eyes of ships entering and leaving Savannah. Water transportation and land-based transportation, therefore, provided a significant number of jobs for free African-American males.

Identifying the free male leaders in black Savannah and listing their property shed additional light on the nature and range of occupations open to male African Americans and the extent of their economic success. One of the most successful free African-American males in land-based transportation was Andrew Marshall, who gained his reputation and respect in the community—and elsewhere—from preaching, but gained his financial security from the dray business. From the late 1820s through the 1840s he was the most financially secure African American in Savannah. In 1824, his real estate was assessed at eighty-four hundred dollars, the highest amount among African Americans,[17] and in 1827, he purchased a gig.[18] Marshall must have rented houses to slaves in the city because the 1850 census listed him as the owner of eight slaves, but the city tax digest did not list him as a slaveholder.[19] Apparently the census taker assumed the slaves on Marshall's premises belonged to him. At the time of his death in 1856, Marshall owned land in Yamacraw containing a single family unit, a "double stone building" and a wooden building: a lot in the village of St. Gall with buildings; a four-wheeled carriage and horses; four shares of stock in the Marine and Fire Insurance Bank of the State of Georgia; and valuable personal items.[20] Indeed, the dray business had been kind to him.

Evans Grate, another preacher who made a living in the dray business, owned real estate in St. Gall that was assessed at eight hundred dollars in 1810;[21] James Oliver, a Virginia native, owned a slave and three lots containing dwellings in St. Gall that were assessed at fourteen hundred dollars in 1837;[22] and Jack Simpson, one of the deacons in First African Church who supported Adam Johnson in the schism, owned real estate valued at eleven hundred dollars in 1848.[23] These draymen were contemporaries of Marshall, and by the 1840s, most of them had died, but by this time a new generation of successful black draymen were entering the field.

One of those new small businessmen was Joseph Andrew Marshall, the older of Marshall's two surviving sons, who by the time he had reached his thirtieth birthday had already surpassed the achievements of his father at a similar period in his life and was well on the way to becoming one of the business leaders in the community when he died in 1853 at the age of thirty-two. At that time, the younger Marshall owned stock in Marine and Fire Insurance Bank (four shares valued at $240), Central Railroad and Banking Company of Georgia (two shares valued at $230), and Savannah Gas Light Company (five shares valued at $150). Joseph Marshall also owned other personal property, including a horse, wagon, buggy, furniture, watch and chain, as well as real estate assessed at $3,000 and $200 cash.[24] He appears to have lived well and had good prospects of living even better, for his father, who was approaching one hundred years of age, had included him in his will.[25] Joseph's friend and brother-in-law, William Pollard, who was also a drayman in the 1850s, owned more real estate but his personal property was not as valuable as Joseph's.[26]

Barbers and butchers were not as numerous as draymen in Savannah, and these black small businessmen generally failed to do as well financially as draymen, with the exception of William (Billy) Goldsmith, a butcher who had acquired real estate assessed at twenty-two hundred dollars in 1810, at a time when no other African American on the tax roll owned real estate that was assessed in the two-thousand-dollar bracket. His real estate depreciated over the next ten years and was worth fifteen hundred in 1820, which still placed the value of his property in the 95th percentile of property owned by African Americans.[27] Saunders Motta, who married into the Dolly family and was the most successful barber of his day, owned two parcels of land that were valued at a total of one thousand dollars in 1810, but he died three years later before having an opportunity to build upon that solid financial base.[28] Emanuel Wand Sr., a barber and leader of First African Baptist Church, owned three hundred dollars in real estate in 1820, but in 1848, he had lost it, although he then owned two slaves; Jackson Ragis, a barber from Martinique, owned one slave but no real estate in 1820.[29]

The building trades attracted a relatively large number of African Americans with enough demand for their services to allow a few of them to own real estate, slaves, and other personal property. In addition to constructing houses, churches, offices, fences, casks, and other wooden facilities and objects, black carpenters and coopers often filled the void created by the absence of undertakers by handling funeral arrangements and making coffins. Prince Candy, Thomas Simpson, and Joshua Bourke were among the successful coopers in the community, and John (Jack) Gibbons was a leading carpenter. In 1809, Candy owned two lots in St. Gall, and by 1820, he had increased his real estate holdings to three lots, all with dwellings, that were assessed at a total of $2,400, and two slaves; three years later he had increased his slave holding to seven,[30] the most of any African American in the city limits of Savannah. Thomas (Tom) Simpson was brought to this country from Africa as a thirteen-year-old in 1804, and within six years of his arrival, he had acquired his freedom and owned real estate in Anson Ward that was assessed at $400, which was a remarkable accomplishment. He was not able, however, to maintain that pace; in fact, he later lost his property and never acquired any more.[31] Joshua Bourke belonged to the young group of African Americans that emerged in the 1850s. His real estate in Oglethorpe Ward, the ward with the highest concentration of African Americans, was assessed at $1,000 in 1854 but had decreased in value to $940 in 1860, the year Bourke died of a "debility."[32] Gibbons owned five slaves in 1823 and his real estate was worth $600.[33]

As a group, the tailors may have been outnumbered by carpenters but there seems to have been a higher percentage of successful tailors than there were carpenters, and there were more émigrés from St. Domingue who established successful businesses in tailoring than in any other vocation. In fact, tailoring was the one occupation where those émigrés at the least held their own against their American-born competitors. The county register of free persons of color does not state when Louis Mirault came to the United States, but he once owned nine slaves. Judging from his account book, he could read and write and had over forty customers, including some of the leading whites as well as Prince Candy, a well-situated free African American. At the time of his death in 1827 those customers owed him the substantial amount of $233.30; if this was representative of debts acquired annually, Mirault did quite well in his trade.[34] Joseph Dubergier, a fellow Haitian and parishioner at Saint John the Baptist Catholic Church, was a real estate owner and slaveholder; in 1806, his taxes were higher than any other African American, including Andrew Bryan.[35] The third member of the St. Domingue trio of tailors, Andrew Morel, also attended the Catholic church, owned valuable real estate, and was the master of slaves. An 1819 newspaper advertisement indicated that his real estate holdings included "A house suitable for a small family, with two rooms on the floor, with out-buildings all in good repair."[36]

By 1850, Morel owned three slaves and real estate that was assessed at $1,600, but further property gains eluded him because he died of dropsy on September 7, 1851, at the age of fifty-nine.[37] Richard Houstoun, one of the American-born tailors, signed a lease in 1807 to rent a lot from Richard M. Stites on which Houstoun would erect a small tailor shop, but later he was released from the agreement upon his request.[38] There is no other information about Houstoun's business transactions. We do not know, for instance, who his customers were, what kinds of transactions were conducted in his shop, or where he bought his materials and clothing. The answers to these and other relevant questions would help to draw a more complete picture of this tailor and his financial dealings. Information is available on his real estate and savings, and from these, it is evident that Richard Houstoun lived comfortably; therefore, he must have done well as a tailor. In his will, Houstoun left his pregnant wife, Nancy, $450 cash; Nancy, their infant daughter, Sarah, and their unborn child were left the family home on the corner of Broughton and Houston Streets in Washington Ward; his mother, Dolly, was left a small house and lot; and his two nephews were left $50 each. A year before his death, Houstoun's two parcels of real estate were assessed at $1,532, and he had two slaves, which his widow retained.[39]

The other successful American-born tailor, Simon Jackson, came to Savannah around 1796 and over the ensuing years established a fine reputation among whites, especially with the prominent lawyer, Richard M. Stites, who handled, and in many instances financed, Jackson's business transactions. In March 1812, for instance, Stites loaned Jackson fifty dollars to pay the fare for his wife, Susan, to travel to Charleston to close the deal on the purchase of property in Reynolds Ward. The next month Stites paid Thomas Young Smith, of Charleston, fifteen hundred dollars to purchase that property, and that May, Stites loaned Jackson ten dollars to pay the return fare for his wife's trip home to Savannah.[40] In the span of three months, therefore, Stites loaned Jackson considerably more than the fifteen hundred dollars needed to buy the property, but only charged him interest (8 percent annually) on fifteen hundred dollars.[41]

Jackson usually purchased his materials, buttons, and garments from New York and sold clothing as well as items that were worn on clothes. On June 11, 1812, he sold pantaloons, cloth, trimmings, buttons, linen, coats, vests, and other items to William H. Noble, a white customer, for $145.50.[42] The clothes were probably ordered from New York, which suggests that men also went to tailor shops to purchase ready-made garments. Jackson's home was always assessed at a relatively high value, when compared to real estate owned by other African Americans, and it stayed in the family until after the death of his widow, Susan, when it was sold in the late 1860s for $10,000.[43]

Most of the early black preachers in the community did quite well financially, but this resulted from their "industriousness," a frequently used term to compliment African Americans during the period, rather than because their churches paid them handsomely. Andrew Bryan, one of the largest black landowners in the Chatham-Savannah area, made his largest acquisition in August 1799 when he bought forty acres of land, with the buildings on them, from

Sarah Evans, a white female, for $428.57. Bryan was surrounded by prominent neighbors—Noble W. Jones and the estate of James Habersham—which suggests that this was choice country acreage.[44] Bryan had eight slaves to work his farm and several buildings that he rented; moreover, he owned a house and lot in Savannah.[45] This black preacher may have hired his slaves from time to time, or may even have allowed some of them to hire their time, a common practice among white slaveholders in the city as well as in the country.

Henry Cunningham did not own as much land or as many slaves as Bryan, but he lived comfortably, probably without receiving much support from his church. He purchased a large lot (sixty feet by ninety feet) at the corner of Broughton and Houston Streets in 1813 for one thousand dollars[46] and subsequently sold the southwest half to Richard Houstoun. When Houstoun's widow was unable to pay the taxes on this property, she sold it back to her pastor for nine hundred dollars and a pledge to pay the back taxes.[47] Cunningham always listed minister of the gospel as his occupation; he did not practice a trade and relied upon income derived from hiring his slaves—he had five at one time[48]—and from renting property, a source of income for many African Americans although none probably relied solely upon it. Since he did not leave a will, it cannot be determined whether he owned shares of stock in major companies in the city, and there are no church records to ascertain his salary.

The most affluent businessman was Francis Jalineau, a merchant from St. Domingue who lived in nearby Coosawhatchie, South Carolina, but attended church in Savannah, which had the nearest Catholic parish, Saint John the Baptist Catholic Church.[49] He owned property in Savannah as well as in Cuba. Since Jalineau did not live in Savannah, he does not appear on the register of free persons. He died on his schooner, en route to Barraca, Cuba, where he was making a permanent move, and left an estate that included a schooner, one lot in Greene Ward, two lots in Carpenter's Row (Trustee Garden), four slaves, and over three thousand dollars in cash.[50] The kinds of merchandise he handled are not indicated in the few extant documents, but his transactions must have required a relatively large amount of cash on hand.

The largest landowner of his day was Anthony Odingsells, although the value of his land was not assessed very high. Odingsells owned Little Wassaw Island, thanks to the generosity of his former owner, Charles Odingsells, who bequeathed the isolated island to him.[51] In addition to owning more land than any other African American, Odingsells was the only African American in the community to have a body of water named after him. When he moved to the island, the deep body of water adjacent to it was unnamed until Odingsells named it the Odingsell River.[52] Odingsells owned two hundred acres of pine land in the country and eight slaves in 1852, but almost a decade later he owned two thousand acres, thirteen slaves, thirty-five milch cows, fifty sheep, and seventy-five swine. Judging from the large number of milking cows, swine, and sheep, Odingsells probably produced milk, meats, hides, and wool commercially, which he may have sold to persons in neighboring settlements on White Bluff or to persons who came from White Bluff, Thunderbolt, Savannah, and surrounding areas, or he may have taken the milk and meats to the city market. Wool from the sheep and the hides may have found their way among the items exported from Savannah. Whether Odingsells exported the wool and hides directly or sold them to merchants cannot be determined, but the weight of the evidence leans toward the latter. These activities and his fishing endeavors probably kept Odingsells too busy to venture into the lumber business, even though the island was loaded with pine trees, which a recent survey has revealed were not subjected to heavy cutting during that period. He managed to keep his slaves until Sherman's army captured Fort McAllister where he had sent them to help build, and his island remained in the family until well beyond the Civil War.[53]

Given the proximity of the water, a number of African Americans fished for both subsistence and profit. Most of the commercial sale of fish, oysters, shrimp, crabs, and other seafoods occurred on the streets and in the city market. These seafoods ran a distant second, however, to the huge amount of garden produce that was sold commercially. In 1859, Chatham County produced more market-garden produce than any other county in Georgia, and much of this was grown by African Americans.[54]

Savannah provided an opportunity for African Americans to earn a living by selling a wide variety of produce which they had either raised on small plots of land or purchased from those who had grown them. A new city market was built on Ellis Square in 1827 to replace the old dilapidated one at the intersection of South Broad (presently Oglethorpe Avenue) and Barnard Streets. Pillars which extended around the four sides of the square supported the shingle roof structure, leaving an uncovered quadrangular space in which live poultry, fish, oysters, shrimp, crabs, and other foods were sold under the four covered sides. Sellers came from as far as fifty miles to market their produce, providing the market with a wide variety and large quantity of food. Beef, pork, and mutton cost $.62½ a pound, eggs $.15 a dozen, spring chickens $.25 a pair, and dressed fowls $.50 a pair. Everyone went to the market.[55]

White butchers who became upset over the presence of African Americans in their trade petitioned the city council to curb the practice, which resulted in the enactment of an 1824 ordinance banning African Americans from selling meats. Free African Americans construed the ordinance to exclude them from stalls in the market but not from selling meats elsewhere, which was a logical assumption judging from the title of the ordinance: "A Bill Entitled an Ordinance to Prohibit Free Persons of Colour From Purchasing Stalls in the Market, and Exposing Meats for Sale Therein . . ." A subsequent ordinance tightened the language to address this circumvention of the intent of the earlier ordinance— to exclude free African Americans as well as slaves from selling meats anywhere in the city—but free African Americans continued to sell meats, contending that the original ordinance permitted them. Finally, in 1829, the city council enacted yet another ordinance addressing the issue, in which they stated unequivocally that the 1824 ordinance prohibited African Americans from selling meats anywhere and that the 1826 ordinance was quite clear on this matter.[56] In spite of this trilogy of ordinances, African Americans continued to sell meats. This issue could not be resolved as long as most white consumers took greater interest in the availability of inexpensive meats than in the color of the butchers.

From time to time, complaints were also lodged against African

Americans who sold groceries. It was a general practice for some slaveholders to allocate small plots of land to their slaves for their personal use, and they had fowls, chickens, cows, swine, and all kinds of garden produce on those plots which provided much of the food consumed in the city. Slaves often sold groceries to free African-American grocery store owners who then sold the groceries to the general public, including many whites.[57] In some instances, however, slaves stole food and sold it to grocers[58] who did not bother to determine whether it had been stolen. Consumers of the groceries were even less interested in how they were obtained as long as they had not been stolen from them and their trade was not being challenged by black competitors.

One of the many legitimate suppliers of groceries was Toby Adams, a native of South Carolina, an ordained minister, member of First African Church, and a former slave who purchased his freedom in 1854. After purchasing his freedom, Adams leased a little farm on the west side of the city across the Ogeechee River on which he planted crops and pastured cattle. He hired a man (probably a slave) to plow the land and kept one regular employee. Adams sold cattle that were subsequently butchered for the market and milk from a wagon that his son usually drove; he cured hides that were picked up daily in Savannah; and he ran a market wagon. In order for Adams to have cleared enough annually to make his efforts worthwhile he had to gross at least $650 because his rent was $150 and the total wages paid his workers (excluding his son) should have been at least $175. These two significant items coupled with his other expenses—for example, food for his animals, supplies, and money for the hides—should have placed his expenses in the $400 range.[59]

William Claghorn had a less diversified business, but he may have had higher profits than Adams. According to the *Savannah Directory*, Claghorn, a charter member of Saint Stephen's Chapel and a master baker, operated a shop on the corner of Liberty and Habersham Streets.[60] If the 1860 census figures are accurate, his four thousand dollars' worth of real estate and two thousand dollars' worth of personal property[61] attest to the success of his bakery; certainly he had no peers in the black community. This thirty-six-year-old businessman was among the new generation of young African Americans who were destined to become community leaders.

Simon Mirault operated a confectionery, which was similar to the type business Claghorn operated, but his shop was located on the western side of Broughton Street near Whitaker Street, two blocks from the city market and on the other side of town from Claghorn's operation.[62] Mirault, the son of Louis the tailor, was thirty-seven years old in 1854 at which time he and his wife, Mary Jane, owned a slave and real estate that was assessed at fifteen hundred dollars.[63] Another young confectioner, James Hanscomb, who was thirty-two years old and a native South Carolinian, was reported to have owned real estate worth four thousand dollars in 1860.[64] Mirault and Hanscomb both pursued an occupation that was also practiced by females.

The economic opportunities of Mirault, Hanscomb, and the other free African-Americans males were very limited, but those of their mothers, wives, and daughters were even more restricted. Those females were in the unenviable position of outnumbering their male counterparts but having almost the same number of occupations available to them. Unlike the situation with many white females, social and economic pressures in free black households often forced nearly every adult free African-American female to work. A serious shortage of free males forced some females either to go unmarried, marry slaves, or become mistresses of white men. This social situation resulted in economic hardships for black females because African-American males were squeezed into the least financially rewarding segment of the economy. The low income earned from working in those jobs drove their wives into the job market to supplement the families' income. Jobs were not plentiful, however, since they were intended mainly for males; furthermore, some professions were not open to African Americans. This spelled additional trouble for free African-American females.[65]

The 49 free African-American males who appeared in the Register of Free Colored Persons in 1823 were listed as employed in eighteen different occupations; whereas the 107 females were listed as employed in twenty—only two more.[66] Hence, although females outnumbered males by a ratio of two to one, they did not possess a comparable range of opportunities in the job market. Even if the female list of occupations was expanded by adding such illegal and unrecognized occupations as teaching and prostitution, or by adding selling milk, which some females did but none listed, this disparity would not have changed significantly. Obviously, the economic burden of free black females was at least as heavy as that of any other group in black Savannah.

Although the size of the free African-American female work force increased and there were shifts among vocations, the nature of those jobs did not change over time, a situation similar to that of their male counterparts. Nevertheless, the dynamics of the job market for black females were more positive than they were for males. Black women fared about as well as their white counterparts, whereas black males did not fare as well as theirs. We learn from the list of occupations which females gave in 1823 that washer-woman (30) and seamstress (26) were the most common vocations; these were followed by cook (17), seller of small wares (11), house-keeper (5), shopkeeper (5), and nurse (4). In none of the remaining occupations were more than two persons employed.[67] The 1860 census contained significant changes in the vocational preferences (which probably resulted from the law of supply and demand): seamstress-dressmaker (121) replaced washerwoman (44) as the most numerous, with the latter moving to a distant second; domestic servant (32) and pastry cook (20) emerged as popular vocations; and the number of nurses (10) more than doubled. Teaching, prostitution, and selling milk were still not listed.[68]

More women sold fruits, cakes, and other foods in the streets and in the market than the figures in 1823 and 1860 reveal. Hawking, the name associated with this practice, was a long-standing popular practice. In 1812, the city council became so annoyed with black females spending time hawking that it passed a resolution indefinitely suspending the issuance of badges and ordered constables to incarcerate all African-American females caught "selling cakes [and] apples" without a badge. The council was evidently concerned that such activities made black women unavailable to nurse whites during the approaching "sickly season of the year," a situation that would have caused great suffering among whites if allowed to continue.[69] This resolution exposed the tenuous position of African Americans and demonstrated one of the ways whites placed their well-being above the concerns of African Americans, even in something as essential as the right to earn a living.

In spite of the disadvantages encountered in the job market, free African-American females were well represented among real estate owners in black Savannah. According to Loren Schweninger, African Americans placed great importance upon owning property, which they perceived as an indicator of prosperity and an important way to gain respect from whites. He further stated that "free women sought to acquire property as means of protection, economic independence, and self-sufficiency." This yearning was partially responsible for real estate ownership among black women in the South exceeding that of their male counterparts. In Savannah, the percentage of women among real estate owners was higher than the average in the South.[70]

The manner in which black women took advantage of the limited economic opportunities afforded may be understood better by identifying some of the successful individuals and the way they earned a living. Susan Jackson, Frances Carley, Phillis Hill, and Nancy Golding were among the early successful pastry cooks in the community. Susan Jackson is just one of several who owned valuable real estate in the city and had a thriving business. She was a charter member of Second African Baptist Church, having been among the initial group to whom Savannah Baptist Church granted dismissal letters allowing them to join Henry Cunningham, a free African-American preacher from McIntosh County, in this new venture. She was evidently a bright person who could handle business negotiations because in 1812 her husband, Simon Jackson, a successful free African-American tailor, sent her to Charleston to close the deal on a house and lot in Reynolds Ward which they were purchasing with a fifteen-hundred-dollar loan secured from Richard M. Stites, a prominent lawyer who handled legal matters for Simon Jackson. After her husband's death, Susan Jackson paid off the balance on the loan (about six hundred dollars), and she paid off a two-hundred-dollar loan that her late husband had contracted, thus allowing her to claim and retain ownership of her home. She earned the money from operating a pastry shop and renting real estate.

Susan Jackson died on January 12, 1862, at the age of eighty-two of heart disease,[71] a rare killer of Savannahians—white and black—during the period because that ailment is generally associated with old age, an experience that is common among today's four-generational society, but was not very common in the nineteenth century. During her long life, this remarkable woman found time to care for the aged mother of an old friend and fellow pioneer member of Second African Baptist Church, Richard Houstoun (a successful free African-American tailor), and to train his younger daughter, Richard Ann (Houstoun) Butler, in the pastry business.

Frances Carley's real estate was assessed at $1,000 in 1854 but it slipped to $700 in 1860[72] at which time she was seventy-five years old and had managed over the years to live comfortably by selling sweets. Phillis Hill owned four slaves in 1823. Nancy Golding, a Liberty County native, moved to Savannah in 1808 and joined the Independent Presbyterian Church in 1841. A huckster who changed to pastry cook, she was so successful that by 1854 her real estate in Yamacraw was assessed at $1,000 and four years later at $1,550, before taking a precipitous decrease in 1860, when the property was assessed at $550.[73] Since Nancy Golding owned the same property during those years, the assessed value reflected a decrease in property value rather than in the size of her holding. She, like Frances Carley, was among a small minority of black property owners whose real estate value declined in 1860, but none as much as Nancy Golding's.

Memories of "delicious ice-cream of the most popular flavors" purchased from Aspasia Mirault's bakery and confectionery on the northeast corner of Bull and Broughton Streets remained with William Harden years later. This shop "was well patronized by the white people" as Harden recalled, which enabled Aspasia, who left revolution-ravished St. Domingue in 1800, to live comfortably; she did experience financial problems at times—for instance, in 1847 when she failed to pay her taxes.[74] Georgia Conrad, the granddaughter of a former Georgia governor, patronized a different pastry cook but her compliments were just as laudatory as Harden's; she described the unnamed female as "the best cake maker and baker . . . whose fruit cakes had such a reputation that they were sent for from many places, England included."[75]

In the 1850s two younger women, Catherine Baty and Richard Ann (Houstoun) Butler, joined this group of older successful pastry cooks. Catherine Baty, who was born in 1801, owned real estate on Pierce Street in Oglethorpe Ward that was assessed at $1,000 in 1854 and at $1,150 in 1860.[76] Richard Ann, the younger daughter of Richard Houstoun, the tailor, was taught to bake by Susan Jackson and later married James Butler, a Liberty County carpenter, in 1842. A year later she gave birth to her only child, a baby girl, Margaret, who died at the age of three.[77] Richard Ann and James Butler must have made a good team because when he died in 1859 they owned the old Houstoun family home on Broughton and Houston Streets, which Henry Cunningham had bought from her mother, and at least three other houses that were rented.[78] She remained a faithful member of Second African Baptist Church throughout her life,[79] and judging from the inventory of her estate she lived a simple life—no gigs, buggies, horses, fine jewelry, or slaves even though she could have afforded them.[80]

Dressmakers, or seamstresses, were in greater demand than pastry cooks. Residents of black Savannah had gained a reputation for lavishly spending money on clothes, especially on so-called "Sunday clothes," which apparently irked whites and drove the local newspaper publisher to comment on how they were driven to "extravagant gratification" to satisfy their desire to dress up. He added "this ambition to dress is absolutely a disease."[81] The publisher probably exaggerated; they enjoyed wearing attractive clothes, but there was nothing abnormal about it.

The absence of a garment industry created a need for dress-makers, and a relatively large group of free black females were drawn to dressmaking. Several did quite well financially. Leah Simpson, a founding member of Second African Baptist Church, owned four slaves and real estate on Farm Street that was assessed at two thou-sand dollars in 1819; she bought a slave in 1820, but the value of her real estate dropped to eight hundred dollars. Catherine Deveaux of Antigua, one of the successful free African-American seam-stresses in the 1820s and 1830s, owned real estate in Greene Ward, the location of Second African Baptist Church, where her husband was a leader, and she subsequently purchased property in adjacent Columbia Ward and in Warren Ward.[82] Her property in Columbia Ward included a "Negro house" on the premises where her slaves, or some other slaves, probably stayed.

Some of the other successful seamstresses of her generation were Betsy Baptist, Manette Tardieu, Betsy Cunningham, Sarah Marshall, and Ann Morel. Betsy Baptist was brought to this country from Africa in 1795, but by 1837, she was free and owned one-half of a lot on which she had built a house assessed at five hundred dollars.[83] Manette Tardieu, who also came to this country in 1795, was a native of St. Domingue. Having come here free, unlike Betsy Baptist, she was able to acquire land more quickly and by 1810 her property was assessed at three hundred dollars.[84] It is difficult to separate the property holdings of the other successful seamstresses from those of their mates since they all had successful husbands. Elizabeth Cunningham was the wife of Henry Cunningham; Sarah Marshall was the third wife of Andrew Marshall; and Ann Morel was the wife of Andrew Morel, a tailor.

By the 1850s a new group of successful free African-American seamstresses in their forties, or younger, had emerged to augment the group comprised of their older contemporaries. Georgia Conrad saved Margaret Blodsett from oblivion when she opined Blodsett's dainty work "was not to be excelled."[85] Louisa Marshall learned to sew while she was single, and this skill became useful after her husband, Joseph Andrew Marshall, died just when his dray business had begun to flourish. Even though she was left in a comfortable state, Louisa's resources were insufficient to support her for the rest of her life at the level of comfort to which she had become accustomed. She was able, therefore, to use the money earned from sewing to supplement the income earned from her husband's estate. In 1858, her home was assessed at fifteen hundred dollars.[86]

Some of the others in this new generation were Hannah Cohen, Georgiana Guard, and Estelle Savage. Hannah Cohen was left in a comfortable financial state by her mother, Maria Cohen, who had inherited seven slaves from her husband, Richard, and had kept most of them until her death in the 1850s. Maria Cohen raised produce in her garden and probably sold it in the market, but Hannah was taught to sew. According to the 1860 census, Hannah's real estate was worth $1,000 and she owned a slave.[87] Unlike Hannah, Georgiana Guard followed the vocation of her mother, June Guard, a former seamstress. A member of the Independent Presbyterian Church, which she joined in 1843 at the age of twenty-three, Georgiana built upon the modest financial resources her mother had left, and in 1860, owned real estate assessed at $1,050 and one slave over twelve years of age.[88] Another of this new generation of seamstresses, Estelle Savage, was the oldest of three children (two girls and a boy) born to Phillis Savage from St. Domingue, but Estelle and her siblings were born in the United States. The two sisters were both seamstresses, but Estelle was more successful. In 1858, Estelle's real estate was assessed at $2,600, while her propertyless sister, Tharsville, and brother, John, lived rent free in houses their older sister owned.[89]

Sarah Black, the youngest of this new generation of successful seamstresses, was only in her mid-twenties in 1860; nevertheless, she owned a large lot outside the city limits on Gaston Street between Jefferson and Montgomery Streets on which she built two "good houses" and two "shanties," which were probably rented. As noted earlier, Sarah lived in a common-law arrangement with an out-of-town white cotton salesman. Living outside the city limits allowed Sarah to keep her cows on the premises; selling milk to the public enabled her to supplement the income received from sewing, her primary occupation.[90]

Rose Jalineau, another of the many émigrés from St. Domingue who came to Savannah and did quite well financially, had a benefactor, Francis Jalineau, who left her property in Cuba. In the 1830s, Rose, a seamstress, probably started to have financial problems, which forced the sale of valuable land in Greene Ward to High Cullen, a white man who paid one thousand dollars for it.[91] This was only a temporary solution to her financial woes; in 1844, failure to pay fifteen dollars in delinquent taxes resulted in the sheriff auctioning her property located at the corner of Congress and Price Streets, which was sold to Orlando A. Wood, Esquire, the highest bidder at three hundred dollars.[92] The seventy-seven-year-old Rose

Jalineau switched occupations in 1848 and turned to washing clothes and other articles for a living, which she continued to pursue until 1864 when she died propertyless at the age of ninety-three. She was buried in the Cathedral Cemetery,[93] along with other deceased Catholics, instead of in the cemetery that had been created for African Americans.

Rose's age was probably the major reason why she was unable to acquire real estate after 1848, but her new occupation, while popular among females, did not produce as many success stories as some of the other occupations, especially in view of the relatively large number of females that practiced it. The marginal skill washing required may account for what appears to have been droves of black women attracted to it, but their numbers kept wages low. Judging from the following description of how washing was done in those days, a rhythmic pounding noise must have filled the air on wash days:

> We took clothes out'n the suds, soaped them good and put them on the blocks and beat them with the battlin sticks, which were made lik a paddle. On wash days you could hear those battlin sticks pounding every which-way . . .[94]

Mary Spiers earned about as much as any washerwoman, and she had accumulated enough money in the 1820s to own five slaves and real estate assessed at four hundred dollars. Another washerwoman, Hannah Pray, owned a house and lot in North Oglethorpe Ward with fig and peach trees in the yard which the neighborhood children (black and white) climbed for their fruits when they were in season. Even though the property was only assessed at seventy dollars in 1847, she did not pay the taxes. In 1860 when the property value had increased to three hundred dollars, she nevertheless paid the higher taxes.[95]

Ann H. Gibbons was the most successful of the post-1850 free black females, but her life is something of a mystery. Although she had a daughter Claudia in 1820 and she owned the most valuable real estate among free African Americans in 1860, neither the father of her child nor the source of the money to purchase her property is known. Whereas her property holdings are listed in the tax digests and censuses, and her daughter is listed in the registers, her occupation(s) is missing from those documents. After appearing on the tax digest in 1833 as propertyless, she started to climb up the economic ladder in the 1840s, and by 1850, she declared two lots with dwellings and four slaves. In 1852, her slaves were assessed at twenty-two hundred dollars, placing her second to Anthony Odingsells, whose nine slaves were assessed at twenty-seven hundred dollars, among the small group of black slaveholders in the Chatham-Savannah area. In 1860, Ann Gibbons owned two lots in North Oglethorpe Ward, one in Middle Oglethorpe (with a total value of nine thousand dollars), and three prime slaves.[96]

In his 1848 census of Savannah, Joseph Bancroft maintained African Americans lived comfortably,[97] but Clement Eaton depicted free blacks in southern towns as living in "miserable shanties" in alleys behind "imposing white residences."[98] Both descriptions contain kernels of truth, but neither is completely accurate. In spite of its proscription by the state,[99] many free blacks owned real estate, with the assistance of their guardians, who usually acted as the primary parties in the purchase transactions. When Fanny Bryan, wife of Andrew Bryan, sold a parcel of land to Andrew Marshall, the following phrase appeared in the indenture: "This indenture made . . . between Fanny Bryan in the county and state aforesaid on the one part and Richard Richardson of the same place merchant on the other part . . ." who paid the fifty-dollar purchase price "for Andrew Marshall as his guardian and trustee . . ."[100] Similarly, when Henry Cunningham purchased the home of the Houstouns, the indenture was made "between James Morison for and on the part and in behalf of Henry Cunningham . . . for whom he is guardian . . . and James M. Wayne Guardian for the heirs of the later Richard Houstoun . . ."[101] If a free black had a steady source of income and desired to own real estate, the opportunity was there to purchase it.

Throughout the period, free blacks took advantage of the opportunity to purchase property, but a higher percentage of these persons did so before 1830 than afterwards, although the value of the real estate owned by African Americans was greater after 1830 than it was previously. In 1820, thirty-six African Americans each owned homes that were assessed at a minimum of $200, and the total value of that property was $31,250. Women homeowners (21) composed a majority of this group, their holdings totaling $17,760, or 56 percent of the total for both groups.[102] In 1823, sixty-four African Americans were homeowners, and the assessed values did not change appreciably.[103] A quarter of a century later, the number had dropped to fifty-seven. The total assessed value of the homes of African Americans in 1848 was $23,190 which was a relatively small amount and reflected the modest sized homes and other dwellings that they owned. Andrew Marshall owned the most valuable real estate, which had an assessed value of $3,750. The median assessed value of homes that year was $200.[104] Within two years, the total value of real estate owned by African Americans increased by $5,660 to $28,850.[105]

The number of free African-American homeowners decreased to forty-three in 1858. This figure included two foreign-born blacks. But whereas the number of homeowners had decreased considerably, the number whose real estate was assessed at a minimum of $1000 increased to eighteen,[106] which continued the large increase of the 1820 figure, which was seven, over the one in 1810, which was four. During the period after 1830, while the number of free African-American (male and female) homeowners decreased, the number of females in the higher bracket increased. For instance, only three females owned homes that were assessed at $1,000 in 1820, one of them, Rachel Marshall, was fronting for her husband, but in 1858 seventeen of the nineteen homeowners in that category were women. They owned real estate valued at a total of $37,750, which was nearly 90 percent of the total assessed value ($41,950) of property owned by this group of black homeowners.[107]

Similarly, there was a wide disparity between mulatto and nonmulatto homeowners. Free mulattoes in Chatham County outnumbered free nonmulattoes 496 to 229 in 1860, but the former outnumbered the latter among homeowners in the one-thousand-dollar-or-more range fifteen to one. Furthermore, the numerical superiority of mulattoes among free African-American property owners in the lower category—property (real and or personal) assessed between one hundred dollars and one thousand dollars—was almost as great as in the one thousand dollar and higher group (which included real estate only) since 84 of the 101 persons in this category were mulatto.[108] In short, mulattoes owned most of the property in black Savannah. In the absence of information to the contrary, mulatto domination of all economic categories may have resulted from a combination of factors: good fortune, generous sponsors, hard work, and, most important, the predilection of whites to patronize them.[109]

Judging from the figures stated above, color made a difference in the life chances of residents in black Savannah. Whether by design or happenstance, it was costly to be black even in the black community. The slave population was overwhelmingly black—in 1860 slightly over 9 percent of the 14,807 slaves in the Chatham County were mulatto. Conversely, the free African-American population of 725 was predominantly mulatto—slightly over 68 percent. That year the census did not classify African Americans in Savannah by color, but it is reasonable to assume that Savannah's slave population of 7,712 included most of the 1,378 mulatto slaves in the Chatham County. There is reason to conclude, moreover, that economic prosperity and manumission were more difficult for blacks to achieve than for mulattoes.

Free African Americans continued to own real estate throughout the period, but a proportionately smaller number owned property in 1860 than in 1823. In the latter year, there were 64 black homeowners among the 572 free African Americans in the general population;[110] in 1860, the population increased to 735, but the number of black homeowners decreased to 36.[111]

What caused this? There are a number of factors which collectively contributed to this situation. For instance, the influx of European immigrants into Savannah during the antebellum period resulted in a shortage of affordable low-priced homes. When demand for a commodity increases but the supply does not keep pace, a price increase ensues. Just at the time when houses were becoming more expensive, hence more difficult to purchase, some African Americans were falling on hard times. Some died intestate, and the state sold their property. Some were victims of one or more of the panics that hit the American economy in 1837 and 1857. Finally, the racial climate became more hostile for African

Americans in the aftermath of the following: the Missouri Compromise debate (1820), which polarized the nation over the slavery issue; the publication of *The Appeal to the Colored Citizens of the World* by David Walker in 1829, which bitterly denounced slavery and called for action to overthrow it, causing the South to become more tense over the slavery issue; and the Nat Turner Slave Revolt (1831), which resulted in the death of sixty whites and led to passage of more restrictive laws in many states. These events collectively contributed to a white backlash in the South that was not favorable to black economic progress.

As alluded to earlier, slaveholders lived in the black community, but the practice was not pervasive. In 1860, for instance, the nine black slaveholders owned a total of 19 slaves, which constituted a small fraction of the 14,807 slaves in the Chatham-Savannah area; except for Anthony Odingsells, who lived on Little Wassaw Island and owned 8 slaves in 1860, no African American owned more than two slaves.

Black slaveholders were interested in owning slaves primarily to help work in their enterprises, which accounts for the seeming anomaly of a slaveholding washerwoman. The available information for Savannah does not indicate that black-owned slaves performed personal services for their master as their primary duty. This was in marked contrast to the situation in Charleston where black-owned slaves were used as personal servants.[112] The differences between the two groups of black slaveholders may have resulted more from socioeconomic differences between the two black communities than from attitudinal differences toward the use of slaves. The black community of Charleston was much older, more affluent, and more aristocratic than its sister community in Savannah, and Charleston's free African Americans had been more successful in narrowing the gap in the standard of living between themselves and whites than black Savannahians had been.

Andrew Bryan was among the minority of black slaveholders who owned relatives. In April 1804, Bryan purchased a female slave named Hannah and her twenty-month-old son named Carolina for $450, and the following August, he sold them to Adam Whitefield, a free African-American butcher and member of First African

Church, for only ten dollars, "Upon the express condition that said Hannah and Carolina shall not be under the control and management of no one but themselves and shall pay no other or further wages per annum to said Adam Whitefield than twenty-five cents."[113] Hannah, Bryan's only child, was Whitefield's wife. A year after purchasing his daughter and grandson, Bryan purchased a slave female named Rachel for $500.[114] This is probably the same female who is listed on the 1809 tax list as the wife of Andrew Marshall,[115] Bryan's nephew and subsequent executor of his estate, and she was purchased as a favor to him. There is no indication that Bryan's five remaining slaves were relatives.

The tax digest for 1810 has information about black slaveholders that did not appear in earlier tax digests and allows a closer look at the identity of the slaveholders and the size of their holdings. In 1810, there were sixteen black slaveholders but none had more than four slaves; the total number of slaves was thirty-two. All the slaveholders were American-born, except African-born Hester Gunn, who owned two slaves.[116] In 1813, the number of slaveholders increased to seventeen, with males outnumbering females nine to eight, but the total number of slaves owned slipped to twenty-nine. Both the number of slaveholders and their total number of slaves increased in 1820, when there were nineteen slaveholders, including five who were foreign-born (three from St. Domingue and one each from Africa and Martinique), and fifty-three slaves.[117] Several years later, the number of slaveholders had increased to twenty-two, including seven who were foreign-born (five from St. Domingue and one each from Africa and Antigua), and sixteen who were females. The total number of slaves was fifty-eight, and seven slaveholders had at least five slaves, headed by Anthony Odingsells who had ten. The black masters worked either in the building trades, or in personal service, except Odingsells who was a fisherman and a farmer; the black mistresses usually were seamstresses, pastry cooks, and washerwomen.[118]

The increases in the number of slaveholders and their slaves ended in the 1830s when slight decreases began to occur and continued in the 1850s and 1860s. The total number of black-owned slaves decreased in 1837 to forty-four, but even more significant decreases occurred in 1850 when both the tax digest and the census recorded eighteen slave owners, and the digest recorded thirty-six slaves. The United States census taker(s) incorrectly reported fifty-eight slaves that year as a result of crediting slaves living in shanties on the property of free blacks as belonging to those persons. In 1860, the number of black slaveholders dropped to one-half the 1850 total.[119]

In the late antebellum period, therefore, African-American slave-holders sustained losses similar to those of the homeowners, and partly for the same reasons, but there was another dimension. The loss of slaves occurred at a time when the demand for slaves was high in Savannah and prices were subject to fewer fluctuations than in Baltimore, Washington, and New Orleans.[120] Obviously there were slaves available to be purchased. While Georgia did not proscribe blacks from owning slaves, the practice was never popular among a segment of whites who did not believe it comported with their image of blacks and reflected badly upon poor whites. Whites did not exhibit much distaste for black homeowners. Hence, black slave-holders experienced more pressures than any other group of black property owners, which took their toll over years, as it became diffi-cult for African Americans in Savannah to purchase slaves just as it was for them elsewhere in the region. Throughout the South, whites were not inclined to sell slaves to blacks. Consequently, there were fewer black slaveholders in 1860 than in 1823, and the total value of the slaves was also down. Black slaveholders were, thus, victims of tightening economic conditions and racial prejudice. Throughout the period, however, two constants prevailed: (1) female slaveholders outnumbered males, and (2) foreign-born blacks were more promi-nent among the slaveholders than among the homeowners.

The origin of slaveholding among black Savannahians is unclear since the first black slaveholder in Savannah has never been identified. Since many black slaveholders in the late 1790s and early 1800s were either African natives or had parents who were African natives, they were probably familiar with seeing blacks owning other blacks, but the circumstances were different. No black in Savannah came to that city as a slave of another black; rather, black slaveholders either received their slaves as a gift, or purchased them.

The largest number of slaves ever received as a gift by an African American in the community was the nine which Charles Odingsells bequeathed to Anthony Odingsells, who was his slave at the time.[121] Jack Harris, a free African American, left his wife three slaves;[122] Jack Gibbons left his wife five slaves; Prince Candy left his wife seven slaves; and Maria Cohen left her daughter a slave butcher and a forty-three-year-old female slave.[123] One of the earliest transactions involving the purchase of a slave by a black after the Constitution was ratified occurred in June 1790, when London Dolly purchased a female slave and her son for five shillings.[124] A little over a decade and a half later, Simon Jackson sold Richard M. Stites a thirty-year-old mulatto cook for $200[125] in one of the rare instances when a black sold a slave to a white. Earlier that year, Francis Jalineau purchased a male slave for $448,[126] and sold him to Jackson for $450 two years later, the same year that Quash Dolly, London's brother, paid $400 for a forty-two-year-old male slave.[127] In June 1811, Henry Cunningham purchased a male slave and subsequently sold him to Andrew Marshall, who kept him until the seventy-year-old slave died in August 1835.[128] This was the last slave that Marshall owned. Louis Mirault purchased a female slave for $800 in 1818, and Anthony Odingsells sold one of his female slaves in 1833.[129]

There is sufficient information to determine the manner in which slaves were acquired, the number of slaves blacks owned, and, in some instances, the age and sex of black-owned slaves. One can also determine from the documents the kinds of work those slaves performed, assuming they worked with their owners when no occupation is given. Determining, however, the treatment of slaves by their black owners is far more challenging.

Black slaveholders in Savannah probably did not mistreat their slaves. Local newspapers and published journals of visitors to antebellum Savannah, which vented their displeasure with other alleged inappropriate behavior among African Americans and could be expected to comment on any abuse of slaves, were silent on the subject.[130] Other circumstantial factors support this conclusion: these slaves were kept in the city where treatment of slaves, generally, was better than in the country; food was plentiful, so slaves should have been well nourished; and slaves in the city were clothed better than their country sisters and brothers.[131]

In spite of their noteworthy accomplishments, the leading property owners in black Savannah were not as affluent as their counterparts in other cities in the South. In fact, a couple of free African Americans in other Georgia communities owned property valued above that possessed by the largest property owners in black Savannah. For instance, Solomon Humphries of Macon owned property valued at twenty thousand dollars, including several slaves; and James Boisclair of Dahlonega, the wealthiest African American in the state, owned the town's largest general store, an ice house, and a gold mine—the Free Jim Mine. Similarly, in Charleston many members of the Brown Society were wealthier than the principal property owners in black Savannah, including Jehu Jones who owned the best hotel in that city. Moreover, William Ellison of Stateburg, South Carolina, the wealthiest African American outside Louisiana in 1860, owned a cotton gin business and over sixty slaves. New Orleans had the largest group of free African-American property owners in the South.[132]

Black Savannah did not have residents who were as wealthy as the persons mentioned above. The diversified economy, access to white consumers, mulatto dominance of wealth, high visibility of women among homeowners, and slight decline in economic fortunes that ensued in the late antebellum period were similar, however, to the general picture Loren Schweninger painted of the Lower South. There was a sufficient flow of income in black Savannah to support community development through the financial assistance provided to the independent black church, civic organizations, and social activities while simultaneously satisfying the ongoing subsistence demands of individuals, thus obviating the need to rely upon whites for assistance. This display of independence caught the attention of whites and fostered self-help. The income generated was spread widely enough to produce a sizable group of free African-American property owners. In short, in spite of the adversity visited upon them by the denial of citizenship, the double standard of justice, and restrictions in the job market, free African Americans gained affluence and autonomy.

CHAPTER IV

A Middle Ground between Slavery and Freedom

They [City Negroes] admit into four classes: family servants, or those who belong to families which they serve; hired servants, or those who are hired out by their owners to wait in families, or to any other service; servants who hire their own time, and work at various employment and pay their owners so much per day or month; and watermen, embracing, fishermen, sailors, and boatmen.

—CHARLES C. JONES, *RELIGIOUS INSTRUCTION OF NEGROES IN THE UNITED STATES*

When plantation slavery is discussed, the slaves usually fall into two categories: field hands and house servants, with the latter being considered as the elite among slaves. There were no field hands among the slaves who lived and worked in Savannah, but many slaves performed manual labor either in their masters' homes, on docks, in small businesses, or in industrial enterprises. Savannah's slaves were given far more latitude and had a wider range of employment options and greater challenges and rewards than their brothers and sisters in the country. Simply mentioning, however, that Savannah's slaves were better off than rural slaves understates the difference in the economic experiences of the two groups of slaves, especially the experiences of a highly visible element of slaves in Savannah who hired their own time. The mechanism of social control was less confining. They were persons more than they were property; they managed their lives instead of having others manage them. Their lives were invigorated, moreover, by living in their own households, which was an improvement over the situation for the rest of the slave population, especially for the country slaves. In short, they occupied a de facto legal status, a middle ground between slavery and freedom.

Slaves in Savannah lived, ate, and were clothed better than those in the country. Consider the dialogue between the slave Patrick Snead and his master over the replacement of the slave's old tools, which resulted in the owner demanding that Snead purchase his own tools since the slave dressed better then he.[1] It seemed to have been out of character for a master to admit that his slave wore better clothes than he; thus this may have been an exaggeration. The slave probably spent more money on clothes than his master wanted him to, and as a means of getting this point across, the master made the slave buy his tools. The master thus sent this message to his slave: the consequences of looking like a freeman is that you must assume the responsibilities of a freeman and buy your own tools. Normally plantation slaves would not have been faced with this problem because their masters provided clothes and tools. This is just one of many differences that existed between city and country slaves.

The slave population of Savannah was quite diverse. It ranged from the "nominal slaves," who were allowed to hire their own time and live almost as freemen away from the supervision of their master, to whom they paid a stipulated sum periodically, to the slaves who lived and worked on the premises of their Savannah masters. Between these two groups were runaway slaves, some of whom formed colonies outside the city limits, while others lived low-profile lives, hiding inconspicuously among the city's black population; and the transient slaves who entered Savannah to perform a specific task, or errand, and left the city immediately after its completion. A relatively small group of slaves accompanied their visiting owners and stayed overnight, or for a few days; a much larger group came to Savannah to embark upon Africa-bound ships of the American Colonization Society, whose length of stay was contingent upon the arrival and departure schedule of the Society's ship; a still larger group of slaves was brought to Savannah to be sold. These slaves (transients, runaways, visiting, and prospective slave trade subjects) were not counted in either the city census reports or those of the federal government, and their number is difficult to ascertain, but not their presence in Savannah.

The slave population of Savannah, therefore, was fluid. Some had roots in the city, and others merely passed through it; some walked the streets by day as they worked, and others, to avoid detection because of their illegal status, came out only at night when it was difficult to see them clearly. Thus, there seemed to have been a constant flow of slaves; some with faces and some, figuratively speaking, without. For the faceless ones, this was more by design than because whites looked past them.

Slaves comprised the overwhelming majority of the residents in black Savannah. In 1810, slaves outnumbered free African Americans four to one (2,195 slaves and 530 free blacks),[2] and in 1850 the ratio had increased to more than nine to one (6,231 slaves and 686 free blacks).[3] If the slaves who were there either illegally, on a visit, or on an errand were added to the officially authorized permanent slave inhabitants of the community in 1850, the combined total of African Americans on a given day would have increased enough to push the black population nearer, if not pass, 8,395, the size of the white population of Savannah. Whites were certainly aware of the situation and complained about the large number of unsupervised slaves,[4] but authorities tolerated the situation, as well they should have since whites had created it.

As late as the 1840s some of the slaves in Savannah had been born in Africa, but the number is unknown. Margaret Stiles, a relative of the Habersham family through marriage, recalled how one of the family's slaves was the daughter of an African king. Another family in the city had two African-born slaves who disliked each other, the female frowning whenever the male was in her presence. After this had continued for a while, her owner asked the slave why she acted that way and she replied: "Him gran'pa eat my gran'pa."[5] Margaret Stiles may not have quoted the female accurately, and if the slave really said so, the incident may have been fictitious, but the hostility between the two slaves and its African origin was probably on the mark, for some of the Old World rivalries and antipathies survived the African deracination.

Savannah was the major slave trading center in Georgia. Most of the speculators came to Savannah the night before the slave auction and stayed at the Pulaski House, which had a slave pen beneath it. Slaves were also placed in a facility on Habersham and Bryan Streets.[6] The other hotels and boarding houses in town where traders may have stayed were the City Hotel, the Mansion House, Susan Platt's Boarding House, and Richardson's Boarding House. The Slave Mart was located in a big building on Bryan Street across from the city market.[7]

One of the major events immediately prior to the antebellum period that had an impact on slave prices was the War of 1812. In February 1815, the average price for 100 slaves sold by the marshal for the District of Georgia was $264.80 each. A year later, the average price for 142 slaves sold in that same district was $312.60 apiece, an increase of roughly 18 percent which was considerable. During the same period, food prices rose 100 percent.[8] Even though the increase in food prices was temporary, the black community probably benefited from it because African Americans were among the major food providers for the city.[9]

Some slaveholders did well from the sale of their slaves, and slave traders did not do badly either since they received a 2.5 percent commission for each transaction. While the following transaction involving slaves of Pierce Butler was the exception, it shows the magnitude of the investment which some masters made in slaves. In March 1859, W. F. Parker, a Savannah slave trader, was commissioned to sell 436 of Butler's slaves and he succeeded in selling 399 for a total price of $287,657 which pleased the trader and, he hoped, Butler. The unsold slaves were taken to Parker's office.[10] The sale price of those slaves was seven times greater than the total assessed value of black-owned property (real and personal) in the community, which was $38,515 in 1852.[11] Even if the personal property owned by slaves in 1852 were added to the total of black-owned property, Butler's payoff in 1859 would still have been seven times greater. This is astounding. Butler's sale was the largest one conducted for an individual by Parker, but the next

January he was commissioned to sell 250 slaves.[12] If this slave trader's volume of slaves was typical, or almost typical, of the kind of business traders handled, Savannah must have buzzed with slave trading at times.

Savannah was an open city to some degree, with African Americans moving in and out during daylight hours apparently with little interference from authorities. Movement within the city was even less inhibited. Evidence of the relative openness of the city is found in the narrative of the fugitive slave Moses Roper, who while admitting that Savannah authorities were "always looking out for run-away slaves," managed to go "through the main street with apparent confidence, though much alarm." Roper was only a temporary resident of Savannah because he succeeded in catching a ship that sailed to the North.[13] Many other runaways stayed longer.

Between 1844 and 1846, an unidentified Savannah hotel registered fifty slaves that traveled to Savannah with their owners. In most instances the owners were female travelers who were accompanied, sometimes, by their children,[14] which probably accounts, in some instances, for the slaves' presence on the trips. During the 1840s and 1850s, moreover, planters traveled to Savannah in wagon trains containing as many as one hundred wagons loaded with cotton and pulled by four- and six-mule teams whose slave drivers looked forward to the four-week trip to Savannah. The slaves usually returned home with salt, other supplies, and tall tales about their stay in the city.[15] M. Dennis, an Eatonton, Georgia, general merchant, frequently sent his slaves to Savannah with wagons to get goods and supplies.[16] Slaves also came in boats with their masters who visited Savannah on business and pleasure trips.[17] These slaves thus joined the legion of others who came for similar reasons as well as those who came to sell produce and small wares, those who came looking for work, those who came seeking transportation to a free region, those who were brought to the Slave Mart, and those who accompanied their masters, or mistresses, on business trips and vacations in swelling the slave population of the city.

The city had a number of conveniences for slaves. Food was inexpensive and plentiful in the city market: rice could be purchased for six cents a quart, flour for four cents a pound, coffee for twelve and one-half cents a pound, and sugar for five cents a pound.[18] Stores were available to buy good clothing.[19] Entertainment and liquor were available in taverns. Although the sale of liquor to slaves was illegal, tavern owners ignored the law.[20] There were confectioneries with tasty ice cream and other sweets; Saturday night amusements: partying, dancing, and female company; rides along the Thunderbolt Road; parades; swimming in the Savannah River; and the opportunity to meet with friends and hang out in the streets, even though complaints from whites made this hazardous at times.[21]

On the negative side was an unusual health statistic that concerned African Americans who permanently resided in the city. Those blacks apparently suffered from a higher rate of malaria attacks than those in the country. According to Richard Arnold, a highly regarded Savannah physician, the only cases of malaria he ever treated among blacks—and it was a mild form—"were solely among city Negroes."[22] Arnold did not state reasons, medical or otherwise, for the difference, but it may have resulted from the greater exposure of city African Americans to carriers of the disease among the throng of people who annually visited Savannah. There is little medical reason to conclude that the few miles that separated country African Americans (free and slave) from city ones could have profoundly affected their immune system.

Urban slavery has received attention from scholars, and the differences between urban slaves and their country relatives have been accurately chronicled. For instance, city slaves dressed, ate, and generally were housed better than country slaves. Furthermore, work was less arduous in the city, slave hiring was more pervasive,[23] women had a lower fertility rate, and children were a greater liability.[24] This was true throughout the South. Slave codes were similar, but implementation varied among slave-owning households. Pragmatism was the guiding principle governing implementation of the slave codes, with some owners giving their slaves more latitude than others. A recurring theme in Savannah was the willingness of masters to forego the services of their slaves in return for suitable monetary compensation from either other whites, or from the slaves themselves. The records have not revealed, however, any instances where free African Americans hired slaves from whites.

Slaves who lived with their masters were provided space in town houses, or they were placed in quarters at the rear of the property near narrow alleys or lanes which the slaves converted into convenient exits when they wished to escape the surveillance of their masters. At night, the lanes and alleys became almost as busy as Bay Street was during the day as slaves moved about the city.[25] The slaves used those lanes and alleys to escape the night patrol that roamed the city looking for African Americans who were not authorized to be out after dark, but it was generally conceded that those patrols were ineffective, and persons composing them were usually indifferent to discharging their responsibilities professionally and conscientiously. Both slaveholders and slaves knew of the patrol's ineptness; still, slaves could not afford to be careless or to press their luck.

The percentage of the legitimate slave population of Savannah that was allowed to live away from their masters is not known, but it was considerable, a situation which consistently concerned many whites. In the early 1780s, the grand jury complained that African Americans had occupied most of the available housing in Savannah, leaving scarcely any for whites,[26] and in 1796, the grand jury recommended that the city act to prevent slaves from living alone in houses.[27] This recommendation went the way of many others that touched on the behavior of African Americans in Savannah—it was ignored—and the practice continued unabated. The practice may have even become more pervasive in the nineteenth century because in 1848 Bancroft reluctantly tailored his census to the actual living arrangements in Savannah:

> In taking the present Census the plan was adopted of enumerating the slave population in their places on abode, without recourse to owners . . . Under the System so much in vogue at the present time of permitting this class of our population to live in streets and lanes by themselves, it has proved more reliable than depending upon owners for returns.[28]

Bancroft conceded that because slaves were allowed to live away from their masters' premises, slave owners knew neither the whereabouts

nor the number of their slaves. A female slave who rented from
Stites was said to have kept "a great many boarders and sels [*sic*]
anything for profit."[29] Apparently the slave was not an angel; in
spite of this, her master did not reassert control over her living
arrangement. Rena Floyd, who enjoyed the privilege of living away
from the supervision of her owner, probably also had boarders
because she rented three shanties that her mistress owned[30] which
collectively exceeded the space this slave needed for her personal
use. Simon Middleton, another of the slaves who can be docu-
mented from the Southern Claims Commissioner's files, rented
from a free African-American female who charged him eight dollars
monthly for her fenced three-acre place with a stable, cook house,
hog pen, and fodder on Montgomery Street near Anderson Street.
The slave kept the buildings in good repair and collected rent from
a white tenant and neighbor for his absentee landlord.[31]

Slaves followed several lifestyles and formed minisocieties such
as campers, who were mainly runaway slaves and who created self-
sufficient camps on the outskirts of the city, and the alley dwellers,
who lived in alleys within the city. The alley dwellers probably were
mainly slaves from outside the city who came there looking for work
and were either unable to afford housing or unable to find any. This
group was augmented by slaves who were in the city temporarily
while awaiting transportation to Liberia. The alley dwellers were
not separated either physically, socially, or economically from other
blacks in the city and did not create separate lifestyles analogous to
those slaves in Washington, D.C., whom James Borchert has
analyzed.[32] The campers, on the other hand, created new societies.
One is tempted to categorize the alley dwellers and campers as
subcommunities within the larger black community, but the
commonality of their color, culture, and church membership indicate otherwise.

Slave campers, who welcomed shelter-seeking runaway slaves
into their minicommunities, bought and sold goods, practiced
trades, and occasionally defiantly used weapons against authorities
who tried to search the camps for runaway slaves.[33] A camp of
runaway slaves established near Fort Jackson in the 1850s was well
provided with beef, pork, whole hogs, and produce, which the slaves

allegedly stole from nearby plantations. The camp also had cooking utensils and musical instruments, which probably were played to entertain camp residents and others who might have come to the camp, as well as a market where food items were exchanged. A police detachment raided the camp in February 1855, arrested four of its slave inhabitants, and placed them in jail until their masters claimed them,[34] but otherwise left the camp undisturbed. This suggests that the authorities, who had the capability to destroy the camp, accepted this style of life among slaves as long as they did not threaten the status quo.

Slaves in the city dressed at least as well as poorer whites, and house servants dressed better than slave millworkers and stevedores.[35] Some slaveholders took extra pride in dressing house servants well because their dress was seen as a status symbol. For example, Coomba Johnson, who was selected from among two hundred slaves on a Bryan County plantation to be Ellen Buchanan Screven's nurse, was subsequently brought to Savannah where her mistress began to "civilize" her. One can sense the pride which swelled in Coomba's mistress as she stated in her autobiography how the slave nurse wore outfits made of calico instead of from the homespun cloth used to make slaves' clothes on the plantation back home. The stately, well-dressed Coomba was often complimented whenever she accompanied her mistress on trips, which seemed to have delighted the mistress.[36]

Living in the city placed slaves in position to work in a wide variety of jobs. There were the usual male jobs: personal services—barber, cook, hairdresser, butler, coachman, waiter, and groom; building trades—carpenter, cooper, sawyer, brickmason, whitewasher, and plasterer; land transportation; and marine occupations—waterman, boatman, fisherman, steward, and pilot. There were also jobs in mills and factories and on the docks. Slave females had numerous opportunities to work as maids, cooks, washerwomen, seamstresses, and midwives.[37] Some of the jobs which slaves worked had become identified as "colored jobs"; hence, they monopolized them.

Georgia was one of the few states that allowed slave fishermen to own boats, which had to be registered annually with the local authorities. The 1790 law required slaves who owned boats or other vessels to register them with the county clerk by giving the size of the vessels and the number of hands that worked on them.[38] At the time the law was passed, Savannah's slaves were its primary beneficiaries because they lived in the state's major seaport town. Those slaves who did not own boats were not shut off from making a living in marine jobs and on the docks. The sight of half-naked slaves toiling in the hot sun rolling hogsheads of rum up the steep incline of the bluff was a common, though depressing, scene in Savannah.[39]

The summer heat may have taken a heavy toil on slave stevedores, but summer was normally the least demanding time for many other slaves. According to a former slave, he worked from 6:00 A.M.–7:00 P.M. in the summer, which was a longer workday than the 6:00 A.M.–6:00 P.M. hours worked in the winter, but he lifted fewer bales of cotton in his master's wholesale store in the summer. In the fall and spring, that slave worked from 6:00 A.M. to midnight.[40] The long hours are indicative of the heavy workload of the slave. Another slave recalled that his master left him to fend for himself in the summer while the master was away from the city. One summer, the slave decided to grow rice on his master's plantation, located about three miles outside the city limits, to earn some money. Since he was a city slave, however, he did not know how to plant and harvest the rice: "All I knew about it, was the little information I could get from seeing the Negroes raise here and there a small piece for themselves." The slave must have been a fast learner because he grew enough rice to make $5.00 to $6.00 from selling it in the city, where his master normally lived, for $1.25 per hundred pounds.[41] Many other Savannah slaveholders left the city in the summer and some of them did just as the owner mentioned above. For instance, Alexander Steel, a Savannah slave, claimed he was the favorite slave of a master who visited the North every summer without leaving any chores for him.[42]

Just as some plantation slaves were allowed to work in their small gardens after chores were completed, so were some city slaves allowed to moonlight after finishing their chores. Sam Knight raised livestock, grew produce, and sold them in the city after he finished his work day.[43] Larry Williams from Beaufort, South Carolina, a patternmaker and millwright, was not allowed to hire his own time, but his master permitted him to work at his trade after the slave had finished working ten hours a day for him.[44] John Cuthbert, a slave carpenter, worked for his master during the day and worked for himself when he had finished with his master's approval. Cuthbert, who made tables and other furniture, "ketched" them to the market where they were sold; moreover, he cultivated a big garden, which his master gave him, and raised pigs and chickens.[45]

Cato Keating and Francis Keaton had uncommon working arrangements. Keating did not moonlight because his work experience was atypical of the kind of working arrangement that is traditionally associated with slaves. Keating's owner paid his slave, a South Carolina native, to supervise a free African-American teenager and the other workers in his three mills. Even after one of the mills had closed, the slave foreman continued to receive his weekly wage. Keating received four dollars each week, which was much less than his master would have paid a white foreman, but it was considerably more than slaves normally received for their labor, and the arrangement was beneficial to both the master and his slave.[46] Keaton, one of mayor Edward C. Anderson's slaves, occasionally received wages from his master, who did something else that was unconventional: during Anderson's absence from the city each summer, Keaton was allowed to hire his own time and keep the wages.[47]

A considerable portion of the slave population did not work on the premises or in the enterprises of their masters but were rented out to work for others who, in turn, compensated the masters for their slaves' labor. An agreement concerning the hiring out of the slave Rebekah Bostic is typical of the formal slave hiring transactions. The slave was given two suits of clothes (one summer and one winter), a blanket, hat, and a pair of shoes by the person who hired him, and that person also paid $25 to Bostic's masters;[48] even though the contract did not state the duration of the agreement, judging from other indentures it probably covered twelve months. Godfrey Barnsley charged $85 for a male slave to work from December 25, 1845, to December 25, 1846, and the hirer had to provide the slave with a summer suit, two winter suits, one hat, one blanket, and two pairs of shoes. Barnsley hired two other slaves for the same length of time but one for $79 and the other $76. Thus, that year those three slaves earned a total of $240.[49] Furthermore, in what must have been an unusual case, an owner sold his slave, then subsequently hired him from the new owner who was paid $30 a month for the slave to perform his old duties of driving the carriage, taking care of the horses and carriage, and occasionally waiting on the family. The new owner had bought the slave to hire him out; the old owner got into a bind because the arrangements for a replacement did not materialize.[50]

In other instances, the agreements were less formal and the compensation varied according to the situation. When Richard M. Stites hired his slaves, they worked for short periods—less than a month—hence the agreements included food and drink but not clothes, blankets, shoes, and other nonmonetary compensation. These agreements were less formal, but just as binding; moreover, he did not charge a standard fee for all slaves. In 1806, he rented a slave carpenter to work at Cedar Hammock for $16.00 plus food and drink. In 1810, Stites hired slaves to Lemuel Kollock on six occasions. The slave, who worked on a wagon and took two loads of rice to town, brought in $4.00 a day for his work, while the one who took a load of manure to Kollock's plantation brought in $2.00 a day. In November 1811, a slave was hired for two days at $.50 a day, but in October 1812, Stites hired a slave boy and a wagon team to Paul Howard, a fellow lawyer, to move his furniture from Bryan County to Savannah and charged $16.00 (including a $1.00 ferry-charge reimbursement) for the three days that Howard employed the boy.[51] Similarly, two female slaves of an unidentified owner were hired out for $2.00 a day, but on another occasion the same slaves earned $4.00 a day; two male slaves of that owner brought in $24.00, but the nature of the work and its duration were not stated.[52] On July 23, 1851, James Sullivan purchased a twenty-one-year-old mulatto slave for $675.00 and hired that slave on several occasions in 1855 for $10.00 a week.[53]

In addition to hiring their slaves to other individuals, slave owners hired them to companies, other types of business enterprises, institutions, and the federal and local governments. The Georgia Central Railroad Company, the city's largest commercial owner of slaves with 125 (118 of whom were males), headed the list of companies that owned slaves, and it was joined by the Upper Steam Rice Mill (66), Steam Boat Company of Georgia (27), Savannah Brick (25), and many other businesses that owned less than 20 slaves. The median number of slaves owned by a Savannah-based company in 1850 was 13, with males constituting an overwhelming majority.[54] These companies often hired slaves to supplement their work force. Nearly all the crew of the Georgia Central Railroad, except the conductors, was composed of slaves; the engineers, firemen, other workers, and construction crews were slaves.[55] Rice mills, cotton mills, sawmills, hospitals, and steamers also hired slaves.[56] The City Hotel of Savannah hired a male slave from June through August 1845, and paid his owner $140.00, plus an additional $7.50 for a female slave that was hired for one and a quarter months.[57] Savannah Medical College hired a slave janitor for $12.00 a month, but later bought him.[58] The federal government hired a slave for seven days between April 17, 1844, and June 21, 1844, to sweep the courtroom of the district court in Savannah and paid its owner, who happened to have been the deputy marshal, $.37½ a day.[59] And the city often hired African Americans, the majority of whom were probably slaves, in the scavenger department until 1853, when the work was contracted out for three-year periods.[60]

Slave hiring, therefore, was a practice which whites generally embraced, but it was quite flexible. All types of slaves were hired—adults and youths, males and females, mulattoes and blacks, artisans and laborers—and the prices charged for the hired slaves varied, with the same slave sometimes bringing in less for one job than for another. The length of time covered by the hiring agreements was as short as a day and as long as a year, with the longer agreements including subsistence compensation to the slaves, for example, clothes, shoes, hats, and blankets. Thus, in slave hiring as in other aspects of the peculiar institution, freelancing was the norm. White slaveholders were adamant and consistent believers in sovereignty. This was as much the guiding principle of slavocracy as it was of state rights. Slaveholders cherished the right to manage their slaves as they pleased, with little interference from government at any level. Laissez faire prevailed, and each slaveholder was left to implement the slave codes in conformity with his best judgment as long as social conventions were respected, the life of the slave was not destroyed, and the actions of the owner did not pose a danger to other whites. A highly individualized slave management structure prevailed, therefore, that worked either to the advantage or to the disadvantage of the slave, depending on the modus operandi of his owner. At times when it worked to the advantage of the slave, the peculiar institution could be very unusual.

In no aspect of urban slavery in Savannah was idiosyncrasy more pervasive than in the situation of the "nominal slaves"; that is, slaves that were allowed to hire their own time. These slaves should not be confused with hired slaves because they merely changed their legal masters for surrogate masters, while on the other hand, nominal slaves enjoyed relatively normal lives. They had full names, family households, jobs, and unsupervised living arrangements that were often better than poorer whites'. These slaves followed the American dream, even though they were not a part of the mainstream: they worked hard, saved their money, and purchased property, while hired slaves received subsistence from their masters. There are no figures on how many slaves fell into this category, but they were probably quite numerous.[61] Although self-hired slaves constituted a minority of the slave population, their number was still considerable. If the slaves that filed claims for property losses at the hands of the Union army comprised a representative sample of the nominal slaves in Savannah, they could have outnumbered free African Americans. If, further, those slaves constituted about 15 or 20 percent of the total number of slaves in Savannah, as many as twelve hundred nominal slaves could have lived in and around Savannah. At no time did the reported free African-American population reach that number. Some nominal slaves had enjoyed the privilege of hiring their time and living away from their masters for ten, twenty, and even thirty years.

Nominal slaves, therefore, were the real slaves without masters in a sense because although they belonged to their masters, those slaves were allowed a de facto status of freedom: they managed their own lives, found their own jobs, and earned their own subsistence. Charles Ball, a slave who came to Savannah seeking employment and was hired by a nominal slave who had hired others to work for him, later wrote a book in which he said, "In Savannah I saw many black men who were slaves and who yet acted as freemen so far that they went out to work where and with whom they pleased, received their own wages, and produced their own subsistence."[62] Had Ball taken a closer look at the situation, he could have reported to his readers that those slaves also lived as freemen. This aspect of urban slavery was the most amazing accomplishment of African Americans, outdistancing the establishment of the black church and the individual achievements of free African Americans, who created viable economic roles for themselves in the Savannah economy, both of which were outstanding accomplishments. Slaves who hired their own time used this hatch in the peculiar institution to escape the more pernicious aspects of slavery and live quasi-free lives. They participated in a wide range of economic activities, often pursuing more than one of them, and through those endeavors, they were often able to hire other members of their nuclear family, set up housekeeping, and compete in the economic arena in many instances on even terms with free African Americans and poorer whites. Theirs is indeed a story that sets urban slavery in Savannah apart from plantation slavery in the country.

City dwellers in Savannah depended upon food grown outside the city limits for subsistence, and slaves produced much of this. In some instances, the slaves worked plots that their masters provided for their personal use[63] and sold the produce in the city, and in other instances, slaves who had hired their time rented parcels of land to grow produce and raise poultry, cattle, and hogs, which they butchered and sold to the general public. A case in point, Cato Keating, took seventy-five cents of the four dollars he received weekly as the overseer of his master's mills to buy provisions, and he saved the rest until enough had been accumulated to buy "stock hogs" that he raised and sold. His wife, Nancy, helped by hiring her own time for five dollars a month, then getting a ten-dollar-a-month job.[64]

Some nominal-slave butchers did about as well in their vocation as free African Americans in that line of work. Sandy Small, a butcher who lived on South Anderson Street just outside the city limits, started hiring his own time in 1844 and continued to enjoy this privilege for the next twenty years. He paid his master twelve to fifteen dollars each month during that period and used his free time to raise hogs that he butchered and sold. In the meantime, his wife, Abigail, sold milk from their cows and homemade sausages.[65] Another butcher, Simon Middleton, who some called one of the best hog butchers in the market, started hiring his own time about the same time as Sandy Small and paid his master twelve dollars each month. Middleton had a large number of customers who contacted him when they wanted to have animals slaughtered; then he went to their homes, loaded the hogs in his wagon, took them to his place to be slaughtered, and returned with meat. When he was not busy doing this Middleton, either hauled wood from the country to the city, or he did the "jabbing" for William H. Davis, the leading butcher in the city and the Confederate butcher during the Civil War.[66] A third slave butcher who hired his own time and went into business for himself was Ulysses L. Houston, pastor of Third African Baptist Church, who traveled throughout eastern Georgia purchasing cattle which he butchered then sold the meat from his residence on the lower story of a building that faced the market; above him in the building was the Slave Mart.[67]

The dray business, popular among free African-American males, enjoyed a similar status among nominal slave males. Charles Verene, April Wolford, Straffon Herb, and William Anderson were among the most successful ones who pursued that business (some of those draymen also followed other lines of work). Verene, a native of Georgetown, South Carolina, initially hired his own time in 1852, upon agreeing to pay his master twelve dollars monthly, which was not too burdensome because he earned well above that amount each month operating two drays, one of which was driven by a slave boy who lived six or seven blocks from Verene.[68] Wolford was also a newcomer to a relatively old practice since he did not start hiring his own time until 1853. Although his agreement was more recent than Verene's, Wolford had a better deal because he paid the same amount as Verene during the busy winter months, but paid two dollars less in the slow summer months.[69] Herb lived on the corner of Anderson and Montgomery Streets in a house that was situated on two and one-half acres of land and rented for four dollars a month. In addition to that expense, Herb was required to pay his master ten dollars monthly but these financial obligations did not present a problem to the slave who earned from twenty-five to forty-four dollars each month hauling in his wagon and running a livery stable under the bluff.[70]

101

A Middle
Ground
between
Slavery and
Freedom

William Anderson, a senior member of the self-hired slave draymen, had been hiring his own time for over a quarter of a century at ten dollars a month by the outbreak of the Civil War. He traveled to the country to get chickens, fodder, potatoes, and watermelons, which were brought to the city and sold; hauled loads; and did odd jobs for whoever hired him. This industrious slave saved enough of his earnings to purchase his freedom, but his owner, George S. Cope, who spoke highly of him, refused to sell him.[71] Cope did not reject the offer because he needed the money that the slave gave him each month, as many other owners did, because during the twenty years he owned the slave after inheriting him from his father, Cope never increased the compensation, even though the price of food, clothes, and other items, the value of the slave, and taxes all increased between 1844 and 1864. If the compensation from the slave was not essential to Cope's financial health, the personal pleasure and social prestige derived from owning a slave in the South and the desire to keep the free African-American population small may have influenced his decision.

Similarly, the compensation which Margaret Dawson paid her master was not essential to his financial stability. Margaret, a nurse whose observation concerning the practice of self-hire supported the view that it was pervasive, said, "there was an abundance of slaves that did that [hired their time]." Margaret claimed that she paid her master $6.50 monthly, and there were times when she did not pay anything because her master "didn't always expect it."[72] Margaret's payments were about average for a female slave, and her master's indifference toward collecting money was consistent, in principle, with the general propensity of masters to make their own rules regarding management of slaves. But this particular type of charity may have been unusual. If this slave was not required to work for her master, if she did not compensate him monetarily in lieu of working for him, and if she did not live on his premises, what was her status? Legally, of course, she was still a slave, but in a practical sense she occupied a middle ground between slavery and freedom.

Edward Hornsby added another dimension to the privileges which masters extended to slaves who hired their own time. This slave carpenter, who had been permitted to hire his time over twenty years for sixteen dollars a month, leased (with a proviso to build a house on the land) a 50-by-180-foot lot at the corner of West Boundary and William Streets from a white man for thirty dollars annually. With the help of a black carpenter, Hornsby built a one-and-a-quarter-story house containing a parlor, kitchen, and two bedrooms downstairs and two rooms upstairs. An agreement between the slave and his landlord allowed Hornsby to reside on the property as long as the owner did not claim it for another purpose. If the owner of the land had terminated the lease, he either would have bought the house from Hornsby or permitted him to move it off the lot.[73] Whites often leased lands and placed buildings on them with their interests being protected by similar stipulations to those of the Hornsby agreement, but few free African Americans were parties to such agreements, and Hornsby's was probably the first one for a Savannah slave. His master was aware of the agreement, the landowner was aware that Hornsby was a slave, the local authorities should have been aware that the slave was building himself a house, and all parties must have known that it was illegal for the slave to own a tenement, yet Hornsby was not molested in his dwelling until, ironically, the Union army destroyed it to get lumber for its use. Those northerners, probably conversant with the slave codes but not with the vagaries related to their implementation, did not believe the slave owned the house. Hornsby was able to enjoy living at that level because he did well economically as a carpenter, and his wife, also a slave, sold milk, which she got from their cows that were kept on the property, to supplement the family income. In this respect, she seems to have had much in common with other nominal-slave wives and with free African-American females spouses who worked to supplement their families' income.

If Hornsby's situation seems strange for a slave, it is probably because scholars have just begun to dig deeply into relevant extant sources. The information uncovered, although it does not reject the old perception of the practice, has revealed an atypical aspect of slavery to which little attention has been paid. The experiences of nominal slaves in Savannah discussed in this chapter are consistent with this view. A most enlightening and fascinating discussion of the Hornsby type slave is found in Loren Schweninger's work, which devotes an entire chapter to property holding among slaves. Included in that discussion is a North Carolina slave who was married to a free African American; he was worth between five and six thousand dollars and owned slaves, which were listed in his wife's name.[74] Similarly, in his work on black slave owners, Larry Koger has a chapter entitled "Neither a Slave nor a Free Person" which identified several slaves who owned other slaves, as well as an even larger number of slaves who owned real estate, were listed as free persons, and paid the capitation tax, which South Carolina required of free African Americans.[75]

Some of the male slaves who hired their own time raised horses to sell, and some ran livery stables. The latter vocation was popular among African Americans, although it was less popular in Savannah than in other urban areas of the South. Daniel Butler, Dennis Smith, and Alexander Steel were among the nominal slaves who pursued those jobs. Butler, a Bryan County native, paid his master twenty dollars monthly for the privilege of hiring his own time, and he leased a livery stable which developed into a profitable venture.[76] Smith raised colts and sold them.[77] Steel also raised horses, but his age and experience enabled him to do much better than Smith. Steel remained on his master's plantation on the Savannah River about nine miles from the city limits, where he entered the horse selling business in 1841 when his master first allowed him to hire his own time. The slave bought a pregnant blooded mare which he subsequently mated with a blooded male horse owned by George P. Harrison, who later was a general in the Confederate army. Steel probably had the finest horses among African Americans in Savannah, and he was among the few persons in the black community to raise a fine stock of horses; he also bought and sold cattle.[78]

Steel's experience was similar to that of Matthew Hayward and William Henry Perkins from the perspective that all three pursued occupations which few blacks followed, but the similarities ended there. While Steel enjoyed some successes raising horses, Hayward did not get very far working in a printing office where his main responsibility was to fold and distribute papers. Blacks were not strangers to working in printing establishments since many of those establishments hired them to set type, cut wooden blocks for engraving, work as pressmen, make paper, deliver newspapers, and to do other jobs, with black pressmen especially being in great demand to handle that physically demanding job. Few free African Americans in Savannah worked in that business, however, and ambitious nominal slaves probably did not follow this line of work because the pay was not sufficient to cover their masters' compensation and other expenses. As matter of fact, besides working in that printing establishment, Hayward worked wherever he could find a job.[79] William Henry Perkins hired his own time and ran a small shop in which he sold molasses cakes,[80] another endeavor that did not reap a large income.

Harriet Dallas, who also hired her own time, washed and ironed, just as many other black women in Savannah did, and pursued other business ventures. Harriet headed a family business whose heavy volume of work forced her, at times, to hire persons from outside the family. She lived outside the city limits "just across the canal" where she and her husband, a self-hired slave pilot, rented about five acres of land on which they kept cows whose milk she sold; in addition to this and the washing and ironing, Harriet sold home-made butter, poultry (which was very profitable during Christmas when many chickens and turkeys were sold), and hauled produce and other items to town. Her husband was hardworking, industrious, and thrifty, according to the testimony of Harriet, and the same words could be used to describe her. It is after reflecting upon Harriet Dallas's resourcefulness that one gets a clearer picture of the term huckster, or seller of small wares, that often appears in the occupation column next to the names of free African-American females. Here was a woman who sold milk as well as butter, a milk by-product, which indicates that she had a pretty keen business sense.[81]

The experience of James Custard, a slave carpenter on one of the nearby plantations, contrasted poignantly with those of the nominal slaves mentioned above. Custard worked in the country three years, building sheds, stables, and houses for his master, but when the work slackened, his master permitted him to go to Savannah to find work; during his stay in Savannah, this slave paid his master twenty dollars monthly. Whenever there was work that needed to be done on the plantation, however, Custard would return and remain as long as the job required. While he was there his master provided him with subsistence but did not pay the slave. Custard only received monetary compensation when he worked in Savannah.[82] Custard's master charged him much more than masters of nominal slaves charged their slaves, and he did not show the compassion of Tony Austin's master who, after charging his slave four dollars a week for twelve years, reduced the payment to three dollars weekly when the slave's family increased and he could no longer pay the original amount.[83] Furthermore, the arrangement which Custard had was charged with uncertainty because he jockeyed back and forth between the plantation and Savannah, whereas some nominal slaves hired their own time for a decade and longer.

The plantation practice of self hire was different, therefore, from the urban practice, although there may have been some plantation slaves who enjoyed the same type of nominal slave status as most city slaves who hired their own time. The agreements which Savannah masters made were mutually beneficial to the slaves and to themselves. Masters received income from the slaves instead of labor, but retained ownership of the slaves. Self-hired slaves, on the other hand, had an opportunity to select their occupation(s), earn incomes from performing them, and set up housekeeping with a reasonable assurance the arrangement would remain in force as long as they abided by the agreements' provisions and did not flaunt social conventions or break the law. Obviously, there was a significant difference between slave-hiring agreements contracted on plantations and those in the city.

Exercising their presumed sovereignty over their slaves, moreover, Savannah masters ignored the proscription on slaves owning property and granted this as a privilege "to encourage faithful and favorite servants."[84] As George Cope testified:

> There was no trouble with persons of his [William Anderson's] character having property of their own—any man who performed

his duty to his master had this privilege and was never interfered with . . . The right to own property was the right that I granted to him.[85]

Cope articulated the presumption of sovereignty in management matters which masters claimed, and implied he was above the law in matters relating to granting property ownership privileges to his slaves. The city fathers, apparently, did not challenge him.

In Savannah, allowing slaves to hire their own time created a middle ground between slavery and freedom for a group of slaves who could not purchase their freedom or gain manumission through other means. Although the vast majority of slaves in Savannah probably lived with their owners, we have it from two highly respected men of their day, Charles C. Jones (Presbyterian minister) and Joseph Bancroft (census taker), that nominal slaves lived away from their masters and provided their own subsistence. These slaves have received little attention from scholars, but this oversight does not negate their presence or detract from their accomplishments. The practice was not unique to Savannah because both Larry Koger and Loren Schweninger identified such practices in other southern states. No other group of nominal slaves in the South may have had the impact on their community, however, which those in black Savannah had. They were a valuable part of its economy, religious community, and social life. In the words of Charles Ball, they "acted as freemen."

CHAPTER V

An African–American Social Melting Pot

*I am living with my third husband. My first husband
was in Virginia. My [Virginia] Master sold me to a
man in Florida. I was married there and lived with
him 20 years. He died here and I married my present
husband.* —CELIA BOISFEILLET

What kind of social life did these African Americans create for
themselves? One would have expected leisure time activities and
social functions to have been scarce at best, judging from African
Americans' inferior legal status and meager financial resources. A
diverse mix of cultures, which at times hindered social interaction
among individuals, and a dearth of civic organizations further
compounded these difficulties. Yet, amid this adversity, African
Americans succeeded in creating a viable social life. The community was an emerging urban area which did not have the wealthy
residents, abundant social activities, and satisfying cultural entertainment of the much older and larger urban areas in the nation.
Social relationships centered around color, just as in other major
cities in the region, but no laws gave this practice legal status, and
no subgroup(s) of free African Americans enjoyed a privileged
status. Social relationships were also determined on the basis of
cultural background. Social classes were nonexistent, however, in
the conventional meaning of the term. Nevertheless, there were
places to go and things to do to avoid boredom.

The first federal census (1790) ever taken of the Chatham-

Savannah area listed the black community at 8,313 persons—112 free African Americans and 8,201 slaves.[1] By 1860, the number of free African Americans in Chatham County had increased to 735, including 705 in Savannah, with the largest increase in their number occurring between 1800 and 1810 when it rose from 224 to 578, a reported increase of 354 persons for that decade. The slave population numbered 14,807 in 1860, including 7,712 in Savannah. A near majority of the slaves lived outside the city limits, whereas most free African Americans lived in Savannah. In 1860, moreover, African Americans (free and slave) slightly outnumbered whites in the Chatham-Savannah area.[2]

Although Savannah had a much smaller free African-American population than Charleston, whose 3,237 was almost as large the total in Georgia (3,500), no other Georgia town approached Savannah's figure, which composed 20 percent of the total in the state in 1860. In fact, whereas a disproportionate number of the state's free African Americans lived in Savannah, the same was not true of slaves and whites, who comprised 3.2 and 5.2 percent, respectively of the state's totals.[3]

The cultural diversity of black Savannah contributed to its social life, as immigrants from at least ten foreign lands and residents of nine states, other than Georgia, had settled in Savannah by 1826. That year, Chatham County registered 828 free persons of color, 64 of whom were from foreign lands and 80 from other states in the United States. St. Domingue had the largest representation among the foreigners (33) while neighboring South Carolina had the largest representation of the American born (53).[4] By the outbreak of the Civil War, however, the cosmopolitan makeup of the black community had changed perceptibly. Only 2 foreign-born persons resided there and three states, in addition to Georgia, were represented in its population: South Carolina (17), North Carolina (1), and Florida (1). On the other hand, seventeen Georgia counties, excluding Chatham County, were represented.[5] The rich cultural diversity present in the 1820s, and perhaps even earlier, resulted from the Atlantic slave trade (prior to its abolition in 1808) and the Haitian Revolution which lasted for over a decade (1791–1804) and claimed an estimated 200,000 victims among the blacks and mulattoes who were adversaries at times.[6] This situation initially created a salad bowl appearance. The abolition of the African slave trade and the creation of a black republic in Haiti ended the large influx of Africans and Haitians into the community. As a consequence, the cultural heterogeneity which graced the black community began to disappear in the late antebellum period and had disappeared by 1860. The multiple aspects of social life—the black family, social events, civic organizations, and education—together with the aforementioned independent black church were the major agents of change which created the homogenization of the previously culturally heterogeneous residents of the community. Black Savannah, thus, was an African-American social melting pot.[7]

In 1788, most of the free blacks were recent arrivals, and this may still have been true in the 1820s; consequently, during much of its early years, black Savannah searched for a social life and an identity. The cultural diversity, multiplicity of skin colors, and African slavery that pervaded the community were obstacles that had to be overcome if the search was to succeed. Over 50 percent of the foreign-born free persons of color were reared in the French culture—thirty-three from St. Domingue and two from Martinique, over 25 percent were born in Africa (17), and most of the remaining foreign born were reared in the British culture.

Indications are that most French-speaking free persons of color in Savannah interacted among themselves and may have kept a social distance from English-speaking ones. Conditions were less accommodating for the former than in New Orleans, however, where a large affluent French-speaking group of free blacks benefited from the cultural legacies of nearly a century of French rule in Louisiana. French was spoken at club meetings and in daily affairs; novels, poems, and newspapers were written in French, creating a barrier between French-speaking free blacks and their English speaking contemporaries.[8] The number of French-speaking free persons of color in Savannah was too small to support cultural events, civic clubs, and a newspaper. Other than at home and at the Catholic church, émigrés had few opportunities to speak French, a situation that portended ill for preserving their cultural identity, especially since the white community was English speaking.

Most free persons of color from St. Domingue attended Saint John the Baptist Catholic Church, whose records, written in French after 1813, revealed the baptism, marriage, and death of black Catholic émigrés.[9] These records furthermore reveal endogamous marriages and persons with French names sponsoring others of that cultural group. Since one does not normally ask a stranger to assume a role that is as special as a godparent, apparently the French-speaking black parishioners of Saint John the Baptist Catholic Church did more than merely worship together. They bonded together in a social network of friends. These social gatherings provided outlets to ventilate frustration and overcome homesickness.

Apparently a small number of first-generation French-speaking émigrés socialized with their American-born contemporaries, but rarely did they intermarry. Clemente Sabatte Sr. settled in Darien where he married Mary Gary, the American-born mother of Clemente Sabatte Jr. and Hetty, both of whom were born in Darien. The elder Sabatte lost touch with his French roots, and even after the family subsequently moved to Savannah where the children were reared,[10] he did not join the Catholic church. Aspasia Mirault, a French émigré and confectionery store owner, had a son by James Oliver,[11] a Virginia native who was married to Rozella at the time; and Andrew Morel, the tailor, had a son by Eve Wallace,[12] who was much younger than he and an American-born free mulatto, while he was still married to his wife, Ann, a native of St. Domingue.

Unlike the first generations, the second generations from the various cultural groups accelerated the assimilation process by inter-marrying. Hence, Tharsville, the youngest offspring of Phyllis Savage, married Alfred Jones. Josephine Mirault married a Bulloch and her son, George, married Sarah E. Houstoun, the granddaughter of Richard.[13] Josephine's younger brother, Simon, who became a widower when his wife, Mary Jane, died in 1854, took a second wife two years later in a ceremony that was performed by the Catholic priest;[14] his daughter Rosa married an Artson,[15] a relative of James Porter; and another daughter Laura married a son of Mary and Robert Woodhouse, and after his death, she married Cyrus Camfield.[16] The husbands of both daughters were prominent members of Saint Stephen's, and as a result their wives became Episcopalians. Conse-quently, through deaths, intermarriages, education, and the termination of the immigration from St. Domingue, visible signs of the French culture, either in speech or close attachment to the Catholic church, disappeared from the black community.

Differences and distinctions made on the basis of color were just as obvious as the early cultural differences, but the color distinctions persisted because the racial climate in Savannah was favorable to the preservation of such distinctions. At the outbreak of the Civil War, for instance, no less than six different terms were used to describe the skin color of African Americans: mulatto, light, yellow, brown, dark, and black.[17] Normally, mulatto denoted African Americans whose skin color was brown or lighter; black, or Negro, denoted those African Americans who carried only the genes of their African ancestors. The classifications were inconsistent—for example, John Cox, pastor of Second African Baptist Church since 1850, was classified as "black" on the 1860 census but as "brown" by the Freedman's Savings and Trust Company.[18]

Because of their biological kinship with whites, mulattoes generally were viewed less negatively than African Americans of the darkest hue. Whites believed very light mulattoes were not immune from yellow fever and could not work effectively in the sun. "With us no man would buy a mulatto for field work,"[19] wrote Dr. Richard Arnold, a white Savannah slaveholder. Arnold implied that mulattoes made good house servants, but inept field hands. African Americans (mulattoes and nonmulattoes), generally accepted the negativism toward blackness which whites harbored, and this created social barriers between mulattoes and non-mulattoes. No caste system existed because there were instances where mulattoes and blacks were married.[20] Mixed marriages between blacks and mulattoes were the exception rather than the rule however, a clear indication that color discrimination was quite prevalent in black Savannah.

A sampling of marital partners further supports this. The Dollys and Baptists, who were black, did not intermarry with the Odingsells, who were mulatto, even though they were among the older free African-American families. Instead, London Dolly married a black woman. William Odingsells' wife, Madeline, was mulatto. Richard Houstoun married a mulatto. Richard Cohen and his wife, Maria, were mulatto. Andrew Marshall, Henry

Cunningham, Jack Gibbons, and Simon Jackson were mulattoes, and they married mulattoes. Furthermore, this practice continued even among the younger generation of successful free African Americans, as Joseph Marshall, his friend William Pollard, and William Claghorn married mulattoes. Richard Ann, daughter of Richard Houstoun, married James Butler, a mulatto. Hannah Cohen (daughter of Richard and Maria) married a mulatto; the Odingsells children, William and Lucy, married mulattoes.[21] All the marriages of free African Americans celebrated in Saint John the Baptist Catholic Church between 1802 and 1813 involved couples of the same color—four mulatto and one black.[22] Furthermore, thirty African-American couples in the 1860 census can be clearly identified as being married, twenty-five of these were the same color and five were not. In every instance the mixed couple involved a mulatto male and a black female.[23] Obviously, color mixing occurred less frequently than either legal status (free African American married to a slave) or cultural mixing.

Ira Berlin introduced the concept of a three-caste system operating in the Lower South in his highly regarded work on free African Americans in the antebellum South. According this thesis, whenever the free African-American population was large "the elevated status of free people of color and the lowly condition of slaves" facilitated development of a system analogous to the one in the West Indies. Free African Americans were given a middle position between slaves and their masters in return for which they were expected to inform on slaves. Berlin states that the three-caste system flourished in Savannah and in other ports of the Lower South where "West Indian émigrés" introduced it. "Occasionally," continued Berlin, "whites granted the most successful free people of color additional rights and quietly allowed them to vote, to testify in court, and ultimately to pass into the white caste."[24]

The three-caste system did not exist in Savannah for three reasons. First, the number of West Indian émigrés was too small, and they were not there long enough as a distinct group to exert the influence required for such a system to have taken root and operated effectively. Similarly, although mulatto émigrés were among the more economically advantaged free persons in the

Chatham-Savannah area, they did not monopolize a vital economic endeavor that could have made whites dependent upon them and vulnerable to demands for special favors. Since many were Catholics in a region where members of that faith were generally suspected and may even have been discriminated against, it is improbable that the city fathers would have catered to them. Consequently, neither the whites nor the coloreds among the West Indian émigrés were in a position to change the status quo.

Second, the other mulattoes were not likely to bargain with whites to enhance their position at the expense of slaves, even if they had been in a position to do so, which they were not. Black churches, which free African Americans were allowed to control, after all, depended upon the support of slaves. As mentioned earlier, black churches had over four thousand members at the height of their popularity, but at no time did the reported free black population reach nine hundred. Clearly, slaves composed a majority in those churches. Two of their members had become pastors of black churches by the late 1850s; William J. Campbell and Ulysses L. Houston, both nominal slaves, headed First African Baptist and Second African Baptist Churches, respectively. Without the support of slaves, black churches would have been less vibrant and influential; without black churches, free African Americans would have lost their surest avenue of advancement in the community.

The third reason is that the large number of nominal slaves did not fit the mold of the typical slave. The population of mulatto slaves exceeded thirteen hundred and included many nominal slaves who were married to free mulatto mates. Nominal slaves probably outnumbered free African Americans in Savannah. Moreover, Savannah's free African-American population was significantly smaller than those in Charleston and New Orleans and similarly represented a much smaller percentage of the total black population than in those cities. The presence of nominal slaves coupled with the relatively small number of free African Americans did not create a situation where the three-caste system could flourish.

Judging from the few relevant extant records, churches facilitated the development of social relationships which often blossomed into marriages. The faithful tended to marry within their faiths. For instance, the Artsons, Bullochs, Camfields, Cohens, Garys, Miraults, Sabattes, and Woodhouses were some of the Episcopalians who married other Episcopalians.[25] The parish register of the Catholic church revealed a similar pattern,[26] but black Catholics may have been influenced as much by their culture as by their faith. The records of the other churches are not available, and if they were, they may have revealed that black Baptists, Methodists, and Presbyterians behaved similarly to other blacks in this regard.

There is also evidence of strong family ties and a desire to pass the names of patriarchs and matriarchs from one generation to the next. John E. Grate, the son of Evans, a contemporary of Andrew Bryan, named a son Evans after his father;[27] and that name remained in the community beyond the Civil War. Three successive generations of Grants named a son Josiah.[28] Similarly, the name Adam was preserved for three generations in the Dolly family.[29] Clemente Sabatte named his son after himself, and that son had nine sons who survived him,[30] probably one of whom was also named Clemente. Robert Woodhouse named a son Robert, and Simon Mirault named his older son after himself.[31] Females also followed this practice. Hetty Sabatte, the younger Clemente's unmarried sister, named her only child Mary, her mother's Christian name;[32] Priscilla Grant, the second Josiah's mother, had a granddaughter named Priscilla;[33] Sarah Houstoun named her daughter Sarah;[34] Elizabeth Porter was named after her mother (James Porter's wife);[35] and the name Mary remained in the Woodhouse family for generations. This practice reflected a sense of pride within free black families.

This strong sense of family often resulted in blacks reaching beyond their nuclear family and bringing distant relatives and, sometimes, friends into the family circle. Julia Wall and her husband did not have any children, so they adopted two girls, Charlotte and Sarah.[36] Estelle Savage adopted Olivia Estelle DeLyons and had a provision in her will leaving all her property to this adoptive daughter, if she survived John and Tharsville.[37] Andrew C. Marshall and Sarah adopted Georgia Houstoun, the daughter of Lucretia, a relative of Sarah Marshall.[38] Susan Jackson housed the impoverished mother of Richard Houstoun and cared for the old lady at the same time Susan trained Richard Ann.[39] This reaching out also occurred among slaves, as evidenced by Margaret Dawson, a nominal slave, who adopted the young Ann Devillers.[40] Even when their relatives were not brought into the households, black families appear to have kept close ties with one other and with cousins, aunts, and uncles. Moreover, friendships spanning decades were quite common.[41]

For the sake of legal convenience, black families were matrilineal—the mother's status determined the status of the children—which is generally reflected in the official documents. In 1861, for example, seventy-two of the free African Americans who registered, as required by law, provided information on their parentage. Two persons gave the names of both parents (Anthony and Madeline Odingsells and Simon and Elizabeth Mirault); three persons gave the name of their father (John Jalineau, twice, and William Claghorn); and the remaining sixty-seven gave the name of the mother. In many instances the document listed black females by their maiden names even when they were married—Josephine Mirault, Estelle and Tharsville Savage, Lucy Odingsells, Hannah Cohen. Some children were listed with their mothers' surname, and some with their fathers', for example, Abraham Cohen (Hannah Cohen's son) and George Bulloch (Josephine Mirault's son). This helter-skelter practice of listing names suggests that the manner in which names appeared in the document depended on the whim of the clerk, rather than an official policy. Moreover, in marriages where the husbands were slaves, their names could not legally appear on the registration form. In spite of what appears to be a state of confusion, the following accurately depicts the situation: (1) black families were never purely matrilineal; (2) the male presence was quite common; and (3) in practical matters families were patriarchal, normally headed by males.

It was not uncommon for African Americans to have had several marital partners during their lifetime, but in addition to death and divorce, some African Americans lost their mates to slave traders. Celia Boisfeillet, whose marital history appears in the introduction of this chapter, was one of the many who lost mates to slave traders. Similarly, Andrew C. Marshall's first wife was sold while they both were slaves; he, too, had three mates.[42] The slave Coomba Johnson remarried after her first husband died, but she deserted the second husband to accompany Ellen Buchanan

Screven to Savannah and become a mistress nurse. This slave's reason for remarrying revealed that she was not above marrying for convenience, a normal human failing then and now: "my first husband I was fond of, but he died, I had to have someone to cut my wood, and bring my water, so I married Cicero."[43] Some remarriages occurred after divorces, but those cases cannot be identified because marriage and divorce records of African Americans were either not kept officially or have been destroyed.

Some African Americans never went to the altar. Charlotte Reed, the mother of Duncan Scott, a future stalwart in Saint Stephen's, was "never married";[44] the same was true of Hetty Sabbatte, who taught school for a short period in Darien after the Civil War, and probably of Sarah Houstoun, who gave birth to a son, Tom Phinizy, in Savannah in 1838, and a daughter, Sarah, in Charleston in 1840; and of Ann Gibbons, the largest black property owner in 1860. Some other women were probably partners in either open common-law arrangements that resulted in children being born or were involved in clandestine affairs. They were a small minority of females in the community.

Marriages between slaves and free African Americans were common, as there was less reluctance to cross the legal status line than the color line. Apparently, free African Americans of both sexes engaged in this kind of mixed marriage, but free African-American females probably did so more frequently than males because of the shortage of free males. Marrying a slave female resulted in the children being born slaves, whereas a free female's children were born free since the issue followed the status of the mother. Consequently whenever a free male took a slave wife he ultimately contributed to perpetuating slavery, and placed free females, who were already at a disadvantage because they outnumbered and outlived the males, at an even greater disadvantage. This may have been the reason why some females were never married. In some mixed marriages, however, both partners were slaves at the time they were married, and one was manumitted after the couple had lived together as husband and wife for a number of years. The prevalence of mixed marriages among free persons of color and slaves supports a conclusion reached earlier: in black Savannah, color was a greater obstacle to social interaction among people of African origin than either culture or legal status.

The absence of public records containing marriage applications and the names of African Americans to whom marriage licenses were issued, as well as the failure of Registrations of Free Persons Color to include slave partners encumber efforts to shed more light on this fascinating subject. Still, existing records reveal a sampling of the marriages involving free African Americans and slaves. Francis Keaton, a slave Baptist preacher, had a free wife, Ellen, who had gained her freedom in 1851 four years before their marriage. Two other slave preachers, William J. Campbell and Ulysses L. Houston, also had free wives.[45] The free wife of the slave James Custard lived on her husband's master's place, where Custard hired his own time, and his wife farmed a plot of land provided by his master for her.[46] Eve Sheftall, who was born free, followed her slave husband to Augusta, Georgia, where she worked as a servant cooking in her husband's master's home.[47] Joseph Sneed, a free African American, had a slave wife who gave birth to eleven slave children (four of whom died), but fortunately he was allowed to hire the time of his entire family.[48] Abraham Johnson, who was free and his wife was slave, was allowed to hire his wife and their two daughters' time for twenty dollars a month (seven each for the wife and one daughter and six for the other daughter).[49] Quash Dolly, who was also free, indentured himself to the master of his slave wife and moved to Augusta to be with her.[50] Finally, Jackson Sheftall, Eve's cousin, who was also born free, married a slave in 1855 convinced that he could purchase her freedom within a relatively short time, but freedom for his wife did not come as quickly nor as inexpensively as he had envisaged. He had to wait seven years and it cost him twenty-six hundred dollars to purchase her and their two daughters.[51]

Marriages between free African Americans and slaves occurred elsewhere in the region, in both the Upper and Lower South. Suzanne Lebsock alluded to the practice in Petersburg, but mentioned only those involving free women, without elaborating further on its pervasiveness.[52] Michael P. Johnson and James L. Roark maintained that free African Americans in Charleston also married slaves, but the practice was restricted to free women, as

"Free men of color clearly opted to marry free women."[53] Larry Koger uncovered information which contradicts this position. He found that Thomas S. Bonneau, a schoolteacher and member of Charleston's mulatto aristocracy, and Mose Irvine, a free African American, were married to slaves.[54] Koger researched a wide range of extant documents, while Johnson and Roark based their conclusion upon an analysis of census data, which, though reliable, apparently did not tell the whole story. Loren Schweninger's finding concerning a Columbia, South Carolina mixed couple supports Koger's. Sally Patterson, a slave woman in the capital city, was married to a free black carpenter.[55] A perusal of the petitions to the Southern Claims Commissioners should shed additional light on mixed marriages between slaves and free people in the South.

Georgia's laws did not sanction slave marriages. Although churches often performed weddings involving one or more slave partners,[56] this did not affect the status of the union in the eyes of the law. Georgia Bryan Conrad has left us a description of one of the two thousand weddings which Andrew Marshall performed. The bride, Conrad's slave maid, was "dressed in some white material with veil and orange blossoms complete" and the groom was dressed in black. The wedding was held in the middle of the parlor of their home. This ceremony was in stark contrast to the "broom jumping" which occurred on many plantations. The reception which followed was held in the basement; the best linen, china, and glass were used, and the choicest food was served to the friends of the bride and groom.[57]

One of the many advantages that blacks living in an urban area enjoyed was the opportunity to see the latest fashions and observe how the upper classes dressed for special social events. Since there were several black seamstresses and tailors, African Americans often wore the latest fashionable clothes on Sundays and special occasions. Although whites did not get upset with the way blacks dressed for work, (for instance, derbies were often worn to work) they became disturbed over what may be described as the ostentatious way many of them dressed when they wore their "Sunday clothes." Young females often shunned turbans, long skirts, and large white aprons for the fancy clothing of the upper classes: bonnets and pantalettes edged with lace.[58] Black males also came under criticism for dressing in fancy clothes, the local newspaper going as far as to declare that slaves dressed better than their masters: "Dick and Jack often leave their more negligent masters far behind."[59]

Black Savannah did not have any theaters, hotels, or lyceums where cultural events could be staged; nevertheless, African Americans found ways to enjoy themselves. In addition to visiting the tipling houses, they held frolics. More wholesome entertainment came at the firemen's parade and during Christmas. Moreover, Sunday rides through the town and surrounding country areas were quite popular. These were some of the ways African Americans entertained themselves.

Saturday nights were the favorite time to enjoy amusements and entertainments, and there were "tipling houses" (dram shops) where an element of the black population purchased whiskey and other alcoholic drinks.[60] Frolics—parties where dancing and other merriments were enjoyed—were probably more characteristic of entertainment held in the country where they lasted until early Sunday morning. A former slave from another county in the state described the Saturday night frolics at which whiskey and lemonade were served, and music was provided by home made instruments that sounded like fiddles, banjos, and flutes.[61] Since these were a part of the slaves experiences on plantations, the slave camps outside Savannah which harbored runaways from near and far and which were known to have had leisure time entertainment probably staged similar events which attracted African Americans from the city and from nearby plantations.

The late night frolics were not allowed in Savannah, although the city fathers did allow blacks to have dances which had to end at 10:00 P.M., and could only be attended by persons with proper authorization. From the language of the ordinance, the dances were intended for free African Americans, but slaves probably were allowed to attend, if their masters approved.[62] The curfew, which the black church probably endorsed since dancing was perceived as sinful, was intended to facilitate monitoring dances which African Americans sponsored in the city rather than to discourage blacks from dancing. Those authorities were aware that dances would be held, either with their blessings, which facilitated proper policing, or secretly, which did not.

The annual firemen's parade was a special occasion for African Americans, large numbers of whom assembled to watch the parade, cheer the black firemen, and enjoy the festivities.[63] The black firemen probably marched behind the white fire companies in the parade. In the absence of horse-drawn fire engines, free black firemen, who were required to serve with the local fire companies in return for their exemption from the city tax,[64] pulled the engines, trucks, and hose carriages, and served as axemen at fires. This spawned friendly competition among the black fire companies to reach the fires first, the winner usually receiving some acclaim.[65] On the way from the fires, the black firemen often sang,[66] a practice that was becoming a tradition among black workers in the region. While the uniforms were similar, each fire company had its own colors, as one observer discerned: "The difference in the customs [uniforms] consisted in the colors used in the uniforms, one for instance having red stripes on the pants and red sailor collars another having blue trimmings, and so on . . ."[67] In addition to wearing uniforms at parades, black firemen wore their uniforms off duty on other occasions; a case in point, at a funeral for a deacon of Third African Baptist Church in 1855, four uniformed fire companies were in the funeral procession.[68]

Christmas was another special occasion in the community. Slave children received candy, nuts, and toys while the adolescents and adults received more substantial gifts.[69] Boys (black and white) gathered in the large squares located throughout the city to soak large balls of tightly twisted cotton in turpentine, light them, and throw them quickly from hand to hand; the fiery balls rushing through the night air created a spectacular sight. This was a favorite amusement.[70] Christmas was also a time to eat heartily, the favorite dishes being all kinds of fowls (mainly chickens and turkeys), rabbits, sweet potatoes, and a variety of other dishes.

African Americans entertained themselves with wheeled vehicles of all sorts—wagons, carts, drays, and buggies. A favorite pastime was Sunday rides through the streets of Savannah and into nearby hamlets such as Thunderbolt and White Bluff, but the city council, which viewed those rides as a nuisance, banned them.[71] In view of the poor track record of enforcing such ordinances, the authorities' action probably did not stop the Sunday rides.

Black Savannah did not have any black Masonic lodges, even though an African lodge under the leadership of Prince Hall had been established in Boston, and from there, chapters had been established in other northern cities. The absence of the Masons did not stop blacks from providing for the needy, which they accomplished by creating benevolent societies and other kinds of associations. These organizations provided financial assistance to the poor and infirm, especially among free African Americans who could not turn to a master in a crisis because one of the consequences of freedom was assuming personal responsibility for subsistence. Furthermore, those organizations loaned money to members, cared for orphans and widows, and helped defray burial expenses of deceased members.[72] In most instances, the organizations were tied to churches; in others, they were either the outgrowth of civic pride and concern, or the result of a group of persons with similar vocational interests joining together, for example, the Porters' Association. These associations were strong manifestations that a sense of community prevailed in Savannah because they focused on areas that the other world–oriented black churches normally did not emphasize. Furthermore, they were another clear indication that black Savannah coveted its autonomy and subscribed to the concept of self-help.

Living in Savannah, an urban area, was more dangerous to the health of African Americans than living in the country.[73] The Board of Health minutes have gaps (the years 1833, 1839–49, and 1856–58 are missing) and records were only kept during May through October each year when epidemics were likely to occur, which prevents giving accurate figures on the causes of deaths among blacks; nevertheless, enough information is available to get a sense of the leading causes of death. The city was more densely populated than the country, thus creating more favorable conditions for the spread of consumption (tuberculosis), typhoid fever, cholera, whooping cough, and other communicable diseases; and being a seaport city, Savannah had a constant influx of visitors, which increased the probability of epidemics. Although living in the city had its advantages—greater economic opportunities, greater freedom of movement, and more leisure activities—it also had its drawbacks, the main one being greater health hazards. As a result of those advantages, blacks in Savannah lived better than those in the country, but they generally did not live as long.

The Board of Health minutes, despite some gaps, are invaluable to any mortality study of Savannah. According to the minutes, the leading killers of adult African Americans between 1834 and 1838 were consumption (18), typhoid fever (14), an assortment of bowel ailments (13), and dropsy (7). In addition to those ailments, blacks (free and slave) died from at least twenty-two others.[74] Since the numbers included only deaths that had occurred during a six-month period in each of those years, they are not as numerous as they would have been if the years' totals were included; nevertheless, the order of the leading causes would have remained unchanged because the diseases were not seasonal. Furthermore, the deaths in those years are probably indicative of those in other years, except during the yellow fever epidemics in 1854 and 1858. Savannah winters were generally mild, which, however, did not preclude nasty weather at times. The weather between October 1834 and February 1835, for instance, was cold, damp, and windy much of the time. Savannah even had snow and sleet that winter.[75] That winter the weather was severe often enough to cause health problems, especially for those persons who did not live in a building or have warm clothing. Conditions were right, therefore, for inhabitants to catch consumption. Of the seventy-five reported nonaccidental deaths, moreover, nearly 70 percent were caused by the four illnesses mentioned above and the remaining 30 percent of the deaths resulted from the twenty-two other ailments.

Excluding the missing years as well as the months when deaths were not recorded, twenty-five persons age twelve and older died from accidents, with drownings (8) being the leading cause of fatal accidents, followed closely by gunshot wounds (6). Those two were responsible for fourteen of the twenty-five reported fatal accidents or for nearly 60 percent of them. Many of the drownings doubtless occurred in the Savannah River, even though it was named only two times; one of the gunshot fatalities was self-inflicted, though it may not have been a suicide, and another gunshot fatality was judged self-defense. There was also one stabbing. Most of the other fatal accidents were nonviolent. "Fell from a window; found dead in a steamboat; died from drinking cold water while overheated; killed by a fallen object"; and an unexplained casualty were the other entries in the minutes.[76] Blacks in Savannah had their arguments and fights, but they apparently seldom resorted to a permanent solution to their temporary personal problems, or if they did, the deaths were not reported. The low incidence of accidental deaths and homicides enhanced the chances of blacks who survived childhood diseases and yellow fever epidemics to live beyond middle age.

A small minority of persons reached the age of 90. In his census, Bancroft reported that "the oldest white person in the city" was a 90-year-old preacher named William McWhir and the oldest African Americans were 91-year-old Andrew Marshall and 100-year-old "Sandy," a slave of William Morel.[77] The minutes revealed that between 1830 and 1864 at least thirty-six African Americans lived to reach their 90th birthday, and twelve of whom lived at least another decade beyond age 90. The oldest Savannahian was a female slave named Hagar who, according to the minutes of the Board of Health, reached 121. If this is accurate, she may have set a record for longevity in the city. A further breakdown of those figures revealed that nineteen slaves (13 females and 6 males) were between ages 90 and 99, but only six free African Americans, all females, were in that age bracket; and eight slaves (6 females and 2 males) were at least 100 years old, while three free African Americans, once again all females, were 100 or older.[78] Obviously, some African-American males did reach that age, as Bancroft reported in 1848; Andrew Marshall was 100 years old when he died in 1857. Even given the minutes' limitations, and the probability that ages may have been off by a few years, the information presented a favorable picture of the free African-American females who comprised 25 percent of the 90-and-over group, even though they constituted less than 10 percent of the total black population. The women in both groups (free and slave) tended to outlive the men, which is consistent with the conclusion reached earlier in this study that among the larger landowners in Savannah, the wives tended to outlive their husbands. "Old age" was listed as the cause of death for most persons in the 90-years-old-and-above group, although lacking knowledge of cancer and heart disease, the accuracy of this is uncertain.

African Americans often had difficulty simply surviving infancy. The infant mortality rate among slaves in 1850 was higher than it was among whites, with 183 of every 1,000 slave infants dying before their first birthday while 146 of every 1,000 white infants died.[79] The major causes of death among black children were different than those of adults. Among children, whooping cough (36), fever (30), infantine (22), and teething (18) were the major causes of death in 1834–38; next came worms (7), scarlet fever (6), lockjaw (5), and spasms (4); there were an additional 18 specific causes, and 13 undetermined causes. Only two children were reported to have died from consumption, and only one child died from dropsy. Furthermore, 2 drowned, 2 fell to their deaths, and 1 died from a wound. Infantine, which was often given as a cause of death, appears to have been the nineteenth-century name for sudden infant death syndrome. For instance, a twelve-day-old slave baby died from no apparent physical ailment, and the physician gave the cause of death as infantine; a similar case exists for a day-old slave baby who died.[80]

Teething as a leading cause of death is more difficult to understand, perhaps because it is a common experience to all human beings and generally is not viewed as life threatening. In 1835, a seven-month-old slave baby died from teething; later that month an eighteen-month-old slave girl died from teething, and the next day a one-year-old slave died from the ailment; in 1837, moreover, a slave infant of Aspasia Mirault died from teething.[81] The real culprit was probably catarrh, inflammation of mucous membrane, which the infants could have contracted while teething. The condition may have gone undetected until it was too serious to cure, or someone may have tried home remedies which did not work. Babies of both races contracted catarrh, and it was life threatening for them. For example, the baby daughter of a friend of the local newspaper publisher contracted a severe case of catarrh while she was teething, but fortunately she recovered from it.[82] Teething, though painful, should not have caused fatalities; unfortunately, black children died from it.

The sizable number of deaths from whooping cough was mainly the result of an outbreak which appears to have lasted from May 25 to July 31, 1836, when 24 black children died from that disease.

Only 6 other black children died from whooping cough the rest of the year (August–October) that the board kept records. White children did not suffer from a similar outbreak. As a matter of fact, the first week of the outbreak (May 25–31) when the disease claimed 5 black victims, no whites died from it. The peak period occurred from June 2–30 when 12 black children died from the disease; an additional 7 children died during the month of July. There were no deaths from whooping cough the following reporting period (May–October 1837), and whooping cough was not among the leading causes of death among black children in subsequent years,[83] indicating that the large number of deaths in 1836 was an anomaly.

Yellow fever was the most dreaded disease among whites and with good reason. Epidemics of the disease struck several times in the nineteenth century. In order to combat the epidemic in 1854, Savannah was filled with smoke twenty-four hours a day throughout the summer; during the day, pine wood was burned, and at night, tar was burned in an effort to purify the air, with little effect. The city looked almost deserted as many stores closed.[84] Once the epidemic had run its course and the cool weather had settled in, 1,040 persons had died from the disease, including 106 African Americans.[85]

The city's mortality figures for the decade after 1854 indicate that proportionately more whites died each year than blacks. According to the figures reported in the 1850 census, there were 15,312 persons in Savannah, including 6,917 African Americans.[86] Although blacks constituted 45 percent of the population, at no time after 1854 did African Americans constitute 45 percent of the recorded deaths in Savannah. In fact, only twice did those deaths exceed more than 40 percent of the total: in 1855 when 318 of the 748 recorded dead were African Americans and in 1857 when 264 of the 642 were blacks. In 1856, blacks composed 38 percent of the deaths; in 1858, they formed a decade low 29 percent; and in 1859 and 1860, the percentages were 38 and 36, respectively.[87] Did the figures after 1854 mirror a reversal in the mortality rates or did they represent an underreporting of mortality figures for African Americans? Mortality figures for African Americans may have been underreported, but why did it happen consistently after 1854? If it happened prior to 1854, why did not it make a significant difference in the life expectancy of the two groups? It is difficult to answer these questions without additional information. Suffice it to say, the minutes contain figures which present a different picture than the conventional one concerning longevity and death among whites and blacks in Savannah. African Americans who survived adolescence tended to outlive their white contemporaries, and beginning in the 1850s (at the latest) the annual number of white deaths was proportionately higher than the figure for blacks. Summarizing the mortality situation simply, black infants died at a higher rate than white, but white elders apparently died at a higher rate than black.

The educational opportunities for blacks, though far more promising than they should have been under the circumstances, certainly did not compare favorably with those that white Savannahians enjoyed. Savannah lacked a professional class of black teachers and up-to-date school buildings. Formal learning was conducted throughout the period in small classroom settings, usually with marginally trained black teachers and a mixed group of free and slave pupils. Public officials made no provisions to educate black children—quite to the contrary. In 1817, the city council passed an ordinance forbidding the teaching of free African Americans and slaves. Twelve years later the state passed similar legislation,[88] but the legislation was discreetly ignored. According to the 1860 census, seven African Americans, all free, attended school that year.[89] This is clearly a misleading figure since there were almost that many black schools operating in Savannah in 1860. These figures do not include Sunday schools.

The goals of Sunday schools and those of the privately run schools were different. The Sunday schools were interested in teaching black children to read the Bible to gain a better understanding of God. This was the same reason why the white Baptist and Methodist churches, the leaders in pushing black education in the early nineteenth century, also favored teaching blacks to read the Bible.[90] The evangelical churches in Savannah subscribed to the position of the seventeenth-century Puritans who encouraged the enactment of the first school laws in the colonies to fortify the faithful against the "old deluder satan."

In the 1730s, long before First African Baptist Church was

established, Dr. Thomas Bray, of the Church of England, and a member of its Society for the Propagation of the Gospel, established a school in Savannah for slaves.[91] Black education continued to operate in a sanguine educational environment until well after the first quarter of the nineteenth century. An 1822 visitor was told that school attendance among children of free African Americans was widespread. Some young slaves learned to read and generally the number of African Americans who could read increased, as children acquired educational skills superior to those possessed by their parents. The favorable educational environment changed late in the 1820s, however, when the state included provisions in its slave codes proscribing teaching slave children how to read, which masters often violated. In many instances masters believed the law was a good one for slaves, except for their favorites. With such lack of enthusiasm for the law permeating the ranks of slaveholders, even free blacks violated the codes, as Charles C. Jones observed in the 1840s:

> Their [free African Americans] advantages for education and conse-
> quently access to the written word of God, are more limited in the
> slave states . . . on account of laws against the education of colored
> persons; but notwithstanding in the slave states the free Negroes do
> have schools for their children, or some private instruction . . .[92]

Free persons of color in Savannah did, indeed, operate schools for black children: Julien Fromantin, of Saint John the Baptist; James Porter and Mary Woodhouse, of Saint Stephen's; Mary Beasley and Jane Deveaux, of Second African Baptist Church; and James M. Simms, of First African Baptist Church, all operated schools where reading, writing, and ciphering were taught; and Porter, with his strong academic background and exposure to the good education available to free African Americans in Charleston, probably taught a secondary curriculum which included grammar, ancient and modern history, orthography, geography, arithmetic, elocution, and music. Even though the existence of black schools in the city was an open secret, pupils devised all kinds of tactics to deceive the police and whites who may have become suspicious and closed their schools. They loitered around the playground, then individually walked off inconspicuously to a designated place; they carried a bucket of some kind as though on an errand; they wrapped their books in newspapers; they picked up chips (the poor used chips for firewood as fuel) on their way to school; and they took circuitous routes to and from school.[93]

Between 1818 and 1860, at least six African Americans operated schools in black Savannah. Fromantin, listed as a carpenter on the 1809 city tax digest, did not list an occupation when he registered with the county in 1826, but by that time he had operated a school unmolested, for almost eight years. Even after the 1829 law was passed, he continued to operate his school, although discreetly, until 1844.[94] Porter, who was well trained for his day, was ostensibly a tailor, but this man with the "bullet-shaped head" and the "bright sparkling eyes, and a pleasant voice" taught school secretly in the evenings in a room with a trap door to escape through in the event of a police raid. Porter's school was raided on one occasion, which forced him to go into hiding temporarily.[95] Mary Woodhouse, a parishioner of Saint Stephen's, taught school in her house on Bay Lane between Habersham and Price Streets, which her mother-in-law, Susan Woodhouse, had purchased in the first decade of the nineteenth century. There were twenty-five to thirty pupils, free and slave, in the school where Mary, assisted by her daughter, Mary Jane, taught the children the basics. According to a pupil, Susan King Taylor, the Woodhouses taught the first two years of school, after which the pupils went to Mary Beasley who taught the remaining years of what could have been considered as an elementary school education.[96] Jane Deveaux had better luck than Porter because she was able to conduct her school for almost thirty years and was never forced to close her doors.[97] James M. Simms was the only teacher of record who was publicly whipped for operating a school, probably because his school operations were less discreet than the others. A stubborn activist, he refused to pay his fine and sailed for Boston where he remained until after the Civil War began.[98]

Whites also violated the law and taught African Americans. In 1855, Sister Jane Frances of the Sisters of Mercy opened a small school for African Americans, defying the ban on such activities.[99] After Susie Taylor had gone as far as Mary Beasley's school could take her, a white playmate, who was a student at a local convent, offered to teach Susie, if the future nun's mother approved and her father was not told. The instructions lasted four months; then the girl joined a convent. Susie's next teacher was the son of her grandmother's white landlord, a high school student, who agreed to teach Susie out of deference to her grandmother; those lessons lasted until he was called to active duty with his volunteer company in 1861.[100] Emily Burke noticed that clerks often taught their slaves, and through that means, those slaves acquired a decent education. The owner of one of the largest Savannah firms taught his young male slave to read, write, and cipher, and using those skills, the slave handled important business matters for his master. The slave read northern newspapers and was conversant with the political issues of the day. Children of slaveholders often taught their slave playmates information which they had learned. An eleven-year-old white boy spent one to two hours daily teaching a slave boy to read without his parents, the slave's owners, being aware of it.[101] A southern congressman justified allowing his slave to learn how to read on the grounds that the slave needed the skill to "know the titles of books, superscription of letters, and other things in performing errands or receiving written orders."[102]

The desire for an education prompted some African Americans to teach themselves to read since attending school was either inconvenient or financially beyond their means. A slave sexton at a local white church taught himself to read by opening the hymnals on the back of the pews and spelling out the words.[103] Andrew Bryan, Andrew Marshall, Ulysses L. Houston, and others learned to read through sheer determination. Marshall used his reading skill to unlock treasures of knowledge through reading the books in his modest library.[104] That may have been the only library in the black community, although a few other blacks may have bought books from time to time.

Although literacy was not widespread among the early leaders of the black community, some could read and write. Since Adam Anderson and Joseph Clay were the only early leaders of First African Baptist Church who could read and write, they were clerks for the church. Both emigrated to Liberia, where Anderson, following in the footsteps of his father, Thomas Anderson, became pastor of a large Baptist church, Caldwell Baptist Church.[105] Simon

Jackson, who could read and write, often handled business matters for persons in Savannah. Louis Mirault and Joseph DuBergier often were sponsors of black parishioners of Saint John the Baptist Catholic Church and signed the parish register acknowledging that baptisms and marriages had taken place.

Quite often, but not always, the younger generation's training was superior to their parents'. This situation occurred because there were more teachers, and they operated more schools than during the previous decades. Andrew Marshall could not write, but his son George, and adoptive daughter, Georgia Houstoun, could; Estelle Savage and her sister could read and write, and probably their brother could also. Simon Mirault Jr. and his step-sister, Susan Cuyler, could read and write, but his step-mother, Elizabeth Mirault, could not. James Porter and his brother, Richard Artson, could read and write, but their mother, Martha (Porter) Artson, could not; Duncan Scott could read and write, but his mother, Charlotte Reed, could not.[106] Richard Houstoun and his daughter Richard Ann could read and write, but Sarah, the other daughter, could not; Josiah Grant II could read and write, but his daughter Eliza (Grant) Habersham could not.[107] Mary Woodhouse, her daughter Mary Jane, and her son William could read and write, but James, another son, could not.[108]

There is strong evidence, therefore, to support claims that African Americans valued education. The harassments which black teachers endured, and the deceptions which pupils devised to pursue their goals are sobering testimonies that the institutionalization of education, unlike religion, had not yet been achieved. Residents of black Savannah worshiped openly, but they were educated secretly. Yet somehow schools survived, even if they may not have thrived. In keeping schools open while keeping their doors closed to muffle the sounds of the eager pupils, the movement to educate blacks that was begun when Georgia was still a British colony remained alive, and a solid foundation was laid for the successful establishment of a black newspaper and an institution of higher education after the Civil War.

A number of conclusions can be drawn from the preceding discussion on social life in black Savannah. First, among the more obvious but little discussed topics on the black experience in Savannah is that the social line between slaves and free African Americans was blurred, unlike the New Orleans and Charleston, which had mulatto aristocracies. This hampered the development of a meaningful system of social stratification. Slaves and free African Americans attended the same social functions, lived in the same dwellings, worked in the same occupations, worshiped in the same churches, and intermarried. Second, color bias was pervasive, just as it was in other urban areas in the region. Blacks predominated among slaves by a wide margin; among free African Americans, however, mulattoes outnumbered blacks by a small margin. The presence of a relatively large number of mulatto slaves, however, (they were almost three times as numerous as free mulattoes) facilitated the popular practice of color-biased marriages.[109] Third, the presence of the black male in the black family was more prominent than public documents indicate. Although slave husbands of free African-American women were overlooked by census takers, who by this very act relegated those black men to the status of phantom husbands, they were the breadwinners of their families. Fourth, black Savannahians were more literate than the census reports and other public documents indicate. Fifth, African Americans created social functions that helped mitigate the confining and oppressive conditions in black Savannah. Sixth, the culturally heterogeneous society of the early 1800s disappeared with the passing of the first generation of émigrés and the abolition of the African slave trade, which resulted in a more culturally homogeneous society in 1860 than prevailed at the turn of the century. Thus, black Savannah was an African-American social melting pot.

Finally, the three-caste system did not flourish in Savannah because, in addition to aforementioned reasons, the key factors which enabled it to flourish in other port cities of the Lower South were not present. West Indians, for instance, did not play the dominant role in the early history of Georgia that they played in South Carolina and Louisiana. Many of the men to whom Charles II granted a charter to settle in the Carolinas owned plantations in the West Indies, and a group from Barbados, called the Goose Creek Men because they settled near Goose Creek, a tributary of the

Cooper River, dominated the government from 1670 to 1712. It is common knowledge, moreover, that South Carolina was the only British colony in North America with a black majority, reminiscent of the situation in the West Indies. This was a clear indication of the British West Indians' influence. Colonial South Carolina had a British West Indian tilt over a century before the arrival of the French West Indian émigrés; however, Berlin is probably wrong about the origin of the practice of the three-caste system in Charleston. On the other hand, Louisiana was a former French colony and many residents from the French-speaking West Indies immigrated there and became successful businessmen. Hence, the French West Indian presence was very strong in New Orleans. In this instance, Berlin is probably right in his assessment of the origin of the three-caste system there. The situation of West Indian émigrés in Savannah was not analogous to either of these. The West Indian influence, either British or French, was negligible in Savannah prior to the arrival of the French émigrés in the late seventeenth century. The émigrés, moreover, adapted to existing practice, rather than changing it.

The relatively small size of the free African-American population and the presence of a large group of nominal slaves worked against the success of the three-caste system. The size of Savannah's free African Americans remained below one thousand, whereas Charleston's exceeded three thousand. For the most part slaves led restricted lives, but a sizable and significant number occupied an anomalous middle ground between slavery and freedom. These slaves had close relationships with free African Americans, who were not inclined toward ruining these relationships by becoming informers, even if the reward could enhance their position. The absence of a strong West Indian influence and the presence of only a small number of free African Americans but a large number of nominal slaves worked in concert to deprive the three-caste system of pillars upon which to stand. This marked another difference between black Savannah and black communities in other cities of the Lower South.

CHAPTER VI

Neighbors, but Not Friends

The first of May all the fire companies paraded, and the city turned out to do them honor. It was a gala day for white and black.

———GEORGIA BRYAN CONRAD,
REMINISCENCES OF A SOUTHERN WOMAN

African Americans in Savannah did not challenge the dominant position of whites. This reduced prospects of racial tension between the two groups who coexisted in a somewhat uneasy, but tolerable, situation. They were residents of the same city, but only whites were enfranchised. They were mostly Christians, but usually attended separate churches. They were neighbors, but only occasionally were they friends. The groups collectively may not have been fond of each other, but individually a different set of attitudes often prevailed. In spite of the seeming contradictions, race relations, though not warm, were not confrontational. In fact, race relations were tolerable enough to spare whites the anguish of experiencing a slave revolt and save African Americans from the humiliation of being subjected to racially segregated beaches and neighborhoods.

Unlike religious and social life in black Savannah, which did not conform to the generalized picture that emerges in the existing literature on the African-American experience in the Old South, relations between blacks and whites in Savannah generally were similar to that in other major cities in the region, except that Savannah was not threatened with a slave attack as New Orleans was in 1811, and it was not rocked by a conspiracy to overthrow slavery as Charleston was in 1822. Social convention proscribed commingling among blacks and whites, and statutes and ordinances were often passed to curb activities and circumscribe social behavior of African Americans. Indeed, race relations may have been the aspect of southern society that was most similar throughout the region—in the Lower and Upper South.

Criticisms of blacks started early and persisted throughout the period. In 1788, the grand jury, upset because free African Americans roamed about the city and surrounding countryside, requested closer supervision. The same grand jury had complained about blacks worshiping on Brampton Plantation.[1] Over the next two decades, whites reduced their harassment of African Americans, as Andrew Byran expressed in a letter to one of his Baptist cohorts,[2] and the legislature stiffened the penalty for killing slaves,[3] but with dubious results because whites were indulgent toward white-on-black crimes.

At the same time, however, the legislature continued to enact antiblack laws. In 1826, for example, in an effort intended to keep black seamen out of Savannah at night, Georgia passed an act that required black seamen to remain aboard their vessels from 6:00 P.M. to 5:00 A.M. This increased the prospects of maintaining peace in the city while it decreased the prospects of slaves running away. The law was stiffened in 1829 when a forty day quarantine was placed on all ships with black personnel. Now black seamen were not allowed in the city, except as inmates in the local jail because the quarantine was lifted only if black seamen were incarcerated in the jail and bond was given to defray their expenses while staying there.[4] The message was clear: white Savannahians did not want black seamen in their midst.

White Savannahians also did not want resident blacks roaming the streets at night. A 9:00 P.M. curfew, enforced by a nightly patrol, was therefore imposed upon them. Each night a bell rang at 9:00 P.M., and all African Americans had to vacate the streets, unless they had written passes. Slaves caught on the streets after the curfew were placed in jail for the night.[5] Slaves feared the patrol, but this did not prevent them from playing pranks. One of the favorite tricks of country slaves was to tie a grapevine across a narrow, dark stretch of road that the patrol normally used. As the

approaching horseback riders hit the grapevine at a gallop, the lead
riders became ensnared in it and were thrown from their horses.[6] All
was far from well between the races, yet the situation was livable.

Compliance with social customs by both groups reduced pressure to structure a rigid, racially stratified society. Some interracial
contact was allowed, but within social customs. Blacks and whites
mingled publicly on the beaches, in some churches, at the city
market, at the firemen's parade, in the work place, and in grocery
stores; and they lived in the same wards.

A certain element of whites, who were frowned upon by other
whites, operated small grocery stores that received most of their food
from slaves and sold it almost exclusively to African Americans.[7]
The choice of customers did not annoy the whites, but the suppliers
of the food did because some allegedly stole the food from their
masters and other whites and exchanged it for money and whiskey.
In this situation the racial dividing lines were blurred because the
white shopkeepers connived with blacks against other whites. It did
not matter to those white shopkeepers that their customers and
suppliers were black, or that in some instances they were dealing in
stolen goods. The shopkeepers formed an alliance of convenience
with the blacks, and both benefited at the expense of other whites.

Some whites conspired with blacks to sell whiskey to other
African Americans. The council had enacted an ordinance prohibiting blacks from selling "spirituous liquors," yet African
Americans were able to evade the ordinance and sell alcohol by
scheming with whites, who obtained licenses and sold them to
blacks, purchased licenses as stand-ins for African Americans, or
purchased whiskey and sold it to black middlemen. Once the
council got wind of this, it closed the loophole in 1834 by rendering
null and void all licenses granted to white persons to retail spirituous liquors which were secured, or used to benefit free African
Americans. White violators of the ordinance were punished.[8]

Apparently at one time, blacks and whites bathed and swam in
the river during daylight hours, which caused the council to pass
an ordinance in 1810 regulating bathing and swimming in the river.
The ordinance did not establish segregated beaches for whites and
blacks, neither does there appear to have been any concern on the
council's part that blacks bathed and swam in the same water with

whites. Perhaps this was because the council's characterization of the acts as "highly improper" reflected the opinion of most well-reared citizens. Thus they were acts in which only blacks and the lower classes of whites would engage. The ordinance prohibited swimming and bathing in the "River opposite the City"—from 7:00 A.M. to sunset. Violators, both blacks (free and slave) and whites, were penalized five dollars, failure to pay which resulted in a whipping not to exceed fifteen lashes.[9] This is one of the few ordinances which treated blacks and whites equally.

Although black Baptists had their own churches, white visitors attended them. "In the afternoon our pastor at the request of the First Color'd African Church attended their meeting house to assist in the Ordination of Jonas one of their Brethren."[10] The pastor of Savannah Baptist assisted Andrew Bryan, who was probably old and feeble. Whites also preached in the black Baptist churches, and white worshipers, especially northern visitors and foreigners, attended services at black churches.[11] Many of those visitors were more interested in being eye witnesses to an uncommon scene in slaveholding states—blacks conducting worship services—than they were in worshiping God. However unorthodox their reason for attending those services may have been, whites worshiped in black churches.

The situation differed slightly in other denominations. There were no black Catholic and Presbyterian churches; blacks and whites of those faiths worshiped in biracial churches. Blacks and whites of the Episcopal faith also worshiped together in Christ Episcopal Church until the black parish, Saint Stephen's, was established. A few blacks still worshiped at Christ Episcopal Church. Similarly, blacks and whites of the Methodist faith worshiped together until Saint Andrew Chapel was organized. Blacks also attended funerals of whites. Black pall bearers served at the funeral of Revolutionary War hero Gen. Nathanael Greene's son, a drowning victim.[12]

Nowhere else in the Savannah, however, was race mixing as pronounced as it was at the city market on Saturday nights. "You will seldom meet anywhere," wrote A. T. Havens, "all sizes and colors from the jet black African to the Mayor of the City, and such confusion of sounds and tongues as one can scarcely imagine."[13] This mixture of races was by no means a collection of strangers in a lonely crowd. It was a collection of residents who knew each other by name. Deference was given to whites, but whites and blacks in the city generally knew each other. On one occasion when William Starr Basinger went to the market, an old black female called him "Marse Tom." When he told her she was mistaken, the old woman replied, "Maybe that's not your name, but I know you are Marse Tom Basinger's son."[14] In this instance, the old black female knew the family, even if she did not know the younger Basinger's first name.

The Savannah Fire Department was manned by males from both races, but they served in racially segregated units. In 1828, the department consisted of 178 slaves, 96 free blacks, and a white company of 17 men, Oglethorpe Company.[15] By the 1840s, another white fire company, Washington Fire Company, was organized. In 1857, the black fire companies in the department were the Axe, Hook, Ladder Company which had 53 firemen, the Hose Carriage Company No. 2 which had 23, both stationed at Fireman's Hall, and Engine Company No. 4 which had 65 and was stationed in Wright Square.[16] All those companies were manned by free African Americans, commanded by white officers, and housed separately from the white companies. In Oglethorpe and Washington companies, white volunteers did the manual work normally reserved for blacks since they did not have any.

Over time the white fire companies probably came to believe they were the true firemen and should be the only ones allowed to wear uniforms. This led Oglethorpe and Washington fire companies to protest against blacks wearing uniforms, a practice the white firemen believed demeaned them. They asked the council to ban blacks from wearing uniforms, which it did.[17] Displeased with this action, the fire department asked the council to rescind its resolution banning blacks from wearing uniforms, citing as its reasons for requesting the action: (1) blacks were allowed to wear uniforms to encourage them; (2) this gave "a more attractive appearance to the whole department"; (3) African Americans had worn uniforms in the past, and no one objected to the practice; and (4) the Fire Ordinance of 1825 gave the Savannah Fire Department control of the city's fire apparatus and empowered it to establish regulations for its management and direction within the limits of city ordinances. The council rescinded the ban, as requested, with a subtle suggestion that the fire department should be sensitive to the feelings of the disgruntled fire volunteers.[18]

Here was a clear example where an element of whites wanted to discriminate against blacks but were overruled by a more responsible element in the fire department, who also happened to have been their superiors, and believed if black firemen were required to do the manual work and face the same dangers as whites, then they should be allowed to wear firemen's uniforms. Besides, wearing the uniforms did not change social customs. After the fires had been extinguished, the smoke had dissipated, and the danger to the city had passed, black firemen returned to their subordinate station in the city. In the meantime, while they performed firemen's duties, they should dress as firemen. Maybe the superiors in the fire department were acting out of self-interest, realizing that succumbing to the wishes of the disgruntled firemen could have led to unhappy lackadaisical black firemen, which could have resulted in inept fire fighting with all its costly ramifications, a price those responsible for directing the city's firefighting efforts were unwilling to pay.

On that issue, the persons in charge sided with African Americans, and the council acquiesced. Similarly, at the Savannah Poor House and Hospital, a white superior sided with a slave against her white supervisor. When the steward, who lived at the hospital and managed it, had a disagreement with the cook, he chastised her. Dr. William Duncan, president of the board, allegedly sided with the cook, which angered the steward, who threatened to resign if the cook was not removed. The board subsequently passed a resolution which placed all servants of the institution, whether owned or hired, under its protection and authorized its president to protect them. All chastisements must have his approval.[19] The steward lost that confrontation, even though he was the best person they had been able to hire in recent years, and the board had approved reappointing him. This must have been unsettling to the steward, and it was inconsistent with the perception that whites presented a united front against blacks.

The races also mixed in the work place. Blacks and whites worked side by side on construction sites of homes, offices, hospitals, military fortifications, churches, and other structures. John Phillips, owner of a brickyard and one of the many employers who hired racially mixed crews, often hired carpenters of both races. Phillips once described a blacksmith whom he had hired to work along with his slaves as a "wild Irishman."[20] It was common knowledge that crews on vessels were mixed, and slave artisans worked with their masters. Mills and factories had racially mixed work crews. While there were laws prohibiting African Americans from working in certain jobs, for example, drugstores, the number of jobs closed to blacks was negligible when compared with those opened to both races, and in such instances, employers tended to follow the most cost-efficient hiring practices.

Savannah was divided into wards, many of which were named either for nationally famous persons or for individuals who had contributed to the development of the city. In 1825, there were eighteen wards, eleven of which had black majorities.[21] In 1848, there were twenty-two wards and three districts (smaller units than wards); blacks constituted majorities in eight of those twenty-five divisions.[22] At no time, however, was any ward inhabited solely by either whites or blacks (see appendixes for the black/white population in 1825 and 1848). Instead, whites and blacks in the city lived in the same houses, blocks, and neighborhoods. Slaves lived in the same dwellings with their owners, or in shanties at the back of the lots on which the masters' premises were located; and some free African Americans worked as live-in servants of whites. Blacks also rented dwellings from whites, and in some instances, these may have been on the same lots with the property owners' homes. In a few rare instances, whites rented from blacks. Thus, black and white homeowners and residents were neighbors; they lived near each other, even if they did not commingle. On occasion, the physical proximity led to whites developing a healthy respect for their black neighbors, or tenants, as the depositions which they gave to the Southern Claims Commissioners indicate.

As a matter of fact, Savannah was less racially segregated residentially in 1848 than it was a century after slavery had been abolished. Savannah, indeed, had its shortcomings in race relations, but the city did not subscribe to Jim Crow housing. In Derby Ward, one of the city's leading business centers with ninety-seven stores (ninety-one of which were brick), 38 percent of the 706 inhabitants were African American. Christ Episcopal Church, the Bank of Georgia,

Central Rail Road and Banking Company, the City Exchange, the Georgia Historical Society, the Pulaski House, and the City Hotel were located in this ward. The ward had forty-six private dwellings in 1848, thirty of which were made of brick; such a high percentage of brick homes was the exception rather the rule in Savannah. The two largest black churches in Savannah, First African Baptist and Second African Baptist churches were located in Franklin and Green Wards, respectively, which had white majorities.[23]

Medical services and health facilities were segregated. Savannah had black nurses, but no black physicians. Whenever blacks became ill, Henry Bourquin Jr. and other white physicians treated free blacks and slaves. Dr. Bourquin administered bleeding to Susan Jackson in April 1811; visited Thomas Lloyd, a free black carpenter, several times between 1811 and 1812 to take care of his children; treated in May 1812, a free African American and his family, who apparently were accident victims because the husband was treated for a hand wound and his wife and child were treated for head wounds; treated one of Andrew Marshall's sons in September 1812; administered bleeding to Jack Gibbons in October 1812; and visited Andrew Morel several times between November 27 and December 2, 1812. Dr. Bourquin also extracted teeth from Simon Jackson's apprentice and several slaves belonging to whites, as well as vaccinating nine of Thomas Gibbons' (a wealthy white) slaves between May 1811 and May 1812. This white physician maintained social distance from his black patients who were listed in his book by their color, sex, and vocation, for example, "taylor"[sic], but rarely was "Mr." or "Mrs." used: "Lloyd (m. m. carpenter), Jackson (taylor), John Gibbons (m. man), Andrew Marshall, and Andrew Morel (taylor)"; whites were listed as "Mr.," "Mrs.," or by some title (e.g., "Colonel," or "Major"). The lone exception to this practice was on one occasion when Simon Jackson, who called on the doctor several times but never for himself, was listed as Mr. Simon Jackson.[24]

Savannah was in the forefront of the nation in providing a health facility and a burial site for African Americans. In 1795, a city-sponsored lottery realized sufficient funds to build a hospital for whites, which became operational between 1809 and 1811. In 1816, Dr. James Ewell introduced the idea of a hospital for African Americans which was received favorably. As a result of the efforts of Dr. John A. Casey, who spearheaded the fund-raising drive and the financial support of Rev. Thomas F. Williams, who bequeathed a portion of his estate to fund the facility, the idea was transformed into a reality. Upon receipt of a request from the executor of the reverend's estate, Richard F. Williams, his brother, the state legislature passed legislation, on December 24, 1832, incorporating the Georgia Infirmary for the Relief and Protection of Aged and Afflicted Negroes (the Georgia Infirmary).[25]

Richard F. Williams, who was elected president of the board of trustees that was created the following January, donated fifty acres of land ten miles outside the city limits on the site where George Whitefield, the Great Awakening evangelist and Anglican priest, had built the Bethesda orphanage in the late 1730s. The Georgia Infirmary remained at the Bethesda site from 1833 to 1838, when it was relocated to within one and one-half miles of the city limits on a site extending from Lincoln Street to White Bluff Road (the present Bull Street). The move addressed concerns of the trustees that remoteness of the facility made it "unfavorable to a faithful supervision on our part, while the inmates, most of whom were from this city, were dissatisfied at the separation it caused from their friends."[26] This was the first infirmary exclusively for African Americans in the United States.[27]

Savannah had long provided a separate burial site for African Americans, but in 1853 the "Old Cemetery" near potter's field was closed and four acres were reserved for African Americans in a new cemetery, Laurel Grove. In 1857, the acreage for African Americans was increased to fifteen.[28] Andrew Bryan and Henry Cunningham were among those persons buried in the "Negro Cemetery" whose bodies were exhumed and removed to what is now called Laurel Grove Cemetery South, where African Americans were buried. But Andrew Marshall was buried in the new cemetery since he died in 1856 after the cemetery was opened. In 1859, the council voted to double the size of the "Colored Cemetery," and build a dwelling there for a caretaker, who would keep the enlarged cemetery in order and protect it and "other adjacent city property from all intruders . . ."[29] Even though it was segregated, the cemetery established for African Americans was superior to burial sites for African Americans in most other cities. In many places blacks were buried in potter's fields.[30]

Whites' attitudes toward blacks may have been more hostile than their actions. In 1822, white butchers petitioned the council to ban the practice of renting stalls in the market to free African Americans because, according to the butchers, blacks should be dependent upon whites "and not independent of them." Responding positively to the petition, the council passed an ordinance which prohibited free African Americans from purchasing stalls in the market.[31] White butchers, obviously, wanted to reduce the number of competitors in the market, and they went after the most vulnerable group. In demanding free African Americans' dependence on whites, those butchers envisaged a situation in which all blacks would be in a servile capacity analogous to slaves. Yet those butchers shared the view of some of their white contemporaries who complained that free blacks were lazy and unambitious. Apparently, they liked the perception of a dependent group of free blacks, but not the ramifications of the reality of such a situation.

A quarter of a century later, the publisher of the *Savannah Republican* criticized the social habits of African Americans, who allegedly smoked cigars in the streets and would not leave the sidewalks to let approaching whites pass. The publisher echoed the complaint of an alleged "very respectful citizen" who was appalled over the authorities' failure to enforce the ordinance which prohibited African Americans from smoking in public. "The colored gentry of this city have, in our opinion, too many indulgences already," lamented the publisher, "and there is risk enough of fires from white people smoking in the streets" without increasing it by permitting blacks to smoke.[32] "Colored gentry," "self-conceited dandies," and "mustached lips" were some of the terms used in the article in reference to blacks. If smoking in public was a fire hazard, it seemed strange that the council allowed it, even for whites, in view of the abundant wooden structures, potential tinderboxes, in the city. The article did not enumerate the indulgences which blacks had to which they were not entitled, but from its tone African Americans had succeeded too well in emulating the lifestyle of whites.

Slaves received their share of harsh criticisms. Some slaveholders believed their slaves were inferior and incapable of showing gratitude and other feelings which whites showed toward each other. Those owners were especially annoyed when family favorites who had been given special consideration to the extent of being treated as other "children" of the family ran away.[33] The other negativisms about slaves have been well chronicled: their dishonesty, mendacity, amorality, and stupidity. John Pierpont Jr., a Unitarian pastor, native of Massachusetts, and recipient of a divinity degree from Harvard, opined, "When I think of the present mental and moral condition of blacks, and their comparative physical uselessness, I tremble at the probable consequence of a state of nominal liberty for them."[34] There were no opinion polls in those days, but if a survey of whites' attitudes had been taken, a consensus probably word have subscribed to the opinion of John Pierpont Jr.

Black Savannahians had the unenviable task of acting as individuals in a society that was wedded to dealing with stereotypes. African Americans seemed to have received mixed reflections in their community looking glass—the white faces surrounding them. Attempts to operate small businesses on city property led to demands to prohibit it because a group of whites wanted them to be dependent on whites. Attempts to accept the dependent role, led to charges that African Americans were useless and incapable of enjoying freedom. Attempts to imitate their white "betters" and walk the city streets smoking, led to acrimonious charges and blame for creating fire risks. Then there was the white hotel owner who was complimented and asked by a guest how he got his black employees to work so efficiently. The hotel owner replied: "I treat 'em just as I would white men; pay them fair wages every Saturday night, give 'em good beds and a good table and make 'em toe the mark."[35] Maxine J. Desverger and several other whites had a different kind of experience with an African American, but with the same positive results; they were neighbors of Abraham Johnson whom they described as a good neighbor, and a skillful, careful, and thrifty farmer.[36] These were the other reflections which African Americans saw in the looking glass. Which of these reflections was accurate?

The mixed reflections are not surprising because whites and blacks were often childhood playmates before they were channeled into the separate worlds mandated by social customs for adult members of their races. As children, whites and blacks often played school together, with the whites being the teachers and blacks the pupils.[37] Margaret Vernon Stiles recalled the relationship which existed between her uncle George Washington Stiles and Frank, the grandson of the family favorite slave, "Mom Violet." The two were born on the same rainy night, and as they grew up, her uncle was encouraged to play the piano, and Frank was given a fife and drum to accompany him. Whenever they played soldier, as children often did, Stiles drilled his two younger sisters, two younger brothers, and Frank, who played the drums while Stiles led the formation with his baton. This companionship lasted until the death of Stiles after the Civil War. Even that war did not disrupt it; Frank accompanied his master, a Confederate officer, to the front lines, and they both returned alive, but Stiles was terribly shaken by his ordeal.[38] Further, Susie Taylor had a white playmate, Katie O'Connor, who lived in the next block and attended a convent.[39]

The anecdote which Georgia Conrad told in her reminiscences conveys very clearly the probable ramifications of close contact between house servants and children. Georgia's uncle, Dr. William Screven, had a tall, solemn-looking, immaculately dressed slave butler who nightly served the family tea and hot buttered toast. One night as Georgia, a lover of toast, tried to take the last slice from the dish, the slave stopped her with a stern admonition that the last piece belonged to Mr. Manners. Georgia was horrified and believed that Mr. Manners was a guest who had not been served. Later that night, as she hovered around the pantry, she spotted the butler eating the toast. When he turned, his eye met Georgia's; the slave bowed and said to her, "I am Mr. Manners." The lesson in politeness remained with Georgia.[40]

Georgia did not ask her uncle to punish the slave for speaking to her sternly. A friendship did not develop, but respect for the slave did. A friendship did develop, however, between Simon Jackson and an Irishman who bequeathed all his earthly possessions to Jackson to show his appreciation for the "many acts of kindness, attention, and friendship" extended to him, a lonely immigrant, who did not have any relatives in the United States.[41] The friendship door swung in both directions; blacks benefited from good deeds as frequently as they performed them. When Simon Jackson expressed interest in purchasing a valuable piece of real estate in Reynolds Ward, which the heirs of a prominent white native of Charleston, South Carolina, owned, Richard Stites, a Savannah lawyer, wrote a letter in Jackson's behalf that stated he was "very generally respected for his industry and correct deportment in life."[42] The letter probably figured prominently in the owner's decision to sell the property to Jackson, and Stites went a step further by lending him the $1,500 needed to buy the property. Unfortunately, Stites could not prevent the sellers from increasing the price from $950, which they had offered the property to him for in 1804.[43] Furthermore, when Confederate authorities seized Sarah Black's six cows, a white female neighbor went to the pen and claimed she owned them. The authorities released the cows to the female who returned them to Sarah.[44]

William Cooper, a white man who often loaned money to Simon Middleton, a nominal slave, was willing to lend him anything else he needed because Middleton, in Cooper's words, was "a man of good credit."[45] Another white Savannahian paid William Anderson, a nominal slave, what must have been the ultimate compliment when he said Anderson "bore as good a character as any man in the city of Savannah," adding he did not "except white men."[46] Furthermore, a white Savannahian stated that Toby Adams was "a very industrious and thrifty man."[47] Charles Green, former owner of Samuel A. McIver and later president of Savannah Bank and Trust Company, applauded the industry and intelligence of his former slave.[48] Harriet Dallas and her husband, a river boat pilot, were described as an industrious family.[49] Even after he was manumitted in 1855, Grant Simpson managed the business affairs of his former owner's widow, including collecting rent from tenants.[50]

White Savannahians did not presume African Americans to be well behaved, industrious, and of good character. Rather, the presumptions were usually negative: they could not manage themselves and were ungrateful, mendacious, and dishonest. Whites were more likely to criticize blacks than to compliment them. Even when Henry W. Smith spoke highly of Anderson, placing him in the elite company that included whites, he probably still had a negative attitude toward most blacks in Savannah. And a similar statement could probably be made about the other whites mentioned above who spoke civilly about African Americans with whom they were familiar. While these persons may have harbored negative attitudes toward African Americans generally, they had different attitudes toward individual African Americans with whom they had positive interactions. In some instances, whites and blacks may have been friends within the limits of social customs, while in others they may have interacted in the economic arena or in the church in more distant relationships. In either situation there may have been a mutual caring for each other that was inconsistent with the mores and folkways of that day, thus could not be admitted publicly; in some instances it even could not be admitted privately. Some whites even may have been unable to admit it to themselves, so completely did racism dominate social conventions.

How does one judge a mistress who freed her slave in 1783, and in her will directed that the blind and sickly former slave should receive an annual annuity for her maintenance?[51] Jack Gibbons was among the well-to-do free blacks of the early 1800s, with his real estate in St. Gall Village and his slaves appearing frequently in the tax digests. What those digests do not reveal is that John Gibbons, a wealthy white Savannahian, gave him the real estate.[52] Dr. Arnold was incensed upon learning that a free black female for whom he served as guardian was ordered arrested in Macon, where she had gone to work for a family, for allegedly failing to register as the law required. Describing the proceedings as "Mean and contemptible . . . a contemptible persecution of a helpless colored woman," Dr. Arnold asked Thomas C. Nisbet, a prominent iron manufacturer in Macon, the woman's employer, to hire a lawyer at his (Arnold's) expense to defend her.[53] These supportive acts of whites on behalf of blacks, while decent and well meaning, appear to have had an aura of paternalism about them. Even so, they were well intentioned and benefited their recipients.

In spite of social pressures against interracial romantic relationships, blacks and whites were romantically involved in Savannah; more often than not, the parties, a white male and a black female, were discreet about the relationship. Sarah Black cohabited with John Robinson, a white cotton salesman from Washington City, for fifteen years and gave birth to nine children—including seven boys—for him. The affair ended when the Union army captured Savannah and Robinson abandoned his black family.[54] Edwin Walton, whose mother was Patience Simpson a free African American, said his father was Thomas Walton, a white man.[55] Patrick Snead claimed that his girlfriend had a white lover, who upon becoming suspicious that he knew of the affair asked Snead if he would like to become his slave. Snead ended the relationship with the female. Subsequently, her white lover changed his attitude, purchased Snead, and hired him out as a cooper.[56] There were probably other interracial liaisons, but they are difficult to document, for obvious reasons.[57]

The role of guardian is less difficult to document. Unfortunately, guardians are among the least studied persons and, perhaps because of this, the least understood persons in the white community from the perspective of race relations. The law required all free African Americans to have guardians, who are often equated with slaveholders. This may have resulted in the general perception that the guardian system was a step above the peculiar institution. Indeed, many of the court appointed guardians, maybe even most of them, were also slaveholders, but was the term guardian a euphemism for slaveholder?

The guardian system and African American slavery were different in a number of ways. Guardians' power over free blacks was much less than slaveholders' power over their slaves. The areas of responsibility were different, and the relationships between guardians and free blacks were different than those between slaveholders and their slaves. Usually, the free black had to indicate the person he wanted as his guardian, the person had to consent to serve in the capacity, and the judge of the ordinary court had to approve the appointment.[58] The court seems to have maintained a very high profile in the relationship between free blacks and their guardians. When guardians were executors of estates of free blacks, they had to submit periodic reports concerning the status of the accounts, and the clerk of the court examined them and reported the findings to the judge, even when the accounts were small, which probably was the rule with most of those accounts. For instance, the estates of Hannah Lewis, which had a balance of $861.82 in 1833,[59] and John (Jack) Gibbons, which had a balance of $2,700.00 in 1837,[60] contained typical amounts.

Being a guardian of a free African American was a demanding and unrewarding obligation, except for the fulfillment that came from having shouldered one's civic responsibility. In order to protect the interest of those estates, guardians were required to post bond. Responding to a request from Cornelia Carter, a free black female from Bibb (Macon) County Georgia, Philip M. Russell agreed to be her guardian, posted bond for seven thousand dollars, and offered Mathias H. Meyer and Charles J. White as his securities. Then, Russell took an oath and received his Letters of Guardian.[61]

Russell and the other guardians were, first and foremost, persons who assumed legal responsibility for free African Americans, handled their legal matters, and reminded them to register each year. Guardians were not paid, and free African Americans were not required to donate free labor to compensate them. Sanguine relationships may have evolved, even if they were tainted with paternalism. Guardians helped African Americans evade what they perceived to have been unreasonable regulations, as when at the urging of white butchers, the city council prohibited free blacks from renting stalls in the market. Some guardians rented stalls and allowed free blacks to use them.[62] Guardians were also the middle-men, and sometimes trustees, in real estate transactions involving free blacks since by law they could not own real estate. If the intent of the lawmakers was to keep blacks propertyless, they were frus-trated because guardians purchased the property as stand-ins for free blacks and later transferred ownership to them.

The guardian system did not encumber the initiative of free African Americans in Savannah. The system may have even spawned benefits for blacks because as a result these powerless persons were provided a conduit to the rich and powerful in Savannah who took a special interest in individual free blacks which they would not have taken without it, and it placed the judicial system at the disposal of their heirs. Dr. Arnold protected the interests of Georgiana Kelly and other free blacks for whom he had consented to serve as guardian. Richard Richardson scrupulously attended to the affairs of Andrew Marshall, as did Richard Stites and Mordecai Myers for Simon Jackson and Jack Gibbons, respectively. As a child, Ellen Arnold visited Georgiana Kelly frequently since her father was that free black female's guardian;[63] and during his boyhood, William Harden was a constant visitor of the "good old Negro woman," Hannah Pray, who happened to have owned trees with delicious fruits and had William's father for her guardian.[64] A peculiar kind of bonding occurred between some free blacks and their guardians that reached beyond those two parties to members of their families. African Americans still faced problems in Savannah, and racism permeated the city, but the guardian system was not a stumbling block in the path of black advancement, nor did it weigh as heavily upon free blacks as the peculiar institution weighed upon slaves.

African Americans were not happy with their situation, but no one appeared who was unhappy enough to lead a revolt against the system. In fact, the community leaders, especially the black preachers, may have been instrumental in keeping the situation cool. In 1829, Henry Cunningham is reported to have turned over to the mayor antislavery literature he had received through the mail.[65] Andrew Marshall, moreover, was described by a white contemporary as having been "especially careful to maintain the cause of law and order in the social relationships by which he was surrounded in his own city and vicinity."[66] This was a polite way of saying he did not rock the boat. We know that Marshall could be stubborn if the occasion demanded it, as when he defied white preachers in the Sunbury Association and when he purchased building materials to construct a large house on his Yamacraw lot; jealous whites whipped him for allegedly buying stolen goods from slaves.

Two major factors present in the lives of Cunningham and Marshall were absent from Denmark Vesey's in Charleston, and they made a difference in those individuals' reactions to race relations in their respective cities: their wives were free, and their churches were allowed to worship unmolested. Conversely, Vesey's wife was a slave, whose freedom he was unable to purchase, and his black church was disestablished after a short-lived independent existence. Cunningham and Marshall, thus, probably believed they had much to lose by conspiring to lead a slave revolt; Vesey, doubtless, believed he had a world to gain. The prominence which closing the black church played in Vesey's decision to revolt against the system further underscored the importance of the independent black church in Savannah, for in addition to its broad ministry it helped to facilitate racial harmony.

In addition to allowing the black church to exist unmolested, the city fathers (prior to the 1850s) did not discourage an exodus of blacks to Liberia. This also facilitated racial harmony because it allowed potential black rebels a peaceful outlet to vent their dissatisfaction. The opportunity to emigrate to Liberia was an important safety valve for ventilating frustrations over the dissatisfaction with conditions in Savannah. In the absence of emigration as an alternative, African Americans had either to accept the status quo or attempt to overthrow the system. With African colonization, however, a new set of alternatives arose: stay in Savannah where the amenities of life were more accommodating than Liberia, or go to Liberia and enjoy freedoms that were unavailable to African Americans in Savannah. Between 1820 and 1850, only 551 black Georgians emigrated to Liberia[67] and the majority of those may have come from the Chatham-Savannah area. Even so, that represented a very small percentage of the African Americans in the area.

Samuel Benedict, who emigrated to Liberia and subsequently became chief justice of its supreme court, did not have any trouble deciding between the two alternatives: "I am often charged with folly and madness," he said, "when I speak of leaving the luxury here to go on to Africa. Yet I am willing to dispense with all those luxury [sic] to go to my rightful inheritance."[68] Liberty and freedom seem to have been the key magnets that attracted black Savannahians to Africa, the most notable of whom were Isaac Roberts, pastor of Third African Baptist Church; Samuel Benedict; Andrew Morel Jr.; Emanuel Wand, a barber; Adam Anderson, son of Thomas Anderson, pastor of Second African Baptist Church; and Jack Simpson and his wife, Sophia.[69]

The peak years of the exodus occurred between 1848 and 1856 when sixteen ships taking 297 free African Americans, 529 slaves, and 58 colonizers left Savannah for Liberia.[70] When the *Howard* departed for Liberia in May 1848, two prominent local white ministers participated in the farewell services at the wharf and between 4,000 and 5,000 persons were present for its departure.[71] When the *Huma* sailed the next May, however, there was so much excitement, white Savannahians became alarmed and pressured the council to ban any future departures from Savannah. Isaac Roberts gave an emotional farewell address; and a large number of relatives and friends of the emigrants, two church choirs, and a band were aboard the steamer which accompanied the *Huma* until it got to Tybee Island, which is just off the Georgia coast.[72]

The colonization-sponsored emigration is another example of the pervasive presence of the independent black church in Savannah. Some of the emigrants were leaders in their churches, and the celebration at the port had religious overtones, as church choirs sang and black preachers delivered moving speeches. It is highly improbable that similar scenes occurred in Charleston and New Orleans when African Americans there departed for Liberia because the independent black church was banned in those cities.

Black Savannahians may have seen the festivities and celebrations surrounding the departure of the *Huma* as a joyous occasion, but whites perceived them differently. The *Savannah Republican* protested "against a repetition of such a scene" and demanded the "intervention of our City Council to adopt such prudential measures, as that no such departure again occurs in Savannah" and called for the grand jury to act. The newspaper described the departure scene as consisting of

> about two thousand negro idlers huzzaing to negro harangues, and shouting to Yankee Doodle from a band of music et. and thus presenting mock-heroic opportunities for negro excitement and idleness.[73]

This depiction contrasted with the one in the *African Repository*:

> An immense crowd assembled this morning at 9 o'clock to witness the embarkation of the emigrants for Liberia . . . Three hearty cheers were given by the one hundred and eighty-one emigrants which were answered by three more from the assembled thousands . . .[74]

Taking its cue from the newspaper article, the grand jury construed the event "as a serious evil, and as a nuisance." That body took a dim view of any outdoor secular "assemblage of Negroes in the city of Savannah," but took special umbrage with the "assemblage" that watched the *Huma* depart for Liberia. Accordingly, the grand jury recommended passage of an ordinance which would prohibit free African Americans from departing for Africa from the port of Savannah.[75] The council agreed in principle with the concerns of the grand jury but, cognizant that such an ordinance would fall within the purview of regulating commerce, stated it did not have authority to enact the ordinance. The cause was not lost, however, as the council was certain existing legislation could achieve the desired results.[76] This was an optimistic prognostication; additional legislation was required.

The *Huma* jubilation scene was a turning point in the attitude of whites toward allowing their city to be a departure site for African embarkation. In the preceding departures, there was less fanfare, and the events went unnoticed, but the back-to-back high-profile celebrations in 1848–49 alerted the city fathers to the changing nature of the departure scene and the potential for civil disturbance it portended. African colonization per se did not appear to have been the issue because at least twice in its harangue about the *Huma* jubilation, the newspaper stated it had no qualms with colonization as long as it was done elsewhere. The perceived frenzied assemblage of spectators who witnessed and participated in the two latest embarkation jubilees was the great concern of whites. Whites did not want that type of show in their town.

Before the near hysteria caused by the *Huma* jubilation had run its course, the council petitioned the state legislature to enact legislation banning free African Americans from the state,[77] upon which that body, uncharacteristically, failed to act. It appears as if the legislature traditionally had shown little regard, at the most, for the welfare of free blacks. Further, the council laid a two hundred dollar tax on free African Americans and slaves who came to Savannah for the purpose of sailing to Liberia, or any other African port.[78]

The council did not believe the American Colonization Society had enough support from African Americans in Savannah to fill Africa-bound ships, which would force the society to abandon Savannah as a site of embarkation, if African Americans (free and slave) from outside Savannah could be discouraged from coming to Savannah to embark for Africa. The council's assessment of the situation was accurate because the tax did discourage blacks from coming to Savannah for that purpose, and the Chatham-Savannah area did not provide enough passengers to continue sending ships to the port, especially since the society was already losing money with the venture. The free African-American population was not large enough to sustain such an effort alone, even if all free blacks favored going to their "rightful inheritance," as Benedict construed it, and there were not enough slaveholders willing to manumit their slaves and pay their passage to Africa, as a few had done. In the same year the tax was laid (1856), the last ship bound for Africa left Savannah,[79] much to the relief of many whites, some of whom had shown greater hostility toward African Colonization efforts than toward any of the slave conspiracies and revolts of the nineteenth century. Even Nat Turner's Revolt failed to produce the diatribes from the press and grand jury that the *Huma* incident spawned.

The overriding fear among whites was a slave revolt; consequently, they eschewed any acts that might have caused one. Naturally, abolitionists were not welcome in Savannah, as S. F. Fisk, a white man, discovered on a cold December night in 1859 when he was tarred and feathered for allegedly cavorting with slaves—he was caught camping with them. A Mr. Schaffer, an alleged abolitionist, fared a little better in that he escaped punishment because he had quick enough wits and feet to escape to the safety of the army barracks; his tormentors vented their anger by destroying his property. Both Fisk and Schaffer fared better than John Brown, the foremost abolitionist of his day who was hanged in Charles Town, Virginia, for leading an assault of the federal arsenal at Harpers Ferry, Virginia, much to the delight of the slave trader W. F. Parker who made the following entry in his diary on December 2, 1859: "Old John Brown hangs today. I wish I was there to see it."[80] The next year, Joseph W. Ribero, a free African American, was whipped and driven from Savannah for allegedly traveling into the countryside in October 1860 and telling slaves there that Lincoln was going to free them, which, to whites, was tantamount to inciting a slave insurrection.[81]

So in the decade before the Civil War, race relations became tense at times over African embarkation, allegations of abolitionists' activities, and the actions of Ribero, who may have been a recent arrival in the area. Nevertheless, the situation did not become unmanageable. The mob action was directed toward whites who had threatened the system. In the past, whites had broached social customs, but these were individual acts of self-gratification, which, though not condoned, were not condemned. Abolitionist activities, on the other hand, were bent upon destroying the peculiar institution, hence were condemned. Even with these occasional tension-filled incidents, there was not a significant change in race relations in the 1850s. The laws passed were no more numerous and burdensome, the regulation of movement about the city was no more confining, and the interaction between the races was no more strained in the 1850s than earlier.

In 1856, Savannah lost one of its pillars of racial harmony: Andrew C. Marshall. William Harden, a white Savannahian, called this highly respected black preacher "the most esteemed colored man who ever lived in Savannah."[82] White preachers in the Sunbury Baptist Association said he was "the leading religious spirit among his colored Brethren."[83] James Simms, who was reared in First African Baptist Church during the Marshall years, said he "was greatly respected by whites, among whom he had many warm and influential friends."[84] The Savannah newspaper said he "was one of the most gifted of his race" and the venerable black preacher "had won the respect and esteem of all who knew him."[85] The epitaph on his vault reads "And like his Master, was by some despised like him, by others loved and prized."[86] These were the reflections which Marshall saw in his community looking glass. If whites and blacks coexisted in an uneasy but tolerable situation, it was partly because Marshall and other black leaders in the community had gained the trust and, in some instances, respect of whites who could count on them to set the proper example.

One may conclude, therefore, that community leaders played a major role in reducing tension between blacks and whites. Black leaders generally did not threaten the status quo, and this reduced the probability of a racial confrontation. White leaders in the community subscribed to the racial practices of their day, but they generally acted responsibly by allowing African Americans to worship in their own churches, own real estate, create social functions, immigrate to Liberia, and move relatively freely throughout the city during daylight hours without being harassed too severely. As a result of the white leaders' actions, a ground swell of uncontrollable discontentment did not form in the black community, and a less tense racial climate existed than might have been expected in light of the oppressive state of affairs that existed in black Savannah.

CHAPTER VII

The Year of Jubilee
has Come

*I attended a meeting of colored people in the Baptist
Church a few days . . . The meeting was opened by
one of the brethren in a prayer of great pathos and
rare power . . . In a strain of rude but hearty elo-
quence, he thanked God that the black people were
free, and forever free . . .*
—GEORGE W. PEPPER, PERSONAL RECOLLECTIONS
OF SHERMAN'S CAMPAIGNS IN
GEORGIA AND THE CAROLINAS

The meeting which George Pepper described above occurred in
Second African Baptist Church on a cold December night in 1864
just days after Sherman's army captured Savannah. That night, a
jubilant group of black Savannahians gathered in an institution,
the independent black church, to celebrate the arrival of an event
for which they had prayed constantly over the years: the Year of
Jubilee. In addition to epitomizing black pride and autonomy,
Second African Baptist Church and its sister black churches in the
city had provided African Americans, free and enslaved, spiritual
nourishment which sustained them during the dark, dreary days of
slavery. Now that the Year of Jubilee had come, it was only fitting
that African Americans would assemble in the independent black
church to commemorate its coming. This marked the first time all
African Americans who gathered in the church to worship were
free. Slavery had been abolished. But how did black Savannahians
arrive at this point?

When the Civil War began, Savannah's large black population must have represented a troubling presence, since in the minds of white Savannahians the Confederate States of America was created to preserve slavery. Word of Lincoln's alleged intent to abolish slavery had circulated among some blacks in Savannah. This may have created sufficient cause for the black population to start an insurrection. Could white Savannahians afford to fight on distant battlefields, leaving their city, homes, and families unprotected from the potential enemy within their midst?

If this question surfaced in the consciousness of whites, it did not linger or become a major cause for concern. As the war progressed, the presence of blacks became a blessing as the Confederate command employed blacks in many nonmilitary capacities, and a small number of blacks, mainly slaves, accompanied local units to the front lines. In fact, white Savannahians feared an attack from the Union forces more than they did a black insurrection. This fear drove Ellen Buchanan Screven's husband, a Confederate officer, to move her from Savannah to Athens, Georgia, in November 1861.[1]

That same month, Gen. Robert E. Lee assumed his first command since joining the Confederate army, when he became commander of the Confederate southern coast defenses in South Carolina, Georgia, and Florida. By that time the Confederate forces had already won a victory over the Union army at Bull Run in the first major battle of the war, and Lee, buoyed by that victory, directed the constructon of fortifications in and around the city to prepare the area for an eventual Union attack. Lee stayed in the area until the next February,[2] which should have disabused Confederate soldiers of their fantasies about a short victorious war. Lee knew better. The war would not be short, and the victory at Bull Run did not portend a Confederate victory.

Confederate troops needed food to sustain them and this responsibility fell to William H. Davis, a successful white butcher who employed at least nine blacks to help him. The blacks subsequently claimed they were forced to work for the Confederates,[3] but Enos Richmond, special agent for the Southern Claims Commissioners, said some of those black butchers were willing contributors to the Confederate cause. According to Richmond, for instance, Jackson B. Sheftall, a "nearly white" butcher, "made money by his service and rendered as much aid and comfort to the Confederacy as a white man under similar circumstances." In the words of Richmond, therefore, Sheftall "was not loyal."[4]

Disputing this allegation, Sheftall said he was forced to work two years for the Confederate army, probably part time, until near the end of the war when he butchered for them full time, in return for which he received the animals' livers, tongues, and hides. Davis provided Sheftall, who apparently was his chief assistant, with forty persons to work under him. Sheftall spent a five to eight day stint at Fort Pulaski, but returned to the city because there was no work for him to do.[5] Sheftall was compensated for his work, which is inconsistent with past experiences of blacks who were pressed into public work. It strains credulity, moreover, to believe Davis placed forty persons under the supervision of someone whom he knew was not loyal to the cause. If Sheftall were the only butcher, or even the best one, in town, then maybe this could have happened. He was neither.

In the question of who was loyal and who was not, the litmus test may be who was compensated and who was not. John Laurence, a free black whose wife and children were slaves, hired his children, lived on Davis's place, and butchered for him, worked in the pens, and salted hides. Whether he was compensated is not known, but Laurence apparently was closely associated with Davis.[6] Sandy Small, who also butchered for Davis, was not compensated because he "did not do it for the good of the cause."[7] Since the Confederates did not compensate all black butchers, those who were compensated must have done something to earn it other than slaughter animals. In light of this, labeling Sheftall and Lawrence as opportunists would be an act of kindness.

There is even less uncertainty about the loyalty of Anthony Odingsells, Savannah's largest black slaveholder. At the beginning of the war, he did quite well selling fish, shucked oysters, meat, and other products to the Confederate troops manning the fortifications on the northern end of Wassaw Island. As the war progressed, the weak Confederate economy was hit with inflation, which caused Confederate officials to pay Odingsells for his products in highly devalued currency. The resulting great hardships were not the worst of his problems, however, as the subsequent forced evacuation of the Confederates led to the Union occupation of the island, an action which prompted Odingsells to send his slaves to Fort McAllister to help build additional fortifications for the impending battle with Sherman's advancing army.[8] The Confederates surrendered the fort on December 13, 1864, and Odingsells' slaves gained their freedom. There was no joy in the Odingsells house, therefore, when the Union army captured Savannah and its surrounding areas.

Odingsells willingly supported the Confederates. There were blacks in Savannah, however, who were forced to support the Confederates. One slave worked for the railroad throughout the war while his master received compensation for his work.[9] One of the real tragedies of the war involved a former nominal slave pilot who had worked hard to earn enough money to purchase the freedom of himself, his wife, and daughter, and shortly after he succeeded in gaining their freedom lost his life piloting a Confederate force down the Savannah River to capture a Union gun boat.[10] The black pilot did not have a choice in the matter; he either had to do as ordered or face what could have been very unpleasant consequences. The Union force which fired on him did not know he was an unwilling accomplice in the confrontation; thus they did not make a distinction between him and the gray coats whom he led down the river.

Free blacks and slaves were pressed into work details building and repairing fortifications. An August 1862 order from Gen. H. W. Mercer, commanding the construction of fortifications, required slaveholders to send 20 percent of their able-bodied slaves to work on fortifications, in return for which the government would pay for the labor of those slaves and underwrite their transportation.[11] The following August (1863) the city council passed a resolution encouraging Savannah slaveholders to send "their slaves as are capable" to work on fortifications to Lt. Col. H. D. Capers "at once and save him the unpleasant task of impressment."[12] Many slaveholders had not complied with the earlier order. Those who had were appalled by the high sickness rate among the Savannah Engineer's slave work force in the wake of a prolonged epidemic which incapacitated sometimes as many as 150 slaves each day. The owners feared their slaves would be overworked, demoralized,[13] or they would escape to Saint Simons Island, where the Union navy had a black settlement, or to some other Union location.[14]

Two slaves from each plantation outside Chatham County were transported into the area to work on building fortifications, thus relieving Confederate troops to fight the war. Slaves from David Ross's plantation in Putnam Country traveled a total of seven days to Savannah and back to work on those defenses.[15] A pair of slaves from the estate of William Dennis in Eatonton, Georgia, who worked on the Savannah fortifications in April and December 1863, earned $76.41 and $89.35, respectively.[16] This influx of slaves into Savannah swelled the already large native black population and could have created security problems in spite of the presence of Confederate soldiers.

The August 1863 city council resolution also ordered free blacks to work on the fortifications without indicating whether they would be compensated.[17] It is also not clear whether free blacks from nearby counties were required to travel to Savannah to build fortifications. Apparently, free blacks were generally unenthusiastic about working on those details; even so, they did as directed.[18] Continuous work on the defenses resulted in the protection of all approaches to the city, as fortifications stretched from the Savannah to the Little Ogeechee River.[19] Ultimately, the effort spent fortifying Savannah was wasted because it merely delayed the Union capture of the city by ten days, which could hardly be considered adequate results for the effort involved. The Confederates hoped to achieve a victory, not delay a defeat.

Although African Americans served in the Confederate army,[20] Savannah did not provide any. According to an anonymous letter to the local newspaper, "April last [1861], sixty odd of the free colored men of this city made a written tender to his Excellency the Governor, of their services in any capacity in which he would employ them," but their services were not accepted.[21] Almost a month later, another article in the newspaper claimed that "a number of our free colored population had tendered their service to the military to aid in the construction of work of defense." The article then listed the names of the twenty-four free black males who allegedly had been honorably discharged from their construction duties.[22] None of the twenty-four was a community leader, and six had close familial ties with black slaveholders—five were sons and one was a grandson. Instead of giving the black volunteers rifles and sending them off to fight, however, the governor assigned them to construction details in the Savannah area. Hence, Gov. Joseph Brown took the same hard-line position against using African Americans as armed combatants that his predecessor took on the issue in the American Revolution. This stance coincided with Jefferson Davis's, until he relented late in the war, in the face of a Confederate defeat.

Some free blacks were loyal to the Confederate cause because they construed it to be in their best interests. Some were doubtless loyal to whatever army was in town, and it happened to be the Confederate army for much of the war. William Sheftall, the brother of Jackson (the butcher), typified this group. He was a drummer in Company 7 (the German volunteers) and before the war, received two dollars for each parade in which he participated. This unit was at Fort Sumter when Gen. P. G. T. Beauregard ordered the artillery fire that started the Civil War, and Sheftall was with them. Sheftall claimed the Confederates compelled him to serve with the Savannah company,[23] but Enos Richmond refuted this, in a sweeping indictment questioning the loyalty of all Sheftalls.[24]

The slave Frank was not at Fort Sumter, but he accompanied his master, boyhood playmate, and lifelong idol, George Washington Stiles, a Confederate officer, to the front lines where, dressed in a Confederate uniform, he played his drum and fife to the men in camp.[25] The slave Ben had a similar wartime experience. His master, Walter Norton, a Baptist minister, was a member of the First Georgia Regiment, Companies A and B, camped in Effingham County. This unit was among the force General Lee took north to Gettysburg where the fortunes of the war turned against the Confederates. Ben survived the war, and he returned to Gettysburg later to "see it again."[26]

These slaves represent a small group that accompanied their masters because they had developed a deep admiration and respect for them. This loyalty was fixed on their masters, however, not on the Confederate States of America. Those slaves did not serve the

Confederate cause for personal gain, glory, or any other compensation, either monetary or emotional. They were victims of a system that had conditioned them to be servile, to identify their masters' interests as paramount, and to give their masters unquestioned loyalty. This blind loyalty rendered them incapable of making the kinds of judgments the Sheftalls should have been capable of making. Thus their actions during the war must be viewed in a different perspective from those of Odingsells, the Sheftalls, James Laurence, Josiah Grant, and others of their ilk.

Black females did not escape having demands placed upon them to aid the Confederate cause. They were ordered to make clothing for the soldiers and to work in the hospital nursing and attending sick soldiers.[27] Those who sewed formed quilting party–like clubs, and they generally displayed the same lack of enthusiasm for their chores which most free black males did.[28] There were exceptions, too, among females because they were products of the same environment as the males; self-preservation is a trait which transcends race, region, sex, and social class.

A number of free African-American females volunteered to make Confederate uniforms.[29] Unlike their male counterparts, however, many of those females were economically advantaged. Ann H. Gibbons, Jane Deveaux, Charlotte Fonnell, and Estelle Savage each owned property assessed at over two thousand dollars in 1860, and the former two were slaveholders; three others in the group had close familial ties to slaveholders (parents, grandparents, or in-laws). Estelle may have influenced her younger sister Tharsville, sister-in-law Eliza Dupon Savage, and Eliza's sister Ann Dupon. These four and most of the other females were seamstresses. One of the female volunteers listed in the local newspaper, Georgiana Kelly, may have been a victim of circumstances since she had very close ties to Dr. Richard Arnold. She may have felt compelled to show public support for the Confederate cause even though privately she supported the Union. Thus, Georgiana Kelly "wore the mask," an expression the black poet Paul Laurence Dunbar used to depict the behavior of African Americans of a later generation.[30]

Some free black females who publicly supported the Confederacy did not experience the anxiety Georgiana doubtless had, nor did they support the cause, as Ann Gibbons did, because a Confederate victory was construed to have been in their best interests. Rather, these females were opportunists. There may have been other black females with defects of character the equal of Rachel Bromfield's, but they have avoided the light. Bromfield, whose husband was among those slaves who accompanied their masters to the front lines, is alleged to have rented a building to the Confederates in 1864 which their signal corps used, and she was among the looters who broke into stores in the city before the Union soldiers arrived in December.[31] An enterprising slave female, Margaret Dawson, is alleged to have kept a boardinghouse where out-of-town blacks who worked on the fortifications stayed. Union officials believed her master was behind the operation,[32] but they were more familiar with the distorted perception of slaves which slaveholders peddled. This female was fully capable of running a boardinghouse, and the black community produced enough food to meet her needs. If black females succumbed to self-preservation less often than the males, this may have resulted from women having had fewer opportunities to work for the Confederate cause since normally they were not compelled to build fortifications and breast-works, were not drummers in units, and did not accompany their masters as personal servants, or qualify to serve in combat units.

Despite these examples of Confederate loyalty, Union sentiment ran strong and deep in black Savannah. Most African Americans who aided the Confederates were compelled to. Those who aided the Union, on the other hand, did so out of conviction as there was not an intimidating Union presence to force the issue. Whatever moved blacks to support the Union cause came from within themselves. They had to be discreet, and except for those who joined the Union army and navy, or were guides and spies, they have been ignored by Civil War historians.

The prospect of gaining freedom for themselves and their families was a powerful attraction among slaves to enlist, as Union recruiters learned early in the war. Most black soldiers hated slavery and wanted to destroy it. Even those who had warm feelings for their masters were able to distinguish between personal relationships and the peculiar institution. They believed the latter was wrong and those who perpetuated it—that is, slaveholders—were their natural enemies.[33] The problem for recruiters, therefore, was getting the message to the would-be recruits, rather than persuading them to enlist.

The first black recruiter was Abraham (or Abram) Murchison, a literate slave preacher who in 1862 assisted in the initial effort to recruit black refugees on Hilton Head, South Carolina. He called a meeting on April 7, and after a brief speech, in which he emphasized the personal responsibility of African Americans to defeat the Confederate forces and apprised his audience that Lincoln was contemplating allowing blacks to bear arms, Murchison asked those who wanted to enlist to stand. All the men stood. After rejecting the old men and young boys, he enlisted 105 volunteers. Within a week the number had increased to 150. They became the nucleus of the First South Carolina Volunteer Regiment, the first official all-black unit of the war.[34]

The premier recruiter and reconnaissance specialist, however, was March Haynes, a large former nominal slave stevedore and Savannah River pilot. Shortly after the Union army captured Fort Pulaski in April 1862, Haynes began smuggling fugitive slaves into the Union camp in a boat he kept hidden in a creek among the marshes below the city. Operations of this kind could not go undetected very long because blacks and whites lived among each other. When it became evident whites were suspicious of his activities, Haynes escaped with his wife to a Union camp. Once his wife had been settled safely, Haynes became a reconnaissance specialist for the Union army, heading an all-black reconnaissance team as it conducted many dangerous missions in Savannah to determine the location of Confederate forts, batteries, and camps. The black reconnaissance team was aided and abetted during its three-day stays, or longer, by black Savannahians who hid and fed the group. Once a mission was completed, the team left Savannah carrying with it as many fugitives as its camouflaged boat would hold. On one mission, when the team was unable to leave until daylight, unlike on other missions, it ran into a six-man Confederate picket which fired on the team. In the ensuing exchange of gunfire, three Confederate soldiers were killed, and Haynes was shot in the leg, but the team managed to escape.[35] In April 1863, Haynes' luck ran out temporarily when Savannah authorities arrested and jailed him for a short period.[36]

Although their contributions were less spectacular and dangerous than Haynes', a number of black pilots facilitated Union operations in and around Savannah by leading the Yankees through the familiar waterways which in peacetime had provided those pilots with a livelihood. Isaac Tatnall, a slave who escaped from the packet ship *St. Mary's* in December 1861, subsequently was employed aboard Union warships, guiding them through the waters between Savannah and Brunswick which he knew so well. He was just one of several slave pilots employed aboard Union warships in the area.[37] In addition to using black pilots, the Union employed blacks to transport cotton. A nominal slave was pressed into service for over two weeks to haul cotton.[38] Blacks, therefore, were employed to move Union soldiers and supplies by land and water.

Unlike the Confederate army, which did not enlist black Savannahians, the Union forces used them in the First South Carolina Volunteers, the 33rd and 120th Massachusetts Regiments, the 138th Colored Regiment, and in other combat units, including naval units.[39] Samuel Gordon Morse, born in McIntosh County July 25, 1832, was the first black from the Savannah area to enlist in a combat outfit. He joined the First South Carolina Volunteers and reached the rank of first sergeant before being honorably discharged from the army a year after the war had ended.[40] A Beaufort, South Carolina–born black claimed that Robert Small, the slave who commandeered the steamer *Planter* from under the noses of Confederates in Charleston Harbor, was his brother, but the former stayed in Savannah during the war.[41] Some fugitive slaves served aboard gunboats.[42] These African Americans joined others from throughout the nation in the fight to set the bondsmen free. Although black Savannahians suffered through servitude without revolting, apparently a desire for freedom and a latent willingness to take risks to attain it were present in the black community.

The official statistics credit Georgia with furnishing 3,486 troops for the Union army, which was well below the median number of 5,462 furnished by the Confederate states. There is no accurate accounting of the African Americans Savannah contributed to the state's total, but the number was probably less than one thousand. The major drawback was they had to leave the city to make those kinds of contributions, and this appealed mainly to slaves who lived with their masters. Most free African-American property owners did not relish abandoning their property and businesses to join the Union army, and the nonpropertied free African Americans did not wish to risk the little they had to join an army that initially showed little interest in them, that also instituted a discriminatory pay policy favoring white soldiers, assigned heavy manual labor work details to black troops, and occasionally assigned them as body servants to white officers.[43] Furthermore, most of the free blacks who normally would have been attracted to taking such risks left the area during the 1840s and early 1850s and settled in Liberia. Even though slaves may have wished to enlist, they had to overcome formidable obstacles to reach a Union camp. In the main, therefore, conditions were not favorable for a mass exodus of African Americans from Savannah to join the Union armed forces.

For these reasons, most African Americans remained in the area throughout the war. Their contributions to the Union cause, nevertheless, spanned a range of nonmilitary activities. As one black Savannahian observed, "Colored people were all Union people; they prayed for the success of the Yankee army."[44] Blacks often uttered this statement to the commissioners. They prayed individually, and in groups, but in both instances it was done privately.[45] Praying was a major part of the belief system of African Americans, who had prayed for freedom long before the Civil War began and never doubted their prayers would be answered. The war encouraged them to remain steadfast and continue to pray. Indeed, the religious faith of black Savannahians was instrumental in their surviving the ordeals of their wretched situation with their sanity intact and their determination undiminished. Without intending for it to be, or perhaps even realizing that it was, religion became therapeutic, and praying was an indispensable part of religious life. It is understandable, therefore, why, when asked about their activities during the war, blacks were not ashamed to respond to the question, in principle, with the quotation given above.

While some blacks formed prayer bands, others formed "bread companies,"[46] which carried bread to the Union army in violation of policy. Black Savannahians were especially kind to the Union soldiers who had been captured and brought to the city. Sarah Ann Black, who refused to attend "meetings to help the Confederates in sewing for them," baked bread and potatoes for the Union prisoners whom she also provided with tobacco.[47] Even though publicly she proclaimed her loyalty to the Confederates and offered to sew for them, privately Georgiana Kelly supervised an operation that occasionally collected as many as three hundred loaves of bread that had been baked in black homes throughout the city for the Union prisoners. The same little black boys who delivered the bread to her home subsequently were dispatched to the stockade to throw the loaves over the wall to the former Andersonville prisoners. Some white women also threw food to those prisoners. This type of activity did not come without risks. One free black female was incarcerated for doing it.[48]

Georgiana Kelly and a female friend also hid a prisoner in their homes for four or five months. They fed the prisoner and cared for him, moving him between the two houses to avoid detection.[49] Hiding escaped prisoners occurred frequently among other blacks. "I stowed away eleven prisoners that came down from Andersonville," said Francis Keaton, who paid for his defiance by being locked in the guardhouse and targeted for being sold as a slave. He gained a reprieve, however, when the keeper fled with the Confederates and left the keys. Keaton took them and freed all prisoners in the facility.[50] Joseph Sneed, who worked for Davis, the Confederate butcher, kept two escaped prisoners in his home, gave them food and clothes, then allowed his eighteen-year-old son to pilot them to a Union gunboat. This showed where Sneed's true loyalty lay. The teenager "guided them around through the marsh to past the steamer *Water Witch,* then directed them on the course for escape."[51] Another black Savannahian had a number of Union troops in his home, some of whom stayed three or four days while others stayed as long as a week before they could escape. His wife prepared meals during their stay.[52] As one free black walked in a sparsely inhabited area, four escaped Union prisoners approached him and asked for "something to wear"; he took them home with him where they remained two months until the Confederates evacuated the city.[53]

Although most blacks stayed home and did not fight in the war, a minority contributed to the Union cause by providing food, clothing, shelter and transportation to Union soldiers—behavior that could have compromised their lives and freedom had they been caught in the act. More than a modicum of courage was required to perform those acts, and much more courage was demanded of those who involved their mates and children in those ventures. The teenager who piloted the prisoners to a Union gunboat exposed himself to an attack from Confederate pickets or a gunboat. The man who allowed his wife to cook for the prisoners whom he harbored placed her in a position to be jailed, as another free black female had been. The ladies who made bread for the prisoners were compassionate, and the boys who picked up and delivered the bread were daring. These were commendable acts.

Blacks on the home front constituted a modern day version of the Trojan horse, in a sense. They did not bear arms, hence did not kill anyone, and the kinds of pro-Union activities they pursued did not figure significantly in the outcome of the war; nonetheless, their efforts were important because they indicated blacks in Savannah generally were loyal to the Union cause. They helped the most vulnerable of the Union troops, those who had survived the horrible ordeal at Andersonville. Most of those soldiers were not in a position to return the favor or to help fight the Confederates if the situation had arisen. In spite of the potentially dreadful consequences, blacks did not turn their backs on the prisoners behind the wall, nor did they lock their doors on those who had escaped. In reaching out to help those troops, blacks demonstrated that carrying weapons, conducting troops through the inlets, and gathering intelligence information may have been the conventional ways of contributing to the war, but they were not the only ways to help the Union cause. When the opportunity arose to aid the cause in unconventional ways, blacks responded.

When blacks in the city decided upon this course of action, they were not aware that Union soldiers would later convert some of the homes in the black community into firewood, and confiscate cattle, poultry, other food, and clothing; or that some of them would be asked to give sworn testimony concerning their activities during the war—their deeds as well as their misdeeds. Union soldiers' subsequent vandalizing of the black community led some blacks to question the actions of those soldiers, but they did not question the wisdom of the actions they had taken earlier on behalf of the Union cause. None of the actions of black Savannahians was taken with an eye toward history—a selflessness that ennobles the acts of those who took risks.

Why did certain African Americans aid the Union cause at the risk of their own personal safety? Their hatred of slavery and their subordinate position in Savannah existed long before Lincoln was elected president in 1860 and Fort Sumter was fired upon in 1861, but the throbbing in their chests was not sufficient reason to take overt action against the oppressive system. While slave revolts had been successful in gaining freedom for slaves in Haiti and to a less extent in Jamaica, none had succeeded in the United States. To the contrary, the conspiracies were often detected before they came to fruition, with the conspirators and many innocent blacks suffering execution, incarceration, or deportation. The war was the catalyst which galvanized long-smoldering desires to strike a blow for "real freedom" because it presented a different scenario for blacks: whites divided and killing each other.

Black churches in Savannah felt the effects of the war. Andrew Chapel lost its minister because he joined the Confederate army, and no replacement was appointed, much to the disappointment of black Methodists in the community. They complained but got no results. The whites subsequently dissolved the board of trustees and sold the property to Trinity Methodist Church.[54] The three independent black churches maintained their memberships in the Sunbury Baptist Association throughout the war and sent delegates to the annual conventions. Those churches were allowed to worship, and memberships actually increased between 1860 and 1862, but later in the war they decreased because masters removed their slaves from the area, and other slaves ran away to Union camps. The war, however, did not cause a change in either the form or order of worship, although black ministers were more guarded than formerly in what they preached from their pulpits, to avoid giving whites an excuse to close the churches.[55]

Savannah's economy also experienced the shocks of wartime. Prices skyrocketed throughout the economy. From June to December 1862, the monthly subscription to the *Savannah Republican* cost four dollars; from January to July 1864, however, a monthly subscription cost fifteen dollars.[56] Coffee sold for thirty-five dollars a pound,[57] which was much higher than previously. Wages also increased but not as much as food prices and newspaper subscriptions did. Slaves were less available in the trade market. A Confederate officer who was in the market to purchase a female slave or a cook searched unsuccessfully throughout the city in 1862. In 1863, slaveholders demanded twenty dollars monthly for the hire of their slaves,[58] and the amount demanded of slaves who hired their own time was also increased. Prior to the war the usual amount was twelve dollars for males and nine for females, but those figures were increased to twenty-one and ten, respectively.[59] Inflationary prices and the labor shortage had become so acute by 1863 that they drove up the prices for slaves and the wages paid black laborers.[60]

The reported number of crimes by African Americans also increased. According to records of the mayor's court, the crime rate among slaves in the city quadrupled between late 1862 and late 1864.[61] The increase in reported crimes may have been related more to the shift in the punishment of slaves from their masters, many of whom were away fighting the Civil War, to the jailer than it was to a significant upswing in crime among African Americans. With increased vigilance of patrols, moreover, lawbreakers were more likely to be apprehended than formerly. In addition to these factors, the fluidity of the slave population, with the constant influx and exodus of slaves hired for work on the fortifications, probably contributed to the increase.

Those conditions apparently did not profoundly affect the social life of blacks. African Americans were accustomed to having their social activities regulated, and the nature of the regulations did not change significantly during the war. Consequently, African Americans continued to congregate in the streets on Sunday afternoons, and whites continued to complain about their refusal to pay proper deference to whites when they approached on the sidewalk and their use of vile language. Blacks still held barbecues, dances, games, and picnics and operated clandestine schools. Marriages were quite popular among slaves. One owner complained about her slaves' penchant for marriages because the supper after the wedding, which the slaves expected, had become too expensive.[62] Engaging in those social activities, which gave the impression of business as usual in the black community, may have given whites a false sense of security. Many whites became careless about observing the actions of individual blacks in the community, as many whites believed blacks generally were too apathetic about serious matters to aid the Union cause. This may have been true of some blacks, but certainly not all blacks.

Blacks were not as naive about current events as whites wished. Whites, for instance, would loved to have blacked out news about the preliminary emancipation the president issued in September 1862, but this did not happen. The news may have been in the community earlier, but nothing was done among blacks until James Simms arrived from Virginia with a copy of the document in late 1862. Several black leaders then asked and were granted permission from the authorities to hold a dinner on January 1, 1863.[63] Granting the request seem strange in light of the mayor's feelings toward the proclamation, which he described as an "infamous attempt to incite flight, murder, and rapine on the part of our slave population." The mayor further characterized the document as an effort to subvert the social system, to destroy the homes of whites, and to "convert the quiet, ignorant dependent black son of toil into a savage incendiary and brutal murderer." The mayor, who shared these views with his father,[64] may not have perceived the responsible free blacks who had asked to hold the supper in the same light he held the slaves. Those persons traditionally had not given whites cause for concern, and they came from the same group who themselves owned slaves in better times.

The supper was held as scheduled on January 1, 1863, at which James Porter was reported to have given an excellent address, the substance of which has been lost, on the Emancipation Proclamation. The only reference to the address appeared in Porter's obituary three decades later. John Cox, the free black pastor of Second African Baptist Church, and Ulysses L. Houston, the nominal slave pastor of Third African Baptist Church, gave prayers, the essence of which was the hope "that God would permit nothing to hinder Mr. Lincoln from Issuing his proclamation."[65] At the time of the supper, news had not reached the community that Lincoln had issued the Emancipation Proclamation on January 1, 1863, abolishing slavery in those areas of the South that were still in rebellion against the Union, but not in the rest of the South.

Black leaders did not repudiate the proclamation or distance themselves from it; neither did they meet secretly to endorse it; rather, they held a public supper at which the major address was devoted to the proclamation, and two of the three leading black preachers offered prayers hoping for its implementation. The black churches' leadership took a prominent role at the supper, which white ruffians, the police, and the marshal did not interrupt, and the participants were not placed in the guardhouse. This was a significant occasion in the history of black Savannah because its leaders supported freedom publicly; whereas in the past, public speeches—mainly sermons—were silent on the subject of the war. Thus, that supper marked a turning point in the history of the black community. Black Savannahians probably did not become defiant or assertive, but they had taken a first step to reconcile their public actions with their private thoughts.

After Lincoln issued the Emancipation Proclamation, the number of free African Americans who registered with the state annually as required by statute increased significantly, commencing with the April term of the Court of the Ordinary. The stream of free blacks who appeared before the court to register and have guardians appointed indicate that the state subsequently tightened its monitoring of the earlier statute, perhaps in an attempt to identify slaves who may have gotten wind of the proclamation and claimed to have become free because of it. Among those who applied to be registered during the spring term in 1863 was Prince Candy, son of a well-to-do free black cooper and slaveholder of the same name in the early 1800s, and among the fourteen who applied to have guardians appointed were Anthony Odingsells and Estelle

Savage. James Porter and his wife, Elizabeth, applied to be registered and have a guardian appointed in the May term. This marked the first time Porter had gone through this procedure even though he had moved to Savannah from Charleston over seven years earlier. By the end of 1863, the Court of the Ordinary had received sixty-five requests to have guardians appointed, ten to register as free persons of color, and ten to register and have guardians appointed, with seventy-six requests receiving favorable treatment, three being rejected, and six being continued with no action being taken.[66]

The steady business continued during the 1864 sessions, although it was not as heavy as the previous year. Included among some of the applicants in 1864 were some who had applied in 1863 and had either been rejected or had their applications continued. Some received better results the second time around. For instance, a man from Washington County who had been rejected previously was allowed to register and have a guardian appointed because he presented "satisfactory evidence" to the court that he was free.[67] The court ended its business abruptly on December 21, 1864, when Gen. William Tecumseh Sherman occupied Savannah and declared martial law.[68]

The Confederate forces evacuated Savannah on December 20, 1864, and about noon the following day, the Union army arrived. In the interval between the departure of the Confederates and the arrival of the Yankees, the city was in an uproar as blacks and whites rushed into the streets looting and plundering.[69] Excitement and disorder were pervasive, but the scene on Bay Street was special. In the mayhem, the ubiquitous Rachel Bromfield and her husband stole rice and molasses from store after store, and on one of her several jaunts across the street with their ill-gained prizes of war, she ran into the path of approaching Union troops and was seriously injured.[70] A female slave who made a special trip to Bay Street to see General Sherman "screeched and screamed" until she lost her voice. As the general approached, she took off her apron and waved it since she did not have a handkerchief.[71]

In the midst of this confusion strode Dr. Richard Arnold, mayor of the city, walking down Bay Street with a big white sheet tied to a pole, as he shouted "peace, peace, for God's sake, peace." The day before, the mayor had led a delegation which met with General Sherman to inform him of the Confederate commander's decision to evacuate the city that night.[72] On December 21, 1864, Bay Street was the focal point of scenes the likes of which Savannah had never experienced as persons from different backgrounds and with different motives for being there intermingled as the most traumatic episode in the history of the city unfolded.

Once the federal troops occupied the city, the plundering subsided and martial law was declared, with the military replacing the civilian authorities. The court was allowed to open to issue marriage licenses, temporary letters of administration, and to probate wills.[73] Fortifications were erected quickly on South Broad (Oglethorpe Avenue), East Broad, and West Broad Streets, and where formerly blacks needed passes to move about the city, whites were now subjected to a similar policy.[74] This was a new experience for whites who had suddenly become quasi prisoners in their own city. Blacks, on the other hand, felt freer than at any other time in their history.

A few days after the troops had arrived and the situation had become calm, an overflow crowd (hundreds were turned away) crammed into Second African Baptist Church to commemorate the great event that had just occurred in the life of black Savannah.[75] Emotions which had been suppressed during the Civil War now were unleashed and shouts of praise and thanksgiving rocked the edifice. After a powerful prayer in which a deacon thanked God that African Americans "were free, and forever free," shouts of "Glory to God! Hallelujah! Praise his name" resounded throughout the building. Then another deacon lined a hymn with the following words:

> Blow ye the trumphet, blow
> the gladly solemn sound
> Let all the nations know
> The year of Jubilee has come.[76]

The hymn liner was so overcome emotionally as he reached the line "the year of Jubilee has come" he could not continue. Soon, the entire church was overcome.[77]

The war and slavery had ended in black Savannah.

Epilogue

*Colored people have not been prevented from opening
business, except to keeping bar-rooms . . . In no other
way has any colored person been prevented from
following any occupation open to any white person.*
—R. D. ARNOLD, DECEMBER 1865

The quotation above is an excerpt from Richard Arnold's reply to
African-American charges of racial discrimination encumbering
efforts to open businesses in Savannah.[1] Having to defend the city
council, which historically had passed discriminatory ordinances
adversely affecting the economic well being of African Americans
without having their actions questioned, must have troubled the
mayor. Col. H. J. Sickler's inquiry into the complaints of African
Americans represented something different in the city; whites could
not do business as usual in the wake of the defeat of the Confederates.

The change in accountability for civil rights abuses was perhaps
almost as distressing to the mayor as the condition of his once beau-
tiful bustling city on the Savannah River. According to one white
Savannahian who wrote in March 1865, seventy-five thousand
Union troops were in the city, and African Americans were being
recruited as soldiers by the "Union Government" and becoming
policemen.[2] This was an exaggerated figure of the number of Union
troops in the city, but their presence was quite visible as well as
unsettling to whites. Another white Savannahian, writing two
months later, said the city "looked very desolate for it was really a

deserted city," with most of the stores closed and the wharves, piers, and bulkheads decaying "and grass and weeds were growing everywhere."[3] The next month, this outpouring of grief over conditions in the city continued as yet another white wrote "such times nobody never before saw or thought could exist in Savannah," where African Americans were "better off than the white folks."[4] The picture painted of black Savannah, on the other hand, was more positive, as thousands of slaves from the interior of the state and South Carolina converged on Savannah in the winter of 1865,[5] concomitantly increasing the black population and bringing in new talent and potential leaders. Black schools operated publicly with government authorization and funding,[6] and the number of black churches increased. Included among the black churches was an African Methodist Episcopal church, the result of Andrew Chapel members shifting to that denomination at the urging of a recently arrived minister of that faith.[7] In the past, the African Methodist Episcopal church had been outlawed in Savannah, but now it joined four black Baptist churches and Saint Stephen's Episcopal church to give the community a total of six black churches by mid-1865.[8] Furthermore, new leadership arose to replace the leaders who had died either during the war or shortly after it had ended,[9] new clubs were organized to augment the prewar organizations, and a feeling of freedom replaced the old desire to be free.

This was the situation in black Savannah during the period immediately following the collapse of the peculiar institution. But what conclusions concerning the independent black church, community development, economic endeavors, social control, and social life can be drawn from this study? Let us begin once again with the independent black church. It was large, influential, and one of the few windows where light might shine on the otherwise dreary situation in black Savannah. The number of black congregations and Protestant denominations represented in the black church increased over time. After establishing its presence in the Baptist faith, the black church subsequently broadened its presence within Protestantism and established chapels in the Methodist and Episcopal faiths. These black churches collectively constituted a beacon of hope, a training center for future community leaders, as well as a cultural melting pot; collectively, furthermore, they constituted the foremost religious institution of its kind in the South and the utmost exemplification of self-help. By 1800, whites in Savannah had determined that an independent black church did not pose a threat to the status quo, and they subsequently permitted the black church to worship free from interference and persecution. This was quite evident in the 1830s when much of the South placed restrictions on blacks assembling for any purpose, including worship, but black churches in Savannah were not bothered, even when an ugly schism occurred in First African Baptist Church. Black Savannah was indeed the cradle of the black church in the region.

The independent black church, community development, and economic endeavors were interrelated. The black community developed slowly. In 1790, it contained 8,313 inhabitants; in 1860, 14,897. The intervening years witnessed the introduction of new churches, businesses, civic organizations, schools, and leisure activities. A community formed within sight of the bluff, and its viability rested upon the independent black church and blacks creating a niche for themselves in the economy. Whites prescribed the occupations its inhabitants would pursue, but did not proscribe black ownership of slaves. More often than not, African Americans were pushed into personal service and manual labor that were not conducive to making them wealthy. The number of vocations opened to African Americans was static, and black Savannah lacked wealthy residents throughout the period. Savannah, for instance, did not have a black who could compare favorably with Jehu Jones, a free mulatto in Charleston who owned perhaps the best hotel in that city;[10] there were several other members of Charleston's Brown Society who were wealthier than Jones. Neither was there a black in the city who could match the wealth of William Ellison of Stateburg, South Carolina, a free mulatto who earned enough money to purchase the home of a former governor of that state and over sixty slaves. In 1860, the number of Ellison's slaves was almost three times as large as the combined total owned by black Savannahians', and his net worth far exceeded the total wealth in black Savannah.[11] Nevertheless, black Savannah evinced affluence and autonomy amid its adversity.

During the period, an increasing number of black schools were operated which taught reading, writing, and arithmetic. Early on, the church was in the forefront of efforts to teach reading skills primarily to foster Bible study. Whites generally frowned upon blacks attending school because they believed education led to obstreperous slaves and arrogant free blacks. The reason African Americans wanted to become literate, however, had little to do with the major reason whites opposed teaching blacks those skills. In spite of laws proscribing them, black schools did not close their doors, except to muffle the sound of children reciting their lesson.

The black codes, or slave codes, shaped the legal system that fostered slavery, the ultimate system of social control. The codes were similar to those in most slave states, but whites did not enforce statutes with the same enthusiasm that they passed them. Hence, even though the laws on the books were often oppressive, casual enforcement—which translated into tolerable race relations—generally made living under them bearable.

As slavery became deeply entrenched in Savannah, slave hiring became increasingly popular. Slaveholders often hired out their slaves to other whites, businesses, and governments at all levels; they also permitted slaves to hire their own time. This latter form of slave hire had become widespread by the late 1830s.[12] The prospect of hiring their own time, enjoying social amenities, and attending church, doubtless attracted slaves from the surrounding countryside and elsewhere in Georgia. The more relaxed form of slavery in the city, moreover, was different from plantation slavery.

The practice of allowing slaves to hire their own time constituted a middle ground between slavery and freedom. Masters who wished to manumit slaves but were discouraged by stringent manumission statutes could circumvent those laws by subscribing to the practice. Slaveholders who wanted to reward favorite slaves could use this mechanism. Owners who desired earning higher incomes from hiring slaves could opt to allow responsible slaves to hire their own time since those slaves paid more annually than owners generally received from hiring out their slaves.[13] Moreover, owners in the city who wanted slaves but dreaded assuming the attendant responsibilities also were attracted to the practice. The major reason the practice gained widespread approval, therefore, was because it benefited slaveholders.

In a backhanded way, white leaders attempted to use the African Colonization Movement as an instrument of social control. Instead of curtailing it, city officials wisely permitted embarkation from the local port and did not harass spectators at the departure site, believing it was in the best interests of the city to let unhappy African Americans depart for Africa in peace. The council only moved to discourage departures from Savannah when departure celebrations portended trouble. African Americans were still free to leave, but not directly from Savannah. By this time most African Americans who wished to leave for Africa had already left the city.

Through social control, whites succeeded in dictating blacks' behavior, but not their innermost thoughts. Throughout their ordeal, African Americans remained steadfast in their desire for freedom. This desire was demonstrated dramatically and fervently in 1849, when thousands of African Americans assembled at the Port of Savannah to bid farewell to persons who were emigrating to Liberia, the land of African Americans' "rightful inheritance," as Samuel Benedict perceived it. Similarly, the large number of runaway slaves in the Savannah area, some of whom established camps on the city's outskirts, reflected this desire. Furthermore, the very existence of ordinances prohibiting liquor sales, banning black education, proscribing many social activities of African Americans, and restricting their movement indicated whites feared that black Savannah too might be the scene of a slave revolt.

Finally let us turn to conclusions concerning social life. In 1788, a diversity of cultures, legal statuses, and colors dotted black Savannah's landscape, but much of this diversity disappeared over time. Cultural diversity was the first to vanish. The African slave trade was abolished in 1808, and large numbers of immigrants from the French-speaking West Indies stopped coming to Savannah by the end of the first decade of the nineteenth century. The end of the influx of blacks from foreign lands and the failure to nurture American-born children of those foreigners in the culture of their parents resulted in the loss of those cultures as distinct entities in Savannah. The capture of Savannah by the Union army ended slavery, and with it the free/slave legal distinction that had existed in Savannah. As 1864 came to a close, therefore, residents of black Savannah generally practiced a common culture and held the same legal status, but the color bias which developed over time remained. The ratio of mulattoes to nonmulattoes was significantly smaller than in any other major southern city; nevertheless, mulattoes dominated the wealth of the community, just as they did throughout the Old South. To depict the situation in Savannah as a mulatto aristocracy, however, would be an overstatement, for reasons that will be discussed later.

There were no social classes in black Savannah in the conventional meaning of the practice. Whereas the long-standing color bias in the community encumbered marriages between nonmulattoes and mulattoes, no difference in their legal status discouraged marriages between free African Americans and slaves. The pervasiveness of marriages between free African Americans and slaves prevented the formation of social classes. In what social class, for instance, would one have placed William Campbell? He was a mulatto nominal slave, pastor of the oldest and largest black church in the city, and the husband of a free mulatto. Moreover, Campbell's income was larger than most free African Americans in the city. What about Ulysses L. Houston? He was pastor of the third largest black church in the city and operated a very successful butchering enterprise that took him away on business trips throughout the state. Houston, a mulatto nominal slave, also had a free mulatto wife and a larger income than most free African Americans in the city. Campbell's and Houston's incomes and vocations normally would have qualified them for upper-class status if they were free, but should slaves be placed in that class? No. After the war when they gained their freedom, both men were among the upper class. Houston was even elected to the Georgia legislature.

Moreover, a number of other factors precluded the formation of social classes. Preachers traditionally were among the upper classes in black communities, but some of the most gifted preachers in black Savannah were slaves. For instance, Andrew Bryan was a slave when he founded First African Baptist Church. Similarly, teachers were generally included among the upper classes, but black teachers in Savannah operated illegally. Hence black teachers could not be included among the upper classes because they operated outside the law, however well intentioned their motives. Successful businessmen were classed in the upper echelon of society, but a number of slaves were successful businessmen. Further, there were no black physicians and lawyers in Savannah because blacks were not allowed to practice those professions. Consequently, conditions in black Savannah militated against the existence of social classes in the conventional sense because the vocations upon which such classes would have been based were either closed to African Americans or were practiced successfully by both slaves and free African Americans. This state of affairs also negated other means of determining status; that is, birth, education, income, and residence. Similarly, the situation precluded the existence of a mulatto aristocracy.

The black community was not leaderless, however, because of the strong personality of black church leaders who emerged as community leaders. These men were often listed among the largest black homeowners and worked in jobs that commanded high financial rewards: barber, carpenter, cooper, drayman, and tailor. Among the women, being a seamstress, pastry cook, or shopkeeper provided the greatest financial rewards, and the persons who practiced these vocations usually owned the most valuable real estate and received the greatest recognition in church and civic organizations. Thus in the aftermath of becoming unfamiliar with the status symbols and social stratification practiced by their African ancestors and being denied access to the professions which their European masters and guardians associated with wealth and power, African Americans developed new status symbols, ones that were inclusive—open to both slaves and free persons.

Blacks ignoring the legal labels used by whites to differentiate between groups of African Americans constituted a major difference between the way residents of the two Savannahs (white and black) viewed the world. Black Savannahians generally did not subscribe to the legal distinctions between groups of African Americans which whites etched into the laws. Accordingly, free African Americans had no qualms about selecting slaves as their religious leaders, mates, neighbors, and business associates. This does not mean that slavery was not despised; it was. What it does show is that the three-caste system did not take hold in Savannah. Herein lies a major difference, moreover, between the way African Americans in Savannah viewed the world vis-a-vis their counterparts in Charleston and New Orleans, where that practice flourished.

The answer to the first major question posed in the introduction, therefore, is that black Savannah was a progressive autonomous community that was in the vanguard of efforts in southern communities to establish an independent black church and black schools. It was the only black community that had an infirmary to provide health care, one of the few communities that had a cemetery to give African Americans a proper burial, and one in which African Americans, free and enslaved, lived together as one people. The answer to the second is much shorter: black Savannah was not a replica of communities in other major southern cities.

Population of the City of Savannah by Ward in 1825

WARD	WHITES			BLACKS		
	Males	Females	Children	Males	Females	Children
Brown	55	72	-	62	77	-
Jackson	52	56	-	87	108	-
Liberty	42	56	77	21	42	59
Anson	51	63	78	47	81	78
Derby	79	60	63	38	77	49
Columbia	27	74	-	28	119	-
Old Franklin	81	42	-	54	64	-
New Franklin	17	12	10	6	8	4
Reynolds	56	39	38	24	75	77
Warren	43	40	-	123	61	-
Washington	74	63	48	32	81	69
Elbert	41	70	-	49	102	-
Greene	79	110	-	111	162	-
N. Oglethorpe	105	115	-	135	224	-
S. Oglethorpe	73	129	-	61	128	-
Heathcote	86	99	59	101	166	-
Decker	68	45	37	19	58	50
Percival	74	105	-	77	136	-
Subtotal	1,103	1,250	410	1,075	1,769	386

Whites	2,763
Blacks	3,230
GRAND TOTAL	5,993

SOURCE: City of Savannah Board of Health Minutes, 1822–27.

Population of the City of Savannah by Ward and District in 1848

WARD	WHITES	BLACKS
Anson	300	300
Brown	223	259
Columbia	257	263
Crawford	101	98
Derby	433	273
Decker	292	100
Ebert	273	224
Franklin (old)	406	201
Franklin (new)	194	39
Greene	252	250
Heathcote	347	334
Jackson	247	252
Jasper	213	131
LaFayette	96	71
Liberty	221	210
Monterey	18	9
Oglethorpe	999	1,327
Percival	275	260
Pulaski	134	136
Reynolds	285	204
Warren	343	201
Washington	422	223
Currie Town District	524	526
Carpenters' Row, Trustees' Gardens, and Gilmerville	182	300
Suburbs	113	122
Subtotal	7,150	6,313

White	7,150	
Blacks	6,313	
GRAND TOTAL	13,463	

SOURCE: Joseph Bancroft, *Census of the City of Savannah,* 1848.

Occupations of Savannah's Free African Americans, 1823

FEMALES		MALES	
Midwife	2	Drayman	8
Vendor of Small Wares	11	Butcher	5
Hairdresser	1	Tailor	7
Washwoman	30	Farmer	1
Nurse	3	Cooper	5
Seamstress	26	Carpenter	6
Pastry Cook	6	Preacher	2
Cook	8	Servant	2
Gardening	1	Barber	3
Mantua Maker	1	Blind Fiddler	1
Servant	3	Physician	1
Spinster (Spinner)	3	Fisherman	1
Shopkeeper	4	Wagoner	1
House Keeper	5	Waiter	1
Baker	1	Laborer	2
Cook and Washer	1	Shoemaker	1
Keeper of Oyster House	1	Carterman	1
Serving Woman	1	Ship Carpenter	1
Market Cook	1		
Subtotal	108		49

Females	108
Males	49
GRAND TOTAL	157

SOURCE: Register of Free Persons of Color, City of Savannah, 1817–29, Georgia Historical Society, Savannah, Georgia.

Occupations of Free African–American Males, 1860

OCCUPATION	NUMBER LISTED	OCCUPATION	NUMBER LISTED
Mariner	21	Sternman on Steamer	2
Carpenter	19	Sawyer	2
Bricklayer	18	Master Baker	1
Laborer	14	Brickmaker	1
Porter	12	Cabinetmaker	1
Cooper	11	Carriage Maker	1
Wagoner	9	Clergy/Cooper	1
Waiter	8	Dray Master	1
Drayman	6	Engineer on Steamer	1
Barber	5	Farmer	1
Butcher	5	Gardener	1
Cotton Sampler	4	Janitor	1
Blacksmith	3	Machinist	1
Carriage Driver	3	Office Boy	1
Hostler	3	Painter	1
River Pilot	3	Patternmaker	1
Tailor	3	Plasterer	1
Confectioner	2	Ship Carpenter	1
Fisherman	2	Stevedore	1
Fireman on Steamer	2	Steward on Steamer	1
Houseboy	2	Assistant to Surveyor	1
Minister of the Gospel	1		

TOTAL   179

SOURCE: United States Office of Census, 1860,
          Georgia, Chatham–Chattahoochee Counties.

Occupations of Free African-American Women, 1860

OCCUPATION	NUMBER LISTED
Seamstress	121
Washing and Ironing	43
Domestic	18
Pastry Cook	15
Servant	131
Nurse	8
Cook	3
House Keeper	3
Midwife	3
Nurse Int. (Intern?)	2
Clear Starcher	1
Mantua Maker	1
Nurse/Seamstress	1
Sausage Maker	1
Seamstress/Pastry Cook	1

TOTAL   352

SOURCE: United States Census Office, 1860,
                  Georgia, Chatham–Chattahoochee Counties.

Black Slaveholders in Savannah, 1823

NAME	OCCUPATION	NUMBER OF SLAVES	
Dolly Bryan	None Listed	1	
Prince Candy	Cooper	7	
Menta Currie	None Listed	1	(Child)
Henry Cunningham	Preacher	1	
Lucy Cuthbert	Washwoman	3	
Maria Cohen	Gardening	6	
Catherine Deveaux	Pastry Cook	1	(Slave Girl)
Papotte Godichan	Seamstress	1	
Juno Guard	Seamstress	1	
John Gibbons	Carpenter	5	
Phillis Hill	Pastry Cook	4	
Susan Jackson	Pastry Cook	2	
Jeanette LaRose	Shopkeeper	1	
Andrew Morel	Tailor	2	
Mursey McIntosh	Washwoman	2	
Mary Motta	Seamstress	3	
Louis Mirault	Tailor	6	
Mary Spiers	Washwoman	5	
Leah Simpson	Seamstress	5	
Mandte Tardieu	Shopkeeper	1	
*Mary Odingsells	Washwoman	2	
*Anthony Odingsells	Fisherman	10	

TOTAL   70

*Did not live in the city; hence does not appear on this register.
  See Chatham County Tax Digest, 1823.

SOURCE: Register of Free Persons of Color, City of Savannah, 1817–29,
            Georgia Historical Society, Savannah, Georgia.

Black–Owned Real Estate
Valued at $500 and Above, 1837

NAME*	ASSESSED VALUE	OCCUPATION
Betty Baptist	$500	Washwoman
Ann Craig	1,500	Pastry Cook
Henry Cunningham	500	Preacher
Prince Candy	600	Cooper
Catherine Deveaux	800	Seamstress
Chloe Gibbons	600	Widow of John Gibbons, Carpenter
Richard and Sarah Houstoun	500	None Listed
Rose Galineau	600	None Listed
Susan Jackson	1,000	Pastry Cook
Andrew Marshall	3,550	Drayman
James and Rozella Oliver	700	Drayman
Mary Roberts	550	Seamstress

*Anthony Odingsells' Property valuation does not appear on this chart because his property was on Wassaw Island, beyond the city limits. His property was valued in excess of five hundred dollars.

SOURCE: City of Savannah Tax Digest 1837,
      Georgia Historical Society, Savannah, Georgia.

Notes

INTRODUCTION

1. Michael P. Johnson and James L. Roark, *Black Masters: A Free Family of Color in the Old South* (New York, 1984), p. 55.
2. Ibid., p. 61.
3. Ibid., p. 38, 88, 176–77.
4. H. E. Sterkx, *The Free Negro in Ante-Bellum Louisiana* (Rutherford, N.J., 1972), pp. 223, 267, 198–99, 272.
5. Richard C. Wade, *Slavery in the Cities: The South 1820–1860* (New York, 1964), p. 115.
6. Larry Koger, *Black Slaveowners: Free Black Slave Masters in South Carolina, 1790–1860* (Jefferson, N.C., 1985), pp. 69–79.
7. Ira Berlin, *Slaves without Masters: The Free Negro in the Antebellum South* (New York, 1974), p. 198.
8. Ibid., p. 214.
9. *Preliminary Report on the Eighth Census, 1860* (Washington, D.C., 1862).
10. Leonard P. Curry, *The Free Black in Urban America, 1800–1850: The Shadow of the Dream* (Chicago, 1981), pp. 174–95.
11. Eugene D. Genovese, *From Rebellion to Revolution: Afro-American Slave Revolts in the Making of the Modern World* (Baton Rouge, 1979), pp. 11–12. Genovese identified eight conditions, some combination of which was required for the success of any large-scale slave revolt. These were absent from Savannah.
12. Curry, *The Free Black in Urban America*, pp. 88–89.
13. Loren Schweninger, *Black Property Owners in the South, 1790–1915* (Urbana, Ill., 1990), p. 86.

HALLELUJAH! PRAISE THE LORD

1. Carter G. Woodson, *The History of the Negro Church*, 3rd ed. (Washington, D.C., 1972), p. 43; Henry Holcombe, *The First Fruits in a Series of Letters* (Philadelphia, 1812), pp. 63–65.
2. Holcombe, *The First Fruits*, pp. 63–65.
3. See Albert J. Raboteau, *Slave Religion: The "Invisible Institution" in the Antebellum South* (New York, 1978); see also J. Ralph Jones and Tom Landers, "Portraits of Georgia Slaves," *The Georgia Review* 21 (spring 1967): p. 128.
4. "Letters Showing the Rise and Progress of Early Negro Churches of Georgia and the West Indies," *Journal of Negro History* 1 (January 1919): p. 78. The quotation earlier in the paragraph also came from this source.

5. Minutes of the Sunbury Baptist Association; see also minutes for the years 1818–21. The term "African Church" was first used in 1822.

6. *Georgia Gazette,* October 23, 1788.

7. "Letters Showing the Rise and Progress of Early Negro Churches," pp. 86–87; George White, *Historical Collections of Georgia* (New York, 1854), p. 313; for the Bryans' connection with Whitefield, see Alan Gallay, "Planters and Slaves in the Great Awakening," in *Masters and Slaves in the House of the Lord,* ed. John B. Boles (Lexington, Ky., 1988), pp. 19–36.

8. "Letters Showing the Rise and Progress of the Early Negro Churches," pp. 82–83; Mary Granger, ed., *Savannah Writer's Project, Savannah River Plantations* (Savannah, 1947), p. 400; Henry C. Holcombe, *The Georgia Analytical Repository,* vol. 1, no. 4 (November–December 1802): p. 186.

9. Deeds. Volume G, 1789–90, Chatham County Superior Court, Georgia Department of Archives and History, pp. 215–16. (Hereafter, all deeds come from Chatham County Superior Court, Georgia Department of Archives and History.)

10. Edgar G. Thomas, *The First African Baptist Church of North America* (Savannah, 1925), pp. 37–38.

11. Ibid., p. 40; Lewis G. Jordan, *Negro Baptist History, U.S.A.— 1750–1930* (Nashville, 1930), p. 48; Jesse L. Boyd, *A History of Baptist in America Prior to 1845* (New York, 1957), pp. 150–51.

12. Holcombe, *The First Fruits,* p. 116.

13. Holcombe, *The Georgia Analytical Repository,* vol. 1, p. 188; Emmanuel K. Love, *History of the First African Baptist Church* (Savannah, 1888), p. 43; Tablet on the tomb of Henry Cunningham, Laurel Grove Cemetery, South, Savannah, Georgia; Joseph D. Waring, *Cerveau's Savannah* (Savannah, 1973), p. 60. Apparently a black Savannahian with the same name was the preacher of African Baptist Church in Philadelphia from 1809–11. See Gary Nash, *Forging Freedom* (Cambridge, Mass., 1988), p. 201.

14. See the minutes of the Sunbury Association for the years since the late 1830s. The convention did not give the same tribute to Cunningham that it gave to Marshall when he died. As a matter of fact, the convention did not mention Cunningham's death. See also Holcombe, *The First Fruits,* p. 116.

15. For a discussion of Marshall's life and work in Savannah see Whittington B. Johnson, "Andrew C. Marshall: A Black Religious Leader of Antebellum Savannah," *The Georgia Historical Quarterly* 69 (summer 1985); and J. P. Tustin, "Andrew C. Marshall, 1786–1856," in *Annals of the American Pulpit,* ed. William Sprague (Charleston, S.C., 1859).

16. Minutes of the Sunbury Association, 1857.

17. Waring, *Cerveau's Savannah,* p. 26.

18. Love, *History of the First African Baptist Church,* pp. 33, 57–58; Claim of Celia Boisfeillet, # 3751, Record Group 217. Southern Claims Case Files, Chatham County, Ga. Her husband spelled his name Boufeulilet. Cambell's testimony in behalf of Mrs. Boisfeillet included an autobiographical sketch. (Hereafter, all claims in Record Group 217 are from Southern Claims Case Files, Chatham County.)

19. James M. Simms, *The First Colored Baptist Church* (Philadelphia, 1888), p. 256; *Savannah Tribune*, June 3, 1893.

20. Tablet on the tomb of Andrew C. Marshall, Laurel Grove Cemetery, South.

21. Thomas, *The First African Baptist Church*, pp. 85–86; Minutes of the Sunbury Association, 1818–62.

22. Charles Joyner, *Down by the River Side: A South Carolina Slave Community* (Urbana, Ill., 1984), p. 160. Joyner gives an excellent discussion of the survival of Africanisms in religious practices of slaves on Waccamac Plantation in Georgetown, South Carolina, a town from which a large number of Savannah slaves were brought.

23. David Benedict, *A General History of the Baptist Denominations in America and Other Parts*, vol. 2 (Boston, 1813), p. 532.

24. Bryan purchased the land from William Bryan in 1790 and sold it to the church in 1797. White trustees, Thomas Polhill, William Matthews, David Fox, and Josiah Fox held the property in trust to circumvent the law proscribing black ownership of real estate. Thomas, *The First African Baptist Church*, pp. 37–38.

25. Ibid., p. 191; "Letters Showing the Rise and Progress of Early Negro Churches," pp. 82–83; Love, *History of the First African Baptist Church*, pp. 2–3; Emily Burke, *Pleasure and Pain: Reminiscences of Georgia in the 1840s* (Savannah, 1978), p. 12.

26. *Savannah Daily Morning News*, May 1861; Thomas, *The First African Baptist Church of North America*, pp. 78–79; Love, *History of the First African Baptist Church*, p. 33.

27. Benedict, *A General History of the Baptist Denominations*, vol. 2, p. 193; Jordan, *Negro Baptist History*, p. 580. Ogeechee African Church was founded in 1803, instead of 1805 as Jordan stated in this work; Berlin, *Slaves without Masters*, p. 73, Berlin has the date of the founding of Third African Church as 1813, but it should read 1833; Holcombe, *The First Fruits*, p. 83; Thomas, *The First African Baptist Church*, p. 29.

28. Letter from E. P. Quarterman, pastor of Second African Church, postmarked October 18, 1981; I had interviewed him in Savannah the previous September, at which time he had promised to send me additional information on the church's founding; Simms, *The First Colored Baptist Church*, p. 57; Mabel Freeman La Far, "The Baptist Church of Savannah, Georgia: History, Records and Register," Georgia Historical Society, Savannah, Georgia, vol. 1, p. 135. In the minutes of August 5, 1808, Richard Houstoun, Charlotte Wall, Susan Jackson, and Hetty Lloyd asked for dismission letters to join "Second Colored Church of this city." Apparently, this quartet attended the black church before being officially dismissed from the white one. This does not alter the position of Reverend Quarterman that those four were among the founders of his church.

29. Benedict, *A General History of the Baptist Denominations*, vol. 2, p. 193.

30. Woodson, *The History of the Negro Church*, pp. 101–2; Simms, *The First Colored Baptist Church*, pp. 123-25, 259–60.

31. Haygood S. Bowden, *History of Savannah Methodism*, (Macon, Ga., 1929), p. 57; Sir Charles Lyell, *A Second Visit to the United States of North America*, vol. 2 (New York, 1868), p. 15. After visiting Andrew Chapel in January 1846, Lyell said that it was "well ventilated," and there were no "disagreeable odors."

32. Christ Episcopal Church of Savannah Parish Register, 1822–51 (microfilm) Georgia Department of Archives and History.

33. Will of Maria Cohen in the Richard Dennis Arnold Papers, Georgia Historical Society, Savannah, Ga.; Register of Free Persons of Color for the County of Chatham, 1826–35.

34. Christ Episcopal Church Parish Register, 1822–51.

35. Charles C. Jones Jr., *History of Savannah, Georgia* (Syracuse, 1890), p. 511.

36. *Journal of the . . . Proceedings of the Episcopal Diocese of Georgia, 1856*, pp. 35–37; Joseph Atwell, *A Brief Historical Sketch of St. Stephen's Parish Savannah, Georgia* (New York, 1874), p. 5.

37. *Federal Writers Project, Savannah* (Savannah, 1937), pp. 49–50; Charles Hoskins, *Black Episcopalians in Georgia: Strife, Struggle and Salvation* (Savannah, 1980), pp. 50–52; George A. Rogers and R. Frank Saunders Jr., *Swamp Water and Wiregrass: Historical Sketches of Coastal Georgia* (Macon, Ga., 1984), p. 57; Henry T. Malone, *The Episcopal Church in Georgia, 1733–1957* (Atlanta, 1960), p. 88; Stiles B. Lines, "Slaves and Churchmen: The Work of the Episcopal Church among Southern Negroes, 1830–60" (Ph.D. diss., Columbia University, 1960), pp. 272–73; Georgia Bryan Conrad, *Reminiscences of a Southern Woman* (Hampton, Va., n.d.), p. 16.

38. *Journal of the . . . Proceedings of the Episcopal Diocese of Georgia, 1856*, p. 45.

39. *Journal of the . . . Proceedings of the Episcopal Diocese of Georgia, 1858*, p. 54.

40. *Journal of the . . . Proceedings of the Episcopal Diocese of Georgia, 1860*, pp. 20, 50–51; Atwell, *A Brief Historical Sketch*, p. 7; William Harden, *Recollections of a Long and Satisfactory Life* (Savannah, 1934), p. 27; Charles L. Hoskins, *Black Episcopalians in Savannah* (Savannah, 1983), p. 14; *Journal of the . . . Proceeding of the Episcopal Diocese of Georgia, 1864*, pp. 50–51.

41. Diary of the Right Reverend Stephen Elliot, Jr., Bishop of the Diocese of Georgia, from May 16, 1858, to December 19, 1867. Diocesan Office, Savannah, Georgia.

42. Christ Episcopal Church of Savannah Parish Register, 1852–73 (microfilm) Georgia Department of Archives and History.

43. St. John the Baptist Catholic Church of Savannah Parish Register, 1796–1816 (microfilm) Georgia Department Archives and History.

44. Independent Presbyterian Church Sessional Minutes, Books 1 and 2, 1828–51 (microfilm) Georgia Department of Archives and History. The record includes a list of the "Coloured Members" stating when they were baptized.

45. "Letters Showing the Rise and Progress of Early Negro Churches," p. 79. This letter was dated January 20, 1788, the same date First African was

established. See also Benedict, *A General History of the Baptist Denomination*, vol. 2, p. 192 for information on slave memberships.

46. Frances Anne Kemble, *Journal of a Residence on a Georgia Plantation in 1858–1859* (New York, 1863), p. 63.

47. Charles C. Jones, *The Religious Instruction of the Negroes in the United States* (Savannah, 1842), p. 176.

48. C. Eric Lincoln, "The Black Heritage in Religion in the South," in *Religion in the South*, ed. Charles Reagan Wilson (Jackson, Miss., 1985), p. 53.

49. Mrs. ———— Smith's Journal, March 17, 1793, Duke University Library, Durham, North Carolina.

50. "Letters Showing the Rise and Progress of Early Negro Churches," pp. 79–80.

51. Lyell, *A Second Visit to the United States*, vol. 2, p. 45.

52. Joshua and Eben Hale to Thomas and Josiah Hale, Savannah, March 17, 1858, Hale family papers, 1858. Georgia Historical Society, Savannah, Ga. Marshall died in 1856; therefore, the writer could not have heard him preach that Sunday in 1858.

53. Lyell, *A Second Visit to the United States*, vol. 2, p. 14.

54. Fredrika Bremer, *The Homes of the New World: Impressions of America*, vol. 1 (New York, 1853), pp. 352–54. Mrs. Bremer said she visited a black Baptist church and believed the name of the preacher was Bentley. William Bentley was a Methodist preacher, who may have been invited to preach at a Baptist church that the writer visited. See Bowden, *History of Savannah Methodism*, p. 97, for information on Bentley being licensed to preach.

55. See Raboteau, *Slave Religion*, pp. 55–68.

56. Mrs. ————Smith's Journal, March 17, 1793; At the church's centennial in 1888, one of the original members told an interviewer that "Daddy Bryan" had baptized her in the river. See Clarence M. Wagner, *Profiles of Black Georgia Baptists* (Atlanta, 1980), pp. 70–71.

57. Holcombe, *The Georgia Analytical Repository*, vol. 1, p. 188; Simms, *The First Colored Baptist Church*, pp. 64–65. Deacons in the black Baptist churches visited shut-ins to administer the Lord's Supper, but they were ordered to stop this practice; apparently, this was one improvisation that the whites would not tolerate. See Minutes of the Sunbury Association, 1843.

58. Bremer, *The Homes of the New World*, vol. 1, p. 352.

59. "One by One They Depart," in *Savannah Tribune*, June 3, 1893. The information was taken from the obituary of Rev. Frank Keating.

60. Ibid., November 13, 1895; Atwell, *A Brief Historical Sketch*, p. 6.

61. Bremer, *The Homes of the New World*, vol. 1, p. 352.

62. Discipline Meeting March 28, 1836, La Far, "The Baptist Church of Savannah, Georgia," vol. 3, pp. 935–36.

63. Minutes of the Sunbury Association, 1839.

64. Minutes of the Sunbury Association, 1840.

65. Bowden, *History of Savannah Methodism*, p. 59.

66. *Journal of the . . . Proceedings of the Episcopal Diocese of Georgia*, 1856, p. 45.

67. Christ Episcopal Church Parish Register, 1852–73.

68. Simms, *The First Colored Baptist Church*, pp. 78–79; Luther P. Jackson, "Religious Instruction of Negroes, 1830 to 1860, With Special Reference to South Carolina," *Journal of Negro History* 15 (January 1930): p. 91; Walter H. Brooks, "The Evolution of the Negro Baptist Church," *Journal of Negro History* 7 (January 1922): p. 17.

69. John W. Blassingame, "Before the Ghetto: The Making of the Black Community of Savannah, Georgia 1865–1880," *Journal of Social History* 6 (summer 1973): p. 474. The title of this article is a little misleading since there was a black community in Savannah before the Civil War; Berlin, *Slaves without Masters*, p. 302; Discipline Meeting May 24, 1805, La Far, "The Baptist Church of Savannah, Georgia," vol. 3, p. 80. Henry Cunningham reported that two black members of Savannah Baptist Church, Charlotte Wall and her servant Cate Wall, were in disorder. Wall, who is listed among the original members of Second African Baptist, apparently did not formally move her membership until later.

70. Simms, *The First Colored Baptist Church*, pp. 68–69; Love, *History of the First African Baptist Church*, p. 44.

71. John B. Boles, "Evangelical Protestantism in the Old South: From Religious Dissent to Cultural Dominance," *Religion in the South* ed. Charles R. Wilson (Jackson, Miss., 1985), p. 17; First African Baptist Church Minutes, Special Collections, Dues, and Funerals, 1871–89; Bowden, *History of Savannah Methodism*, p. 77. At the second quarterly conference for 1846, three members of Andrew Chapel were expelled.

72. Bowden, *History of Savannah Methodism*, p. 94.

73. March 21, 1871 Conference, First African Baptist Church Minutes Special Collections, Dues, and Funerals, 1871–89.

74. "Appendix A," Minutes of the Sunbury Association, 1839.

75. Minutes of the Sunbury Association, 1832; see also Tustin, "Andrew C. Marshall, 1786–1856," in *Annals of the American Pulpit*, ed. Sprague, p. 257.

76. "Appendix A: Digest of Letters," Minutes of the Sunbury Association, 1843; Love, *History of the First African Baptist Church*, pp. 51–52; Berlin, *Slaves without Masters*, pp. 308–9.

77. Minutes of the Sunbury Association, 1859.

78. Lillian Foster, *Wayside Glimpses, North and South* (New York, 1860), p. 109; Thomas, *The First African Baptist Church*, p. 141; Milton C. Sernett, *Black Religion and American Evangelicalism* (Metuchen, N.J., 1975), p. 138.

79. Howard H. Harlan, *John Jasper: A Case History in Leadership*, vol. 14. (Charlottesville, Va., 1936), p. 14; Benjamin Quarles, *Black Abolitionists* (New York, 1969), p. 69; Berlin, *Slaves without Masters*, p. 300; Lawrence N. Jones, "They Sought a City: The Black Church and Churchmen," *Union Seminary Quarterly Review* 26 (spring 1971): p. 255.

80. William Boufeuilet and Bancers, November, 1865. Record Group 105. Bureau of Refugees, Freedmen, and Abandoned Lands. Affidavits, Miscellaneous Records, Contracts, 1865–72, Savannah, Georgia. Box 30 National Archives, Washington, D.C. (Hereafter, all claims in Group 105 are from

Bureau of Refugees, Freedmen, and Abandoned Lands in the National Archives.)

81. William H. Sinclair to Agent of Bureau of Refugees, Freedmen, and Abandoned Lands in Savannah, Georgia, Galveston, Texas, September 12, 1866, ibid. Box 28.

82. "Letters Showing the Rise and Progress of Early Negro Churches," pp. 86–87.

83. Independent Presbyterian Church African Sunday School (microfilm) Georgia Department of Archives and History. The extant minutes of the Sunday school begin September 15, 1833, and they have a short history of the school.

84. Jones, *Suggestions on the Religious Instructions of the Negroes*, pp. 25–26; see also J. S. Law, *Essay on the Religious Oral Instruction of the Colored Race* (Penfield, Ga., 1846), p. 11.

85. *Journal of the . . . Proceedings of the Episcopal Diocese of Georgia, 1854*, p. 28.

86. Thomas, *The First African Baptist Church*, pp. 47–48; Harlan, *John Jasper*, p. 10; Richard H. Haunton, "Savannah in the 1850s" (Ph.D. diss., Emory University, 1968), pp. 339–40; Minutes of the Sunbury Association, 1831, 1857.

87. *Journal of the . . . Proceedings of the Episcopal Diocese of Georgia, 1857*, p. 36.

88. Carter G. Woodson, *The Education of the Negro Prior to 1861* (Washington, D.C., 1919), p. 85; Curry, *The Free Black in Urban America*, p. 195.

89. Jackson, "Religious Development of the Negro," p. 175.

90. Blassingame, "Before the Ghetto," p. 477; William E. B. Du Bois, *Black Reconstruction in American, 1860–1880* (New York, 1969), p. 507; *Savannah Tribune*, November 13, 1895; Ethel M. Christler, "Participation of Negroes in the Government of Georgia, 1867–1870" (master's thesis, Atlanta University, 1932), pp. 7, 62.

91. Brief of Evidence in *Richard Baker et al., Complainants vs. Peter Houston, et al., Defendants* (March, 1881), First African Baptist Church Minutes, Special Collections, Dues, and Funerals, 1871–89.

92. Ibid.

93. Evelyn Brooks Higginbotham, *Righteous Discontent: The Women's Movement in the Black Baptist Church. 1880–1920* (Cambridge, Mass., 1993), pp. 1–3. Higginbotham argues that women played a crucial role in helping the black church to become "the most powerful institution of racial self-help in the African-American community." She therefore supports my position.

94. Article IV, Constitution of the Sunbury Baptist Association. This document is in the minutes of the Sunbury Association, 1823.

95. Ibid.

96. Minutes of the Sunbury Association, 1823.

97. Ibid., 1824.

98. Simms, *The First Colored Baptist Church* (1881); Love, *History of the*

First African Baptist Church (1888); Thomas, *The First African Baptist Church* (1925). For the present status of the debate between the two congregations over which is the real heir of Andrew Bryan see *The Atlanta Constitution,* February 27, 1988, 2C, p. 1E.

99. Savannah City Council Minutes, 1828–31 (microfilm) Georgia Department of Archives and History, p. 240.

100. La Far, "The Baptist Church of Savannah, Georgia," vol. 3, pp. 722–23.

101. Ibid., pp. 723–24.

102. Robert F. West, *Alexander Campbell and Natural Religion* (New Haven, 1948), p. 226. This passage gives the position of Campbell that had the most direct bearing on Marshall's troubles with the association.

103. Minutes of the Sunbury Association, 1832.

104. Love, *History of the First African Baptist Church,* p. 18.

105. See Sunbury Association Minutes for the years 1818–25. During those years, First African Church did not have a permanent pastor, and Adam Johnson, Josiah Lloyd, Adam Sheftall, Jack Simpson, and Evans Great (1822) represented the church; Great's only appearance, in 1822, was probably as a minister.

106. Thomas, *The First African Baptist Church,* pp. 50–51.

107. Minutes of the Sunbury Association, 1833.

108. Tombstone of Adam A. Johnson, Laurel Grove Cemetery, South.

109. Minutes of the Sunbury Association, 1837.

110. Ibid.

111. Minutes of the Sunbury Association, 1844.

112. Bowden, *History of Savannah Methodism,* p. 118.

113. This percentage was based upon the total African-American population in Chatham County (19,470) since the black churches drew a sizable number of worshipers from the nearby plantations and those figures were probably included in the membership figures. See the *Sixth Census of the United States, 1860* for the population figures for Chatham County.

114. The census did not include church membership until 1890. This, however, has not precluded scholars from giving estimates. The percentage I gave was taken from Edward Pessen, *Jacksonian America: Society, Personality, and Politics* (Homewood, Ill., 1978), p. 68.

115. *Fifth Census of the United States, 1830; Sixth Census of the United States, 1840.*

116. Minutes of the Sunbury Association, 1854.

117. Minutes of the Sunbury Association. See the minutes for the years 1850–60.

CITIZENSHIP DENIED; JUSTICE COMPROMISED

1. See a discussion of the enslavement crisis in South Carolina in Johnson and Roark, *Black Masters: A Free Family of Color in the Old South,* pp. 159–67.

2. "Petitions of Heirs of Adam Sheftall" #9, Record Group 233. House of Representatives of the United States, 1871-80. Claims Disallowed by Commissioners of Claims, National Archives, Washington, D.C. Emanuel Sheftall, a butcher, was the son of Adam Sheftall. (Hereafter, all claims in Record Group 233 are from Claims Disallowed by Commissioners of Claims in the National Archives.)

3. Claim of Samuel A. McIver, #6609, Record Group 217.

4. Claim of David Moses, #15448, Record Group 217. S. P. Millege, a slave friend of Moses, made the statement.

5. Claim of Celia Boisfeillet, #3751, Record Group 217. See the depositions of her husband, Mitchel, and William Campbell, pastor of First African Baptist Church.

6. Sidney Weeks, "The History of Negro Suffrage in the South," *The Political Science Quarterly*, 9 (December 1894): p. 675.

7. W. McDowell Rogers, "Free Negro Legislation in Georgia," *The Georgia Historical Quarterly* 16 (March 1932): pp. 35–36.

8. Lucius Q. C. Lamar, *A Compilation of the Laws of the State of Georgia . . . Since the Year 1810 to the Year 1819, Inclusive* (Augusta, Ga., 1821), p. 815. This law was circumvented with the complicity of whites in a manner that will be included in a discussion of white guardians.

9. *Acts of the General Assembly, 1824* (Milledgeville, Ga., 1825), p. 125.

10. Edward Sweat, *Free Blacks and the Law in Antebellum Georgia* (Atlanta, 1976), pp. 3–4.

11. Edward G. Wilson, *A Digest of All the Ordinances of the City of Savannah . . . Which Were of Force on the First of January, 1858* (Savannah, 1858), pp. 174, 305.

12. Ibid., p. 181.

13. Howell Cobb, *A Compilation of the General and Public Statutes of the State of Georgia* (New York, 1859), p. 851.

14. Ibid., p. 614; Wilson, *A Digest of All the Ordinances, 1858*, p. 175.

15. Savannah City Council Minutes, September 13, 1819.

16. Ibid., June 5, 1820.

17. Wilson, *A Digest of All the Ordinances, 1858*, pp. 181–82.

18. Ronald Killion and Charles Waller, eds., *Slavery Time When I Was Chillun Down on Master's Plantation* (Savannah, 1973), p. x; Burke, *Pleasure and Pain: Reminiscences of Georgia in the 1840s*, p. 23; Jones, *Religious Instruction of the Negroes in the United States*, pp. 121–22. South Carolina had a similar law, which forced Daniel Payne to close his school in Charleston and move to Philadelphia, where years later he became an African Methodist Episcopal bishop. Daniel Payne, *Recollections of Seventy Years* (New York, 1968), pp. 35–36, 38.

19. See Savannah City Council Minutes, September 3, 1818, and those for April 1, 1824.

20. Savannah City Council Minutes, August 15, 1839.

21. Savannah City Council Minutes, April 6, 1846.

22. Savannah City Council Minutes, November 21, 1860.

23. Savannah City Council Minutes, February 18, 1814.

24. Savannah City Council Minutes, February 17, 1848; Joseph Bancroft, *Census of the City of Savannah*, (Savannah, 1848), pp. 13–20.

25. Ralph B. Flanders, *Plantation Slavery in Georgia* (Chapel Hill, N.C., 1933), p. 35.

26. W. McDowell Rogers, "Free Negro Legislation in Georgia Before 1865," *The Georgia Historical Quarterly* 16 (March 1932): p. 33.

27. Wilson, *A Digest of All the Ordinances, 1858*, p. 174.

28. *Columbian Museum and Savannah Advertiser*, September 1799.

29. *Republican and Savannah Evening Ledger*, February 11, 1813.

30. Wilson, *A Digest of All the Ordinances, 1858*, p. 175.

31. Ibid., p. 172.

32. Ibid., p. 7.

33. *Report of R. D. Arnold Mayor of the City of Savannah for the Year Ending September 30, 1860* (Savannah, 1860), p. 22.

34. *Eighth Census of the United States, 1860.*

35. Frederick Douglass, *Frederick Douglass: The Narrative and Selected Writings,* ed. Michael Meyer, (New York, 1984), p. 353. The speech was delivered November 16, 1855.

36. Deeds., p. 235, vol. 3K, 1852.

37. Ibid., p. 111; vol. 3H, 1849–51. The deed was recorded February 17, 1851.

38. Chatham Court of the Ordinary Minutes, 1830–38 (microfilm) Georgia Department of Archives and History. During those years Joseph Kelton was apparently the only black to apply for registration and to have a guardian appointed.

39. Chatham County Court of the Ordinary Minutes, 1862–67.

40. Ibid., p. 33; Flanders, *Plantation Slavery in Georgia*, p. 233; Sweat, *Free Blacks and the Law*, pp. 4–5.

41. Rogers, "Free Negro Legislation in Georgia," p. 33.

42. Haunton, "Law and Order in Savannah," pp. 2, 6, 16. Savannah had over two hundred liquor stores, including the more than one hundred located on the east side.

43. Savannah Board of Health Minutes, 1830–64, Georgia Department of Archives and History. The information was compiled from all the volumes which covered those years.

44. Haunton, "Law and Order in Savannah," p. 10. This lower black-inmate population resulted in part from masters often administering personal punishment to their slaves, thus obviating the need for the state to punish them.

45. Sweat, *Free Blacks and the Law*, pp. 4–5; Rogers, "Free Negro Legislation in Georgia," p. 34.

46. Daniel J. Flanigan, "Criminal Procedure in Slave Trials in the Antebellum South," *Journal of Southern History* 40 (November 1974): p. 556.

47. Haunton, "Law and Order in Savannah," p. 17; *Savannah Republican*, March 3, 1855. An article detailing the escape of four prisoners from the jail

said two were black and two were white; Chatham County Jail Records, 1805–15 (microfilm) Georgia Department of Archives and History. In January 1810, a free black who allegedly deserted from his schooner and a free black who owed a debt were incarcerated.

48. Wade, *Slavery in the Cities,* pp. 184–85; Haunton, "Law and Order in Savannah," p. 17; see also Helen H. Catterall, *Judicial Cases Concerning American Slavery and the Negro,* vol. 1 (Washington, D.C., 1926), p. 145. The condition existed in a Virginia jail, but they very well could have described Savannah's.

49. William Grimes, *Life of William Grimes, the Runaway Slave* (New Haven, 1855), p. 42.

50. Catterall, *Judicial Cases,* vol. 3, p. 18. The case was *Cooper and Worsham, by their Next Friend v. Mayor and Aldermen* (1848). These two free blacks were arrested in 1847 for violating section five of the 1839 ordinance.

51. Savannah Ordinance, July 1810. Georgia Historical Society. The Society has an engrossed copy of the ordinance.

52. Edward Ayers, *Vengeance and Justice: Crime and Punishment in the Nineteenth-Century South* (New York, 1984), p. 103.

53. *The Daily Georgian,* February 12, 1842.

54. Wilson, *A Digest of All the Ordinances,* 1858, pp. 7, 172.

55. Ibid., pp. 174–75.

56. Wade, *Slavery in the Cities,* p. 187; Kenneth M. Stampp, *The Peculiar Institution: Slavery in the Ante-Bellum South* (New York, 1956), p. 186; Grimes, *Life of William Grimes,* p. 31; Haunton, "Law and Order in Savannah," p. 16; John P. Jewett and Benjamin Drew, *North-side View of Slavery: The Refugee* (Boston, 1856), p. 104.

57. "Letters Showing the Rise and Progress of the Early Negro Churches," pp. 77–78; Love, *History of the First African Baptist Church,* p. 38; Thomas, *The First African Baptist Church of North America,* pp. 33–34.

58. Love, *History of the First African Baptist Church,* p. 53; Thomas, *The First African Baptist Church of North America,* p. 46; Simms, *The First Colored Baptist Church,* 242; Woodson, *The History of the Negro Church,* pp. 112–13.

59. Wilson, *A Digest of All Ordinances,* 1858, pp. 181–82.

AFFLUENCE AND AUTONOMY AMID ADVERSITY

1. John A. Eisterhold, "Savannah: Lumber Center of the South Atlantic," *Georgia Historical Quarterly* 57 (winter 1973): pp. 538–39; Clement Eaton, *The Growth of Southern Civilization, 1790–1860* (New York, 1961), p. 199; *Eighth Census of the United States, 1860: Manufactures* (Washington, 1865), vol. 8. See also, Whittington B. Johnson, "Free Blacks in Antebellum Savannah: An Economic Profile," *The Georgia Historical Quarterly* 64 (winter 1980): pp. 418–31. The author thanks the *Georgia Historical Quarterly* for allowing him to use information in that article throughout this chapter.

2. *Report of Edward Anderson Mayor of the City of Savannah for the Year Ending October 31, 1856* (Savannah, 1856), p. 13.

3. Eisterhold, "Savannah: Lumber Center," pp. 539–40.

4. Ibid., 533–34; Charles Seton Henry Hardee, *Reminiscences and Recollections of Old Savannah* (Savannah, 1926), pp. 121–24.

5. Bancroft, *Census of the City of Savannah*, pp. 34–36.

6. *Seventh Census of the United States, 1850.*

7. *Savannah Morning News*, September 29, 1859.

8. *Eighth Census of the United States, 1860.*

9. Register of Free Persons of Color, City of Savannah, 1817–29.

10. Bancroft, *Census of the City of Savannah*, p. 13. Preachers were overlooked in Bancroft's survey; Lorenzo Greene and Carter G. Woodson, *The Negro Wage Earner* (Washington, D.C., 1930), p. 14. These authors quoted Bancroft and made the same mistake.

11. *Eighth Census of the United States, 1860.*

12. This conclusion is based upon information previously cited in notes 9, 10, and 11 above.

13. Hardee, *Reminiscences and Recollections*, pp. 121, 124.

14. Charles Colcock Jones Collection, 1749–1909, Hargrett Rare Books and Manuscripts Library. The Jones Family owned a cotton plantation in Liberty County and shipped their cotton to Savannah for export to foreign markets. Among the charges were the drayage expenses.

15. *Savannah Daily Republican*, February 11, 1848; *Savannah Morning News*, September 19, 1859.

16. Hardee, *Reminiscences and Recollections*, p. 79.

17. City of Savannah Tax Digest, 1824.

18. City of Savannah Tax Digest, 1827.

19. *Seventh Census of the United States, 1850.*

20. Will of Andrew Marshall, 1857. Central Records Office, Chatham County Courthouse. The Georgia Department of Archives and History has extant county records for this period on microfilm.

21. City of Savannah Tax Digest, 1810; Register of Free Persons of Color for the County of Chatham, 1826–35.

22. City of Savannah Tax Digest, 1837.

23. City of Savannah Tax Digest, 1848.

24. Estate of Joseph A. Marshall, 1853. Central Records Office, Chatham County Court House. (Hereafter, all estates are from Office, Chatham County Courthouse.)

25. See note 19 above. The will was made in 1852, but Andrew Marshall died in 1856.

26. *Directory of the City of Savannah, 1858; Eighth Census of the United States, 1860.*

27. City of Savannah Tax Digest, 1810, 1820.

28. Austin D. Washington, "The Dollys: An Antebellum Black Family of Savannah, Georgia," *Savannah State College Bulletin, Faculty Research Edition* 26 (December 1972): p. 102; City of Savannah Tax Digest, 1810; Tombstone in Laurel Grove Cemetery, South.

29. City of Savannah Tax Digest, 1820, 1848.

30. City of Savannah Tax Digest, 1809, 1820, 1823.

31. Register of Free Person of Color for the County of Chatham, 1826–35; City of Savannah Tax Digest, 1810.

32. City of Savannah Tax Digest, 1854, 1860; Savannah Board of Health Minutes, 1859–64.

33. City of Savannah Tax Digest, 1823.

34. Estate of Louis Mirault, 1827. See also Register of Free Persons of Color, City of Savannah, 1817–29, and the city tax digests for the years 1809–27.

35. Ruth Blair, ed., *Some Early Tax Digests of Georgia* (Atlanta, 1926), p. 28.

36. *Daily Georgian,* December 4, 1819.

37. City of Savannah Tax Digest, 1850; Edward F. Sweat, "Free Negroes in Antebellum Georgia" (Ph.D. diss., Indiana University, 1957), p. 171. Sweat used the 1850 federal census which erroneously credited Morel with owning three slaves. See also Savannah Board of Health Minutes, 1850–55.

38. Rental Lease Agreement between Richard M. Stites and Richard Houstoun, Savannah, October 21, 1807. Wayne-Stites-Anderson Papers.

39. Estate of Richard Houstoun, 1814; City of Savannah Tax Digest, 1813.

40. Richard M. Stites to William Drayton, Esquire, Savannah, October 7, 1811. Wayne-Stites-Anderson Papers.

41. Simon Jackson Account, Wayne-Stites-Anderson Papers. See also Richard M. Stites to William Drayton, Esquire, Savannah, December 3, 1811, in the same collection.

42. Clothing Bill for George Anderson, September 3, 1810, and Bill and Receipt of William H. Nicoll, June 11, 1812 in the Wayne-Stites-Anderson Papers.

43. See the tax digest for the appropriate years; Estate of Susan Jackson, December 1869.

44. Deeds. Volume 2E, 1812–16, p. 63.

45. "Letters Showing the Rise and Progress of Early Negro Churches in Georgia," pp. 86–87.

46. Deeds. Volume 2E, 1812–16, p. 245.

47. Deeds. Volume 2G, 1816–17, p. 14.

48. Chatham County Tax Digest, 1833.

49. Elizabeth was baptized on December 18, 1803, and her brother Simon Francois on June 9, 1807. They were the children of Francis and Rosette Jalineau, "a free negro woman." Saint John the Baptist Catholic Church Parish Register, 1796–1816.

50. Estate of Francis Jalineau, 1824.

51. Estate of Charles Odingsells, 1800.

52. Joseph Parsons, "Anthony Odinsells: A Romance of Little Wassaw," *Georgia Historical Quarterly* 55 (summer 1971): p. 212.

53. Chatham County Tax Digest, 1852; *Eighth Census of the United States, 1860:* Schedule 2, Slave Inhabitants of the White Bluff District, Chatham County Georgia; Sweat, "The Free Negro in Antebellum Georgia," pp. 193–94; Parsons, "Anthony Odingsells," p. 219.

54. James David Griffin, "Savannah during the Civil War" (Ph.D. diss., University of Georgia, 1963), p. 26.

55. Hardee, *Reminiscences and Recollections*, pp. 17–18, 61–64.

56. Savannah City Council Minutes, 1828–31, p. 66.

57. Thomas Statom, "Negro Slavery in Eighteenth-Century Georgia" (Ph.D. diss., University of Alabama, 1982), pp. 138–39; *Savannah Morning News*, May 28, 1851.

58. Richard H. Shryock, ed., *Letters of Richard D. Arnold, M.D.*, *1808–1876* (Durham, N.C., 1929), p. 44.

59. Claim of Toby Adams, #3928, Records Group 217; First African Baptist Church Minutes 1871–89.

60. *City of Savannah Directory, 1859*.

61. *Eighth Census of the United States, 1860*.

62. Harden, *Recollections of a Long and Satisfactory Life*, pp. 48–49. Simon Mirault was not Aspasia Mirault's husband, as Harden stated.

63. Chatham County Tax Digest, 1864.

64. *Eighth Census of the United States, 1860*.

65. For a more extensive discussion of free African-American women in Savannah see Whittington B. Johnson, "Free African-American Women in Savannah, 1800–60: Affluence and Autonomy Amid Adversity," *The Georgia Historical Quarterly* 76 (summer 1992): pp. 260–83.

66. Register of Free Persons of Color, City of Savannah, 1817–29.

67. Ibid.

68. *Eighth Census of the United States, 1860*.

69. Savannah City Council Minutes, 1812–22, p. 10.

70. Loren Schweninger, "Property-Owning Free African-American Women in the South, 1800–1870," *Journal of Women's History* 1 (winter 1990): p. 30; see also Schweninger, *Black Property Owners in the South*, pp. 84–87. The situation for free African-American women in Savannah was better than it was for their counterparts in Petersburg, Virginia, where there was never more than seventy men for every one hundred free African-American women, but women comprised only 45.9 percent of the real estate owners. See Suzanne Lebsock, *Free Women of Petersburg: Status and Culture in a Southern Town, 1789–1860* (New York, 1984), pp. 99, 102–4.

71. La Far, "The Baptist Church of Savannah, Georgia," vol. 1, p. 135; Simms, *The First Colored Baptist Church*, p. 57; Simon Jackson Account, Wayne-Stites-Anderson Papers; Richard M. Stites to William Drayton, Savannah, December 3, 1811. Wayne-Stites-Anderson Papers; Deeds, vol. K, 1832–34, p. 508; vol. 2R, 1832–33, pp. 508–9; Chatham County Court of Ordinary Inventories and Appraisement, 1862–74 (microfilm) Georgia Department of Archives and History, p. 96; Savannah Board of Health Minutes, 1859–64; City of Savannah Tax Digest, 1860; Susan Jackson is not listed in the 1860 Census.

72. Chatham County Tax Digest, 1854; *Eighth Census of the United States, 1860*.

73. Register of Free Persons of Color, City of Savannah, 1817–29, 1826–35; Chatham County Tax Digest, 1854; City of Savannah Tax Digest, 1858, 1860.

74. Harden, *Recollections,* pp. 48–49; City of Savannah Tax Digest, 1847.

75. Conrad, *Reminiscences of a Southern Woman,* p. 16.

76. City of Savannah Tax Digest, 1854, 1860.

77. Register of Free Persons of Color for the County of Chatham, 1837–49.

78. City of Savannah Tax Digest, 1858.

79. Account of Richard Ann Butler, #638, Registers of Signatures of Depositors in Branches of the Freemen's Bureau Savings and Trust Company, National Archives, Washington, D.C. (Unless otherwise indicated, all the accounts are from the Registers of Signatures of Depositors.)

80. Estate of Richard Ann Butler, December 1869. See also Inventories and Appraisement, 1862–74 Chatham County Court of Ordinary. She sold a lot for six hundred dollars in 1868; therefore that lot does not appear in the appraisement. Deeds. Volume 4A, 1868.

81. *Savannah Republican,* June 6, 1849.

82. City of Savannah Tax Digest, 1810, 1820, 1824.

83. Register of Free Persons of Color for the County of Chatham, 1826–35; Chatham County Tax Digest, 1837.

84. Register of Free Persons of Color for the County of Chatham, 1826–35; City of Savannah Tax Digest, 1810.

85. Conrad, *Reminiscences of a Southern Woman,* p. 16.

86. City of Savannah Tax Digest, 1858.

87. Register of Free Persons of Color for the County of Chatham, 1826–35; *Eighth Census of the United States, 1860.*

88. Independent Presbyterian Church Sessional Minutes; Register of Free Persons of Color for the County of Chatham, 1826–35; City of Savannah Tax Digest, 1860.

89. Register of Free Persons of Color for the County of Chatham, 1826–35; City of Savannah Tax Digest, 1858; Estate of Estelle Savage, 1891.

90. *Eighth Census of the United States, 1860;* Claim of Sarah Ann Black, #18222, Record Group 217.

91. Estate of Francis Jalineau, 1824; Deeds. Volume 2V, 1837–38, p. 100.

92. Deeds. Volume 3B, 1843–44, pp. 329–30.

93. Register of Free Persons of Color for the County of Chatham, 1837–49; see tax digests for the years 1848–64; Savannah Board of Health Minutes, 1859–64.

94. Interview with Sally Hunt of Commerce, Georgia. Ex-Slaves Interviews—W.P.A., Hargrett Rare Books and Manuscripts Library.

95. Register of Free Persons of Color, City of Savannah, 1817–29; City of Savannah Tax Digest, 1820; Chatham County Tax Digest, 1847, 1860; *Eighth Census of the United States, 1860;* Harden, *Recollections,* p. 49.

96. Register of Free Persons of Color for the County of Chatham, 1837–49; City of Savannah Tax Digest, 1809, 1833; Chatham County Tax Digest, 1852; City of Savannah Tax Digest, 1860; Estate of Ann H. Gibbons. Claudia B. (Anderson) Gibbons, Ann's daughter, was her sole heir.

97. Bancroft, *Census of the City of Savannah*, p. 54.

98. Eaton, *The Growth of Southern Civilization*, p. 248.

99. Lamar, *A Compilation of the Laws of the State of Georgia*, p. 815; Ralph B. Flanders, "The Free Negro in Ante-Bellum Georgia," *North Carolina Historical Review* 9 (July 1932): p. 267.

100. Deeds. Volume 2L, 1821–24, p. 19. The property was sold in 1812, but the transaction was not recorded until 1821.

101. Deeds. Volume 2G, p. 143.

102. City of Savannah Tax Digest, 1820.

103. City of Savannah Tax Digest, 1823.

104. City of Savannah Tax Digest, 1848.

105. Sweat, "The Free Negro in Antebellum Georgia," p. 154.

106. City of Savannah Tax Digest, 1858.

107. City of Savannah Tax Digest, 1850.

108. *Eighth Census of the United States, 1860.*

109. Whites in Charleston preferred to do business with mulattoes. Johnson and Roark, *Black Masters*, p. 61. The same practice probably occurred in Savannah.

110. City of Savannah Tax Digest, 1823; *Fourth Census of the United States, 1820*, Book I (Washington, 1821), p. 28.

111. *Eighth Census of the United States, 1860*; City of Savannah Tax Digest, 1860.

112. Will of Thomas S. Bonneau, Will Book G, 1826–34, Charleston County Courthouse, Charleston, South Carolina; Koger, *Black Slaveowners*, pp. 83, 97.

113. Deeds, Volume 1Y, 1803–5. For a discussion on how Adam Whitfield gained his freedom see Austin Washington, "Some Aspects of Emancipation in Eighteenth-Century Savannah, Georgia," *Faculty Research Edition, Savannah State College Bulletin* 26 (December 1972): p. 105.

114. Deeds, vol. 2B, 1806–9, p. 64.

115. City of Savannah Tax Digest, 1809.

116. City of Savannah Tax Digest, 1810.

117. City of Savannah Tax Digest, 1813, 1820.

118. City of Savannah Tax Digest. 1820.

119. City of Savannah Tax Digest, 1837, 1850, 1860.

120. Claudia Dale Goldin, *Urban Slavery in the American South, 1820–1860: A Quantitative History* (Chicago, 1976), pp. 114–22

121. Estate of Charles Odingsells, 1800. Anthony was eligible to receive the slaves upon reaching his majority; in the meantime, income earned by the slaves was to be used to finance his education.

122. Wills. Volume E, 1808–17, pp. 292–93.

123. See City of Savannah Tax Digest, 1837 (for Chloe Gibbons' property), 1847 (for the estate of Prince Candy); Will of Maria Cohen, Richard D. Arnold Papers, Georgia Historical Society.

124. Washington, "The Dollys," p. 102.

125. Simon Jackson to Richard M. Stites, Savannah, August 5, 1897. Wayne-Stites-Anderson Papers.

126. Bill of Sale, State of South Carolina, January 16, 1807. Wayne-Stites-Anderson Papers.

127. Bill of Sale, State of South Carolina, April 5, 1809. Wayne-Stites-Anderson Papers; Francis Jalineau to Richard M. Stites, Coosawatchie, South Carolina, April 7, 1809 in the same collection; Washington, "The Dollys," p. 102.

128. Deeds. Volume 2D, p. 155; Savannah Board of Health Minutes, 1834–38.

129. Carter G. Woodson, *The Negro in Our History*, 2d ed. (Washington, D.C., 1922), p. 127.

130. *Savannah Republican*, May 17, 1849 contains a complaint about blacks gathering to celebrate the departure of friends for Liberia; The *Savannah Republican*, June 6, 1849, contains a complaint concerning the ostentatious dress and smoking habits of blacks and their refusal to yield sidewalks to whites; *Savannah Daily Morning News*, June 4, 1861, contains a complaint about blacks lack of support of the Confederate cause. The following are just a few of the contemporary accounts of life in antebellum Savannah: Bremer, *The Homes of the New World*; Burke, *Pleasure and Pain*; Conrad, *Reminiscences of a Southern Woman*; and Lyell, *A Second Visit to the United States*.

131. This characterization of black slaveholders is different than the experience of William Ellison, a Stateburg, South Carolina, planter and owner of over sixty slaves, who allegedly did not feed and clothe his slaves properly, but Ellison's situation was different than that of his Savannah contemporaries. See Johnson and Roark, *Black Masters*, 107–52.

132. John Hope Franklin, *From Slavery to Freedom* (New York, 1967), p. 224; W. S. Yeates, S. W. McCallie, and Francis P. King, "A Preliminary Report on a Part of the Gold Deposits of Georgia," *Geological Survey of Georgia Bulletin* No. 4-A (1896); David Williams, "Georgia's Forgotten Miners: African-Americans and the Georgia Gold Rush," *The Georgia Historical Quarterly* 75 (spring 1991): p. 85; Will of Thomas S. Bonneau, 1826–34; Johnson and Roark, *Black Masters*, pp. 126–27; Schweninger, *Black Property Owners in the South*, p. 17.

A MIDDLE GROUND BETWEEN SLAVERY AND FREEDOM

1. Jewett and Drew, *North-Side View of Slavery*, p. 102.

2. *Third Census of the United States, 1810*. There were 2,195 slaves and 530 free African Americans in Savannah that year.

3. *Seventh Census of the United States, 1850*. The slave population of Savannah was 6,231 and the free-black population was 686.

4. Ayers, *Vengeance and Justice*, p. 103.

5. Margaret Vernon Stiles, *Marse George: Memories of Old Savannah* (Savannah, 1959), pp. 8–9.

6. Interview with George Carter, Ex-Slaves Interviews—W.P.A., Hargrett Rare Books and Manuscripts Library. This slave formerly belonged to Dr. Richard Arnold, and his is the only interview of a Savannah slave in this collection; see also Killion and Waller, eds., *Slavery Time When I Was Chillun*, pp. 156–57. The interviews in this work were taken from the above collection.

7. Charles C. Coffin, *Fours Years of Fighting* (Boston, 1866), pp. 423–24.

8. Statement of the Average Price of Negroes and Produce Years 1815–16–17, Keith Read Collection, Hargrett Rare Books and Manuscripts Library.

9. A discussion of African-American food providers will appear later in this chapter and elsewhere in this study.

10. The dates were March 3–4, 1857. W. F. Parker—Diary, 1859–60, Hargrett Rare Books and Manuscripts Library.

11. Chatham County Tax Digest, 1852.

12. The date was January 14, 1860, W. F. Parker—Diary, 1859–60.

13. Moses Roper, *A Narrative of the Adventures and Escape of Moses Roper from American Slavery* (London, 1838), pp. 88–91; William A. Byrne, "The Burden and Heat of the Day: Slavery and Servitude in Savannah, 1833–1865" (Ph.D. diss., Florida State University, 1979), p. 112.

14. Unidentified Hotel Ledger, 1844–46, Georgia Historical Society.

15. Jones and Landers, "Portraits of Georgia Slaves," p. 523.

16. M. Dennis Ledger, 1855–67, Hargrett Rare Books and Manuscripts Library.

17. John Soloman Otto, *Cannon's Point Plantation, 1794–1860: Living Conditions and Status Patterns in the Old South* (Orlando, Fl., 1984), p. 155.

18. Claim of Simon Middleton, #20084, Record Group 217.

19. Jewett and Drew, *North-Side View of Slavery*, p. 100.

20. Statom, "Negro Slavery in Eighteenth-Century Georgia," pp. 146–47.

21. Savannah City Council Minutes, 1838–44, p. 202.

22. Shryrock, *Letters of Richard D. Arnold*, p. 66.

23. See Wade, *Slavery and the Cities*; and Goldin, *Urban Slavery in the American South*.

24. Goldin, *Urban Slavery in the American South*, pp. 59–60, 63–64.

25. Byrne, "The Burden and Heat of the Day," p. 122.

26. Statom, "Slavery in Eighteenth-Century Georgia," p. 145.

27. *Columbia Museum and Savannah Advertiser*, October 21, 1796. One of the local newspapers always published the grand jury's report.

28. Bancroft, *Census of the City of Savannah*, p. 3.

29. Martha(?) Hill to Richard M. Stites, Savannah (?), 1806. Wayne-Stites-Anderson Papers.

30. *Summary Reports of the Southern Claims Commissioners, 1871–1874,* (Washington, D.C., 1876), vol. 1, p. 461. This four-volume document contains the disallowed claims.

31. Claim of Simon Middleton, #20084, Record Group 217.

32. James Borchert, *Alley Life in Washington: Family, Community Religion, and Folklife in the City, 1850–1970* (Urbana, Ill., 1980).

33. Statom, "Slavery in Eighteenth-Century Georgia," p. 62.

34. *Savannah Republican,* February 16, 1855.

35. Byrne, "The Burden and Heat of the Day," p. 123.

36. "Autobiography of Ellen Buchanan Screven, 1841–1915," Hargrett Rare Books and Manuscripts Library, p. 53.

37. Greene and Woodson, *The Negro Wage Earner,* p. 11.

38. *Columbia Museum and Savannah Advertiser,* January 8, 1802; Statom, "Slavery in Eighteenth-Century Georgia," pp. 117–19.

39. Mrs. ———— Smith's Journal, 1793; see also the testimony of a slave stevedore in John W. Blassingame, ed., *Slave Testimony: Two Centuries of Letters, Speeches, Interviews, and Autobiographies* (Baton Rouge, 1977), pp. 330–33.

40. Jewett and Drew, *North-Side View of Slavery,* pp. 99–100.

41. Grimes, *Life of William Grimes,* pp. 37–38, 46.

42. Claim of Alexander Steel, (no number), Record Group 217.

43. *Summary Reports of the Southern Claims Commissioners, 1877–78,* vol. 3, p. 211.

44. Claim of Larry Williams, #14157, Record Group 217; see also Claim of Lido Brown, #18225, Record Group 217.

45. Claim of John Cuthbert, #18096, Record Group 217.

46. Claim of Cato Keating, #20689, Record Group 217.

47. Claim of Francis Keaton, #16975, Record Group 217.

48. Contract for Slave Labor, Keith Read Collection, Hargrett Rare Books and Manuscripts Library.

49. Godfrey Barnsley Papers, 1805–72, Hargrett Rare Books and Manuscripts Library.

50. Grimes, *Life of William Grimes,* p. 161.

51. Wayne-Stites-Anderson Papers.

52. Unidentified Cash Book, 1834–36, Georgia Historical Society.

53. Hynes-Sullivan Papers, 1811, 1850–56, Hargrett Rare Books and Manuscripts Library.

54. *Seventh Census of the United States, 1850.*

55. William E. B. Du Bois, *The Negro Artisan* (Atlanta, 1902), p. 17; Claim of Anthony Owens, #18095, Record Group 217. This slave was hired to a railroad company which allowed him to visit his slave wife whenever the train stopped at the station near where she lived.

56. *Savannah Republican,* February 16, 1826, February 18, 1848, and January 10, 1851; *Savannah Morning News,* September 29, 1859; Savannah Medical College Faculty Minutes, 1852–62, Hargrett Rare Books and Manuscripts Library.

57. Settlement of Accounts at City Hotel Savannah, Harden-Jackson-Carithers Collection, 1779–1919, Hargrett Rare Books and Manuscripts Library.

58. Savannah Medical College Faculty Minutes, 1853–62, Hargrett Rare Books and Manuscripts Library. The information was taken from a transcript of those minutes by Anna Stowell Bassett in 1932.

59. Harden-Jackson-Carithers Collection, 1779–1919. This is the same Bancroft who took the city council–funded census in 1848.

60. Savannah City Council Minutes, 1817–22, p. 393; *Report of Edward C. Anderson, Mayor of the City of Savannah for the Year Ending October 31, 1856*, p. 4; Haunton, "Savannah in the 1850s," p. 290.

61. Wade, *Slavery in the Cities*, p. 49; Ayers, *Vengeance and Justice*, p. 103. Ayers estimates that nearly 60 percent of the slaves in Savannah lived away from the control of their masters; Jones, *The Religious Instruction of Negroes*, p. 139. He does not state how many slaves were hired out but seems to suggest that the number was considerable.

62. Charles Ball, *Slavery in the United States: A Narrative of the Life and Adventures of Charles Ball, A Black Man* (New York, 1837), pp. 391, 368–69; Wade, *Slavery in the Cities*, p. 49. Slaves were also employed by free African-Americans—see Jewett and Drew, *North-Side View*, p. 101.

63. Shryock, *Letter of Richard Arnold*, p. 44.

64. Claim of Cato Keating, #20689, Record Group 217.

65. Claim of Sandy Small, #3931, Record Group 217.

66. Claim of Simon Middleton, #20084, Record Group 217.

67. Coffin, *Four Years of Fighting*, pp. 423–24; Dorothy Sterling (ed.), *The Trouble They Seen: Black People Tell the Story of Reconstruction* (Garden City, 1976), p. 31.

68. Claim of Charles Verene, #13364, Record Group 217.

69. Claim of April Wolford, #16007, Record Group 217.

70. Claim of Straffon Herb, #16244, Record Group 217.

71. Claim of William Anderson, #18285, Record Group 217.

72. Claim of Margaret Dawson, (no number), Record Group 233.

73. Claim of Edward Hornsby, #13, Record Group 217.

74. Schweninger, *Black Property Owners in the South*, p. 46.

75. Koger, *Black Slaveowners*, pp. 69–79.

76. "Testimony of Daniel Butler," Claim of Alexander Steel, (no number), Record Group 217.

77. Claim of Dennis Smith, #18603, Record Group 217.

78. Claim of Alexander Steel, (no number), Record Group 217.

79. Claim of Matthew Hayward, #9204, Record Group 217.

80. *Summary Reports of the Southern Claims Commissioners, 1879–80*, vol. 4, p. 86.

81. Claim of Harriet Dallas, #15213, Record Group 217.

82. Claim of James Custard, #6978, Record Group 217.

83. "Testimony of Tony Austin," Claim of Edward Hornsby, #13, Record Group 217.

84. *Summary Reports of the Southern Claims Commissioners, 1875–76*, vol. 2, p. 50.

85. "Testimony of George Cope," Claim of William Anderson, #18285, Record Group 217.

1. *First Census of the United States, 1790* (Philadelphia, 1791), p. 55.

2. *Population of the United States in 1860: Georgia, Eighth Census* (Washington, D.C., 1864), pp. 58–59; *Second Census of the United States, 1800,* p. 2n; Aggregate Amount of Persons Within the United States in 1810, pp. 80–81; see also censuses for the years 1820, 1830, 1840, and 1850.

3. *Population of the United States in 1860: Georgia,* pp. 71, 74; *Preliminary Report of the Eighth Census, 1860,* p. 280.

4. Register of Free Persons of Color for the County of Chatham, 1826–35.

5. Register of Free Persons of Color for the County of Chatham, 1861–65.

6. For an interesting discussion of this event, which at times degenerated into civil wars, see Martin Ros, *Night of Fire: the Black Napoleon and the Battle for Haiti* (New York, 1994). The casualties figures cited are found on page 197 of that work.

7. The culture which emerged from the melting pot had distinctive features of black Savannahians' African heritage, but it was not purely African.

8. John Blassingame, *Black New Orleans, 1860-1880* (Chicago, 1973), pp. 155–56.

9. St. John the Baptist Catholic Church Parish Register, 1796–1816.

10. Account of William Gary, #2353.

11. Account of Robert Oliver, #1391.

12. Account of Benjamin Morel, #2204.

13. Estate of Sarah Houstoun, 1872.

14. Estate of Simon Mirault, December 1875.

15. Ibid.

16. Register of Free Persons of Color for the County of Chatham, 1861–65; Saint Stephen's Church Parish Register, 1868–1901. Saint Matthew Parish, Savannah, Ga.

17. Register of Free Persons of Color, City of Savannah 1860-73.

18. Account of Reverend John Cox, #578; *Eighth Census of the United States, 1860.*

19. Shryock, *Letters of Richard D. Arnold,* p. 32.

20. *Seventh Census of the United States, 1850; Eighth Census of the United States, 1860.* I am making a distinction between color discrimination and a caste system. The two are not synonymous. Mulattoes and blacks performed the same jobs, attended the same churches, and enjoyed the same leisure activities.

21. Register of Free Persons of Color, City of Savannah, 1817-29; Register of Free Persons of Color for the County of Chatham, 1837–49;

22. Saint John the Baptist Catholic Church Parish Register, 1796–1816.

23. *Eighth Census of the United States, 1860.* The slave mates do not appear in the census, which restricts the size of the population and prevents a more

accurate determination of the practice. Savannah was not unique in this regard (it was common throughout the region) neither did it disappear with ratification of the Thirteenth Amendment; rather color bias pervaded black communities well into the twentieth century. See Willard Gatewood, "Aristocrats of Color, South and North; the Black Elite," *The Journal of Southern History* 54 (February 1988). Gatewood focuses on the upper classes, but their lower class brothers and sisters shared their view of blackness.

24. Berlin, *Slaves without Masters,* pp. 198, 214.

25. St. Stephen's Church Parish Register, 1868–1901; Christ Episcopal Parish Register, 1822–51, 1852–73.

26. Saint John the Baptist Catholic Church Parish Register, 1796–1816.

27. Account of John Grate, #2437.

28. Account of Josiah Grant, #1405.

29. Account of Adam Dolly, #47.

30. *Savannah Tribune,* April 9, 1887. Sabatte, who had recently returned to Savannah after having lived in Darien for a number of years, died at the home of his mother-in-law, Elizabeth Mirault.

31. *Seventh Census of the United States, 1850*; Account of Simon Mirault Jr., #238.

32. Account of Hetty Sabatty (Sabatte), #6028.

33. Account of Josiah Grant, #1405.

34. Register of Free Persons of Color, City of Savannah, 1860-73.

35. Account of Elizabeth S. M. Porter, #6226. Elizabeth was only seven years old when her father opened the account in 1871.

36. Account of Julia Walls, #3678. (See also #14338)

37. Estate of Estelle Savage, 1891.

38. Account of Georgia Benton, #1313.

39. Register of Free Persons of Color for the County of Chatham, 1826–35.

40. Claim of Margaret Dawson, #9, Record Group 233.

41. Claim of Alexander Steel, (no number), Record Group 217.

42. Claim of Samuel A. McIver, #6609; Claim of Francis Keaton, #16975; Claim of Josh Cuthbert, #18096; Claim of Sarah Ann Black, #18222; Claim of David Moses, #15448. All the claims are in Record Group 217.

43. Johnson, "Andrew Marshall" p. 191; "Autobiography of Ellen Buchanan Screven," pp. 54–55.

44. Account of Charlotte Reed, #2717.

45. Claim of Francis Keaton, #16975 Record Group 217: see also Claims of Celia Boisfeillet and Edward Hornsby cited previously.

46. Claim of James Custard, #6979, Record Group 217.

47. Deposition of Eve [Sheftall] Waters in Petition of Heirs of Adam Sheftall, #9, Record Group 233.

48. Claim of Joseph Sneed, #3927, Record Group 217.

49. Claim of Abraham Johnson, #3920, Record Group 217.

50. David Robinson to John Gibbons, Savannah June 10, 1792. Telfair Family Papers, 1806–1909. Georgia Historical Society.

51. Claim of Jackson B. Sheftall, #9, Record Group 233.

52. Lebsock, *Free Women in Petersburg*, p. 104. Limiting the study to women probably resulted from the nature of her study. Lebsock seems to have little regard for those marriages because they were not legal in the eyes of the law. This did not detract from their importance, however, to the parties involved. In this regard, Lebsock is less perceptive on this issue than on most of the others discussed in the study.

53. Johnson and Roark, *Black Masters*, pp. 209–11.

54. Koger, *Black Slaveowners*, p. 172.

55. Schweninger, *Black Property Owners*, p. 47. See also page 46 of this study for a mixed marriage alluded to in the previous chapter. There were doubtless other marriages; for information on these, read pages 29–60.

56. Killion and Waller, *Slavery Time When I Was Chillun*, p. x.

57. Conrad, *Reminiscences of a Southern Woman*, p. 16

58. Byrne, "The Burden and Heat of the Day," p. 126; Coffin, *Four Years of Fighting*, pp. 414, 421; *Savannah Republican*, June 6, 1849.

59. *Savannah Republican*, June 6, 1849; Jones, *The Religious Instruction of the Negroes*, pp. 145–46.

60. *Columbian Museum and Savannah Advertiser*, October 21, 1796.

61. Ex-Slave Interview—W.P.A., Interview of Washington Browning.

62. Savannah City Council Minutes, 1822–25, p. 4.

63. Sweat, "Social Status of Free Negroes in Antebellum Georgia," p. 130.

64. Sweat, "Social Status of the Free Negroes in Antebellum Georgia," pp. 129–31; *Report of James P. Screven Mayor of the City of Savannah for the Year Ending September 30, 1857* (Savannah, 1857), pp. 29–30.

65. Mrs. Paschal N. Strong Sr., "Glimpses of Savannah, 1790-1825," *Georgia Historical Quarterly* 33 (March 1949): p. 28; *Report of James P. Screven Mayor of the City of Savannah*, pp. 29–30.

66. Charles Olmstead, "Savannah in the 40s," *Georgia Historical Quarterly* 1 (September 1917): p. 248.

67. Conrad, *Reminiscences of a Southern Woman*, pp. 17–18.

68. Foster, *Wayside Glimpses*, p. 109.

69. Jones and Landers, "Portraits of Georgia Slaves," p. 409.

70. Conrad, *Reminiscences of a Southern Woman*, p. 18.

71. Savannah City Council Minutes, 1844–50, p. 19.

72. Berlin, *Slaves without Masters*, p. 310; Tustin, "Andrew Marshall," p. 257; William H. Grimshaw, *Official History of Free Masonry Among the Colored People in North America* (New York, 1969), p. 265. The first black Masonic chapter in Georgia as not organized until 1870.

73. Edward Meeker, "Mortality Trends of Southern Blacks, 1850–1910: Some Preliminary Findings," *Explorations in Economic History* 13 (January 1976): p. 29.

74. Savannah Board of Health Minutes, 1834–34. For a description and discussion of the causes of those diseases see Ann S. Lee and Everett S. Lee, "The Health of Slaves and the Health of Freedmen: A Savannah Study," *Phylon* 38 (June 1977): pp. 173–77. The authors based their analysis solely on

William Duncan, *Tabulated Mortuary Records* (Savannah, 1870). Failure to expand their research to include information from the Board of Health minutes has compromised their findings.

75. Minutes of the First African Sabbath School, from 1826–December 27, 1835.

76. Savannah Board of Health Minutes. This information is taken from minutes covering the years 1830–64, which are contained in several volumes of the minutes.

77. Bancroft, *Census of the City of Savannah*, p. 9.

78. Savannah Board of Health Minutes. The information was taken from several volumes commencing with the one for 1828–32.

79. Lee and Lee, "The Health of Slaves and the Health of Freedmen," p. 171.

80. Evelyn Ward Gay, *The Medical Profession in Georgia, 1733–1983* (Fulton, Mo., 1983), pp. 232–33; Savannah Board of Health Minutes, 1834–38.

81. Savannah Board of Health Minutes, 1834–38.

82. Israel Keech Tefft Papers, Georgia Historical Society.

83. Savannah Board of Health Minutes, 1834–38.

84. Edmund ——— to Francis B. Hacken, Savannah, August 29, 1854, Savannah Yellow Fever, 1854, Hargrett Rare Books and Manuscripts Library. The letter was written by an unidentified employee of J. E. DeFord Drug Shop on the corner of Broughton and Barnard streets.

85. Lee and Lee, "The Health of Slaves and the Health of Freedmen," p. 173; Thomas Gamble Jr., *A History of the City Government of Savannah, Georgia from 1790 to 1901* (Savannah, 1901), p. 232; William Harden, *A History of Savannah and South Georgia*, vol. 1 (Chicago, 1913), pp. 411–12; Haunton, "Savannah in the 1850s," p. 289.

86. *Seventh Census of the United States, 1850*.

87. *Report of R. D. Arnold, Mayor of the City of Savannah for the Year Ending September 30, 1860* (Savannah, 1860), p. 35.

88. Killion and Waller, *Slavery Time When I Was Chillun*, p. x.; Williard Range, *The Rise and Progress of Negro Colleges in Georgia, 1865–1949* (Athens, Ga., 1951), p. 4; Savannah City Council Minutes, August 25, 1817.

89. *Statistics of the United States (Including Mortality, Property, etc.) in 1860* (Washington: Government Printing Office, 1866), p. 507.

90. Woodson, *The Education of the Negro Prior to 1861*, pp. 118–19.

91. Henry A. Bullock, *A History of Negro Education in the South: From 1619 to the Present* (Cambridge, Mass., 1967), p. 12; Julia Floyd Smith, *Slavery and Rice Culture in Low Country Georgia, 1750–1860* (Knoxville, Tenn., 1985), pp. 141–42.

92. Jones, *Religious Instruction of the Negroes*, pp. 121–22; Jeremiah Evarts Diary, 1822. Georgia Historical Society. Evarts was told that "children of free Negroes in Savannah generally attend school."

93. Sister M. Julian Griffin, *Tomorrow Comes the Song: The Story of Catholicism Among the Black Population of South Georgia, 1850–1978* (Savannah, 1978), pp. 17–18; *Savannah Daily Republican*, July 12, 1865. The newspaper article lists the courses on which the pupils at Porter's school were examined.

94. Waring, *Cerveau's Savannah*, pp. 66–67; Robert E. Perdue, *The Negro in Savannah, 1865–1900* (New York, 1973), pp. 124–25.

95. Hoskins, *Black Episcopalian in Savannah*, p. 14; *Savannah Tribune*, November 13, 1895; Coffin, *Four Years of Fighting*, p. 420.

96. Susie King Taylor, *Reminiscences of My Life in Camp* (Boston, 1902), p. 5; see also Jewett and Drew, *North-Side View of Slavery*, p. 99 for the experiences of Patrick Snead.

97. Griffin, *Tomorrow Comes the Song*, p. 18; Superintendent's Monthly Report of Schools, Record Group 105.

98. Perdue, *The Negro in Savannah, 1865–1900*, pp. 70–71.

99. Griffin, *Tomorrow Comes the Song*, pp. 17–18.

100. Taylor, *Reminiscences for My Life in Camp*, p. 5.

101. Burke, *Pleasure and Pain*, p. 23.

102. Nehemiah Adams, *South-Side View of Slavery; or Three Months at the South in 1854* (Richmond, 1855), pp. 56–57.

103. Coffin, *Four Years of Fighting*, p. 428.

104. Simms, *The First Colored Baptist Church in North America*, p. 80; Love, *History of First African Baptist Church*, p. 54.

105. William Allen Poe, "Georgia Influence in the Development of Liberia," *The Georgia Historical Quarterly* 57 (spring 1973): p. 9; Simms, *The First Colored Baptist Church in North America*, p. 80.

106. Account of George Marshall, #4490; Account of Mrs. Martha Artson, #8816; see citations given earlier for Accounts of Tharsville Savage, Simon Mirault Jr., and Georgia Benton; Account of Elizabeth Mirault, #6131; Account of Richard Artson, #2444; Estate of Estelle Savage; Account of Duncan Scott, #362; Account of Charlotte Reed, #2717.

107. See Will of Richard Houstoun and Account of Richard Ann Butler; Estate of Sarah Houstoun, 1872; see Accounts of Josiah Grant and Eliza Ann Habersham.

108. Estate of Mary E. A. Woodhouse, December, 1884. James made his mark with the customary X. Account of William H. Woodhouse, #225.

109. There were 1,378 mulatto slaves in Chatham County in 1860, the majority of whom probably lived in the city (Savannah); on the other hand, there were only 496 free mulattoes in Savannah that year. *Eighth Census of the United States, 1860.*

NEIGHBORS, BUT NOT FRIENDS

1. *Georgia Gazette*, October 23, 1788.

2. Holcombe, *The First Fruits*, p. 16.

3. H. Stebbin to Reuben Champion, Savannah, February 15, 1816. Champion Family Letters, 1816–69, Hargrett Rare Books and Manuscripts Library.

4. F. N. Boney, ed., *Slave Life in Georgia: A Narrative of the Life, Suffering, and Escape of John Brown, A Fugitive Slave* (Savannah, 1972), p. 32n.

5. Conrad, *Reminiscences of a Southern Woman*, p. 18.

6. Jones and Landers, "Portraits of Georgia Slaves," p. 270.

7. Shyrock, *Letters of Richard D. Arnold*, p. 44.

8. Savannah City Council Minutes, 1834–42, p. 15.

9. Savannah Ordinance, July, 1810. Georgia Historical Society. This is the engrossed original copy of the ordinance.

10. La Far, "The Baptist Church of Savannah, Georgia," p. 282.

11. Ibid., p. 347; A. T. Havens, Journal of a Trip to Georgia and Florida, 1842–43, November 28, 1842, Hargrett Rare Books and Manuscripts Library. The Library has the manuscript; see also Holcombe, *The First Fruits*, p. 160.

12. Mrs. —— Smith's Journal.

13. Havens, Journal of a Trip to Georgia and Florida, October 22, 1842.

14. "Savannah Volunteer Guards, Reminiscences," William Starr Basinger Collection, Hargrett Rare Books and Manuscripts Library, vol. 1, p. 58.

15. Waring, *Cerveau's Savannah*, p. 27.

16. *Report of James P. Screven, September 30, 1857*, pp. 29–30.

17. Savannah City Council Minutes, 1844–50, p. 305. The resolution was received at the October 26, 1848, meeting.

18. Ibid., p. 82. This action was taken at the December 7, 1848, meeting.

19. Savannah Poor House and Hospital Minutes, 1836–76. Georgia Department of Archives and History. The action was taken at the February 7, 1858, meeting.

20. John Phillips Diary, 1853, Hargrett Rare Books and Manuscripts Library.

21. Savannah Board of Health Minutes, 1822–27.

22. Bancroft, *Census of the City of Savannah*, pp. 15–20.

23. Ibid., p. 17. Bancroft placed those black churches in the wrong wards.

24. Henry Bourquin Jr. Papers, 1810–12. Georgia Historical Society.

25. Gay, *The Medical Profession in Georgia*, pp. 229–30. Gay said Thomas F. Williams was a merchant and that the infirmary was opened on Lincoln Street in 1832. *Daily Georgian*, February 6, 1833, p. 2, col. 5 and 6. The paper noted that the facility would soon be opened.

26. Georgia Infirmary Collection, #301, Minute Book 1, 1833–91. Georgia Historical Society; *Exercises at the Unveiling of the Bronze Tablet Commemorating the One Hundredth Anniversary of the Georgia Infirmary* (Savannah, 1933), pp. 19–27. The author thanks Jan Flores, Archivist of the Georgia Historical Society, for calling his attention to this collection and the centennial pamphlet.

27. *Federal Writers Project, Savannah* (Savannah, 1937), p. 52.

28. Gamble, *A History of the City Government of Savannah*, p. 207.

29. Savannah City Council Minutes, 1857–62, pp. 54–55.

30. Curry, *The Free Black in Urban America*, p. 193. In some cities blacks formed benevolent societies which operated cemeteries, and in others, churches had small cemeteries.

31. Savannah City Council Minutes, 1822–25, p. 41.

32. *Savannah Republican*, June 6, 1849.

33. H. Stebbin to Reuben Champion, February 15, 1816, Champion Family Letters, 1816–19, Hargrett Rare Books and Manuscripts Library.

34. George H. Gibson, "The Georgia Letters of John Pierpont, Jr., To His Father," part 1, *The Georgia Historical Quarterly* 55 (winter 1971): p. 575.

35. Sidney Andrews, *The South Since the War: As Shown by Fourteen Weeks of Travel and Observation in Georgia and the Carolinas* (Boston, 1866), p. 367.

36. Claim of Abraham Johnson, #3920, Record Group 217.

37. Bullock, *A History of Negro Education in the South*, p. 10; Burke, *Pleasures and Pain*, p. 78.

38. Stiles, *Marse George*, pp. 2–3, 13-14.

39. Taylor, *Reminiscences of My Life in Camp*, p. 5.

40. Conrad, *Reminiscences of a Southern Woman*, p. 16.

41. Estate of Daniel Huguenin, 1811.

42. Richard M. Stites to William Drayton, Esq. of Charleston, S.C., Savannah, October 7, 1811. Wayne-Stites-Anderson Papers.

43. J. Sanford Baker to R. M. Stites, Charleston, S.C., October, 3, 1804. Wayne-Stites-Anderson Papers. At the time Stites was interested in purchasing the property.

44. Claim of Sarah Black, #18222, Record Group 217.

45. Deposition of C. G. Cooper in the Claim of Simon Middleton, #20084, Record Group 217.

46. Deposition of Henry W. Smith, in the Claim of William W. Anderson, #18285, Record Group 217.

47. Claim of Toby Adams, #3928, Record Group 217.

48. Deposition of Charles Green, in the Claim of Samuel A. McIver, #6609, Record Group 217.

49. Claim of Harriet Dallas, #15213, Record Group 217.

50. Claim of Abraham Johnson, #3930, Record Group 217.

51. Chatham County Record Book, vol. 1-H, 1790–91, p. 831.

52. Chatham County Court of Ordinary Estate Records, vol. E, 1808–17, p. 346.

53. Shryock, *Letters of Richard D. Arnold*, p. 72.

54. Claim of Sarah Ann Black, #18222, Record Group 217; Account of Richard Lewis, #9684; Account of Matthew Lewis, #6645.

55. Account of Edwin Walton, #391.

56. Jewett and Drew, *North-Side View of Slavery*, p. 101.

57. Interracial couples lived without molestation elsewhere in Georgia. An interesting account of miscegenation in Hancock County and Sparta, where successive generations of Hunt women cohabitated with wealthy white men, is discussed in Adele Logan Alexander, *Ambiguous Lives: Free Women of Color in Rural Georgia, 1789–1879* (Fayetteville, Ark., 1991). See also Kent Anderson Leslie, *Woman of Color, Daughter of Privilege: Amanda America Dickson, 1849-1893* (Athens, Ga., 1995). David Dickson, another white slave-holder in Hancock County, Georgia, left his entire estate to his mulatto daughter with whom he had a close relationship even though he had raped her slave mother. Her inheritance made Amanda the richest African-American female in the South.

58. "Guardianship Papers for Free Persons of Color," Keith Read Collection. See the appointment of a guardian for Joseph Kelton, March 7, 1837.

59. Chatham County Court of the Ordinary Minutes, 1830–38, p. 129.

60. Ibid., p. 197.

61. Chatham County Court of the Ordinary Minutes, 1862–67, p. 68.

62. Savannah City Council Minutes, 1822–25, p. 41.

63. Deposition of Ellen Cosens, in the Claim of Georgiana Kelly, #15586, Record Group 217.

64. Harden, *Recollections*, p. 49.

65. Waring, *Cerveau's Savannah*, p. 29.

66. Tustin, "Andrew Marshall," p. 255.

67. Poe, "Georgia's Influence in the Development of Liberia," p. 3.

68. Randall Miller, "Georgia on Their Minds: Free Blacks and the African Colonization Movement in Georgia," *Southern Studies* 17 (winter 1978): pp. 356–57; Samuel Benedict to Ralph Gurley, Savannah, May 30, 1833, American Colonization Records.

69. *The African Repository*, vol. 24 (June 1848): pp. 188–90; 25 (June 1849): pp. 218–19.

70. James M. Gifford, "The African Colonization Movement in Georgia, 1817–1860" (Ph.D. diss., University of Georgia, 1977), p. 89.

71. *The African Repository*, vol. 24 (June 1848): pp. 162–63.

72. Ibid., pp. 185–87; Gifford, "The African Colonization Movement in Georgia," p. 56; Poe, "Georgia's Influence in the Development of Liberia," p. 11.

73. *Savannah Republican*, May, 17, 1849.

74. *The African Repository*, vol. 25 (June 1849): pp. 185–86.

75. Chatham County Superior Court Minutes, 1847–50, pp. 281–82; see also *Savannah Republican*, May 22, 1849, p. 2, col. 5.

76. Savannah City Council Minutes, 1844–50, p. 417.

77. Ibid., p. 260. This action was taken at a special meeting on January 14, 1850.

78. The text of the ordinance was printed in *The African Repository*, vol. 32 (July 1956): pp. 283–84; see also James M. Gifford, "Black Hope and Despair in Antebellum Georgia: The William Moss Correspondence," *Prologue* 8 (fall 1976): p. 158.

79. Gifford, "The African Colonization Movement in Georgia," pp. 89.

80. W. F. Parker—Diary, 1859–60; see entries for December 2, 1859, and Saturday, December 3, 1859.

81. Shryock, *Letters of Richard D. Arnold*, p. 98.

82. Harden, *A History a Savannah and South Georgia*, vol. 1, p. 497.

83. Minutes of the Sunbury Association, November 1857.

84. Simms, *The First Colored Baptist Church in North America*, p. 79.

85. *Savannah Morning News*, December 11, 1856.

86. Laurel Grove Cemetery South.

1. Autobiography of Ellen Buchanan Screven, 1841–1915, p. 2, Hargrett Rare Books and Manuscripts Library.

2. Lee and Agnew, *Historical Record*, p. 82; Harden, *Recollections*, p. 101.

3. The following black butchers worked for William Davis: George Gardener, Josiah Grant, John Laurence, John Monroe, Sandy Small, Jackson Sheftall, Joseph Sneed, Abraham Stewart, and Alexander Steel. See the deposition of Enos Richmond, Special Agent, in the Claim of John A. Laurence, #3926, Record Group 217.

4. *Summary Reports of the Southern Claims Commissioners*, vol. 4, p. 89.

5. Heirs of Adam Sheftall (Jackson B. Sheftall), Report #9, Record Group 233.

6. Claim of John A. Laurence, #3926, Record Group 217.

7. Claim of Sandy Small, #3931, Record Group 217.

8. Parsons, "Anthony Odinsells," pp. 218–19; Sherman's army captured Fort McAllister on December 13, 1864. Emory M. Thomas, *The Confederate Nation, 1861–1865* (New York, 1979), p. 280.

9. Claim of Anthony Owens, #18095, Record Group 217.

10. Claim of Harriet Dallas, #15213, Record Group 217.

11. T. Conn Bryan, *Confederate Georgia* (Athens, Ga., 1953), p. 132.

12. Savannah City Council Minutes, August 4, 1863.

13. Bryan, *Confederate Georgia*, p. 133; Clarence L. Mohr, *On the Threshold of Freedom: Masters and Slaves in Civil War Georgia* (Athens, Ga., 1986), p. 178.

14. Clarence L. Mohr, "Before Sherman: Georgia Blacks and the Union War Effort, 1861–64," *Journal of Southern History* 45 (August 1979): p. 335.

15. Interview of Della Briscoe, Ex-Slave Interview—W.P.A., Hargrett Rare Books and Manuscripts Library.

16. M. Dennis Ledger, 1855–67, pp. 257, 272, Hargrett Rare Books and Manuscripts Library.

17. See August 4, 1863, Savannah City Council Minutes cited in note 15.

18. Claim of Josiah Grant, #14912; Claim of Joseph Sneed, #3927; Claim of Samuel McIver, #6609, Record Group 217. These are just a few of the records which have complaints of free blacks about being forced to work on the fortifications.

19. Luis F. Emilio, *A Brave Black Regiment: History of the Fifty-Fourth Regiment of Massachusetts Volunteer Infantry, 1863–1865* (New York, 1969), p. 289.

20. Thomas, *The Confederate Nation: 1861–1865*, p. 262.

21. *Savannah Daily Morning News*, June 6, 1861, p. 1, col. 2; see also Benjamin Quarles, *The Negro in the Civil War* (Boston, 1969), p. 36. Quarles says fifty-five men volunteered.

22. *Savannah Daily Morning News*, July 3, 1861.

23. Heirs of Adam Sheftall (William Sheftall), Report #9, Record Group 233.

24. *Summary Reports of the Southern Claims Commissioners*, vol. 4, p. 89.

25. Stiles, *Marse George*, p. 13.

26. Blassingame, *Slave Testimony*, p. 635.

27. Bryan, *Confederate Georgia*, p. 131.

28. For the reaction of one free black female to those orders, see the Claim of Sarah Ann Black, #18222, Record Group 217.

29. *Savannah Daily Morning News*, July 26, 1861.

30. Claim of Georgiana Kelly, #15586, Record Group 217; see "We Wear the Mask" in Paul Laurence Dunbar, *The Complete Poems of Paul Laurence Dunbar*, ed. W. D. Howells (New York, 1946), pp. 112–13.

31. Claim of Rachel Bromfield, #13361, Record Group 17

32. *Summary Reports of the Southern Claims Commissioners*, vol. 4, p. 65; Claims of Margaret Dawson, Report #9, Record Group 233. The printed volumes summarize the findings of the commissioners.

33. Mohr, "Before Sherman," pp. 339, 341.

34. Quarles, *The Negro in the Civil War*, pp. 109–10; Mohr, "Before Sherman," p. 349.

35. Frederick Denison, *Shot and Shell: The Third Rhode Island Heavy Artillery Regiment in the Rebellion, 1861–1865* (Providence, R.I., 1879), p. 261; Mohr, "Before Sherman," p. 340.

36. Mohr, "Before Sherman," p. 340. The reason(s) why Haynes was released is not given.

37. Mohr, *On the Threshold of Freedom*, p. 84; Quarles, *The Negro in the Civil War*, p. 93.

38. Claim of Charles Verene, #13364, Record Group 217.

39. Claim of Joseph Sneed, #3927; Claim of Toby Adams, #3928; Claim of Alexander Steel (no number), Record Group 217; Record Group 105. See Box 30 which contains arrears of pay and bounty given to Brazil King and Paul Weary; also see citations in notes 39 and 40.

40. Tombstone of Samuel Gordon Morse (1832–75), Laurel Grove Cemetery, South.

41. Claim of Larry Williams, #14157, Record Group 217.

42. Bell Irvin Wiley, *Southern Negroes, 1861–1865* (New York, 1938), pp. 310–11, 320–24.

43. Claim of Sandy Small, #3931, Record Group 217. Small claimed two of his cousins went into service on a gunboat.

44. Claim of Harriet Dallas, #15213.

45. Claim of Alexander Steel, (no number), Record Group 217.

46. Claim of Lido Brown, #18225, Record Group 217.

47. Claim of Sarah Ann Black, #18222, Record Group 217.

48. Claim of Georgiana Kelly, #15586, Record Group 217.

49. Ibid.

50. Claim of Francis Keaton, #16975, Record Group 217.

51. Claim of Joseph Sneed, #3927, Record Group 217.

52. Claim of David Moses, #15448, Record Group 217.

53. Claim of Larry Williams, #14157, Record Group 217.

54. Bowden, *History of Savannah Methodism*, pp. 120–21.

55. In 1862, First African Baptist Church had 1,815 members, Second African, 1,146, and Third African, 288. Minutes of the Sunbury Association, 1862; Simms, *The First Colored Baptist Church*, pp. 132–33.

56. Godfrey Barnsley Papers, 1805–72, Hargrett Rare Books and Manuscripts Library.

57. Claim of Josiah Grant, #14912, Record Group 217.

58. Colonial Dames of America, S. R. Atkinson Papers. Georgia Historical Society.

59. Claim of Moses Stikes and Binah Butler, #17563, Record Group 217.

60. Bryan, *Confederate Georgia*, p. 130; Wiley, *Southern Negroes*, pp. 89–90. Wiley says while the price of slaves increased throughout the period, their value in gold decreased.

61. Mohr, *On the Threshold of Freedom*, p. 207.

62. Bryan, *Confederate Georgia*, p. 132; Mohr, *On the Threshold of Freedom*, pp. 208–9.

63. *The Savannah Tribune*, November 13, 1895.

64. James L. Roark, *Masters without Slaves: Southern Planters in the Civil War and Reconstruction* (New York, 1977), p. 75.

65. *Savannah Tribune*, November 13, 1895.

66. Chatham County Court of Ordinary Minutes, 1862–67. The figures were compiled from all the 1863 terms. See specifically pages 78–79, 88.

67. Ibid. See minutes of the July 1864 Term.

68. Ibid. See minutes of the December 1864 Term.

69. See deposition of Samuel Bogans in the Claim of Josiah Grant, #14912; also see deposition of Enos Richmond in the Claim of Rachel Bromfield, #13361, Record Group 217.

70. See Enos Richmond Deposition cited in note 61.

71. See deposition of Delia Rivers in Claim of Georgiana Kelly, #15586, Record Group 217.

72. Harden, *Recollections*, p. 117; Blassingame, *Slave Testimony*, pp. 635–36.

73. Chatham County Court of Ordinary Minutes, 1862–67. See minutes of the December 1864 Term.

74. Blassingame, *Slave Testimony*, pp. 635–36.

75. George Pepper, *Personal Recollections of Sherman's Campaign in Georgia and the Carolinas* (Zanesville, Ohio, 1866), p. 290; Coffin, *Four Years Fighting*, pp. 422–23.

76. Pepper, *Personal Recollections*, p. 290.

77. Ibid.

EPILOGUE

1. Richard D. Arnold, mayor to Col. H. J. Sickler, Savannah, December 1865. Record Group 105. This letter is located in Box 28 of Letters Received, Unentered, (Savannah, Georgia).

2. A. Champion to ?? Savannah, March 24, 1865. Champion Family Letters, 1816–69.

3. Edwin Rhodes Papers, 1865. Georgia Historical Society. The information comes from his diary.

4. Susan Bogardus Papers. Georgia Historical Society. The letter was written to Susan on June 13, 1865.

5. Blassingame, "Before the Ghetto," pp. 463–64; Alan Conway, *The Reconstruction of Georgia* (Minneapolis, 1966), p. 30.

6. Conway, *Reconstruction of Georgia*, pp. 86–87; Christler, "Participation of Negroes," p. 67.

7. Leon Litwack, *Been in the Storm so Long: The Aftermath of Slavery* (New York, 1979), p. 467; Bowden, *History of Savannah Methodism*, p. 128.

8. *Savannah Daily Republican*, June 3, 1865.

9. A number of the well-to-do free black females died in the 1860s including Susan Jackson, Sarah Marshall, Ann H. Gibbons, and Richard Ann Butler. See Savannah Board of Health Minutes, 1859–64; Estate of Ann H. Gibbons, Central Records Office; Tombstone of Richard Ann Butler, Laurel Grove Cemetery, South.

10. *Charleston Directory and Strangers Guide 1816* (Charleston, S.C., 1816), p. 46; Will of Jehu Jones (microfilm), South Carolina Department of Archives and History, Columbia, South Carolina; Marina Wikramanayake, *A World of Shadow: The Free Blacks in Antebellum South Carolina* (Columbia, S.C., 1973), pp. 107, 110; Horace E. Fitchett, "The Traditions of the Free Negro in Charleston, South Carolina," *Journal of Negro History* 21 (April 1940): p. 143.

11. For a revealing look at the property owned by William Ellison and how he acquired it, see Johnson and Roark, *Black Masters,* pp. 105–52.

12. See Ball, *Slavery in the United States* (1837); Jones, *Religious Instructions of Negroes in the United States* (1842); and Bancroft, *Census of the City of Savannah* (1848).

13. Slaves were hired out for an annual sum of seventy-five to eighty-five dollars; whereas slaves who hired their time paid their masters about twelve dollars monthly.

Bibliography

PRIMARY SOURCES

MANUSCRIPTS

Central Records Office, Chatham County, Georgia, Courthouse

    Estate of Ann Gibbons.
    Estate of Richard Houstoun, 1814.
    Estate of Sarah Houstoun, 1872.
    Estate of Daniel Huguenin, 1811.
    Estate of Susan Jackson, 1869.
    Estate of Francis Jalineau, 1824.
    Will of Andrew C. Marshall, 1857.
    Estate of Joseph A. Marshall, 1853.
    Estate of Louis Mirault, 1827.
    Estate of Simon Mirault, 1875.
    Estate of Anthony Odingsells, 1881.
    Estate of Charles Odingsells, 1800.
    Estate of Estelle Savage, 1891.
    Will of Mary Woodhouse, December 1884.

Charleston County, South Carolina, Courthouse

    Will of Thomas S. Bonneau.

Diocese of Georgia

    Diary of the Right Reverend Stephen Elliot Jr.

Duke University

    Mrs. _____ Smith's Journal.

First African Baptist Church

    Minutes, Special Collection, Dues and Funerals, 1871–89.

Georgia Department of Archives and History

    Chatham County Court of Ordinary Estate Records. Deeds, 1849–64.
    Chatham County Court of Ordinary Estate Records. Wills, 1808–63.
    Chatham County Court of Ordinary Inventories and Appraisement, 1852–74.
    Chatham County Court of Ordinary Minutes, 1830–67.

Chatham County Jail Records, 1805–15.
Chatham County Record Book. Deeds, 1790–1868.
Chatham County Superior Court. Minutes, 1847–60.
Chatham County Tax Digest, 1810–60.
Christ Episcopal Church of Savannah Parish Register, 1822–74.
Independent Presbyterian Church Sessional Minutes, 1828–51.
Minutes of First African Sabbath School, 1826–35.
Savannah Board of Health Minutes, 1830–64.
Savannah City Council Minutes, 1812–62.
Savannah Poor House and Hospital Minutes, 1836–76.
City of Savannah Tax Digest, 1810–60.
Saint John the Baptist Catholic Church of Savannah Parish Register, 1796–1816.

Georgia Historical Society

Richard Dennis Arnold Papers.
Susan Bogardus Papers.
Henry Bourquin Jr. Papers, 1810–12.
Brief of Evidence in *Richard Baker, et al., Complainants vs. Peter Houston, et al., Defendants* (March 1881).
Colonial Dames of America, S. R., Atkinson Papers.
Jeremiah Evarts Diary, 1822.
Georgia Infirmary Collection, 1833–91.
Hale Family Papers, 1858.
Hynes-Sullivan Papers, 1811, 1850–56.
Mabel Freeman La Far. "The Baptist Church of Savannah, Georgia: History, Records, and Register." 3 vols.
Register of Free Persons of Color, City of Savannah, 1817–29, 1860–63.
Register of Free Persons of Color for the County of Chatham, 1826–35, 1828–47, 1837–49, 1863–64.
Edwin Rhodes Papers, 1865.
Savannah Ordinance, July 1810.
Israel Keech Tefft Papers.
Telfair Family Papers, 1806–1909.
Unidentified Cash Book, 1834–36.
Unidentified Hotel Ledger, 1844–46.
Wayne-Stites-Anderson Papers.

National Archives

Bureau of Refugees, Freedmen, and Abandoned Lands. Affidavits, Miscellaneous Records, Contracts, 1865–72. Savannah, Georgia. Record Group 105.
House of Representatives of the United States, 1871–80. Claims Disallowed by Commissioners of Claims. Record Group 233.

Office of the Comptroller of the Currency. Registers of Signatures of Depositors in Branches of the Freedmen's Savings and Trust Company, 1865–71. Record Group 101.

United States General Accounting Office. Southern Claims Case Files. Chatham County, Georgia. Record Group 217.

South Carolina Department of Archives and History

Will of Jehu Jones.

Saint Matthews Parish

St. Stephen's Church Parish Register, 1868–1901.

University of Georgia: Hargrett Rare Books and Manuscripts Library

American Colonization Society Records.
Autobiography of Ellen Buchanan Screven, 1831–1915.
Godfrey Barnsley Papers, 1805–72.
William Starr Basinger Collection.
Brampton Plantation. Appendix.
Champion Family Letters, 1816–69.
M. Dennis Ledger, 1855–67.
Ex-Slave Interviews—W.P.A.
Harden-Jackson-Carithers Collection, 1779–1919.
A. T. Havens—Journal of a Trip to Georgia and Florida, 1842–43.
Charles Colcock Jones Collection, 1749–1919.
Minutes of the Sunbury Baptist Association, 1818–1938.
W. F. Parker Diary, 1859–60.
John Phillips Diary, 1853.
Keith Read Collection.
Savannah Medical College Faculty Minutes, 1853-62.
Savannah Yellow Fever, 1854.

GOVERNMENT DOCUMENTS

United States

Catterall, Helen H. *Judicial Cases Concerning American Slavery and the Negro*. 5 vols. Washington D.C.: Carnegie Institution, 1926.

Preliminary Report on the Eighth Census, 1860. Washington D.C.: Government Printing Office, 1862.

Summary Reports of the Southern Claims Commissioners, 1871–1880: Disallowed Claims. 4 vols. Washington D.C.: Government Printing Office, 1876–81.

United States Census Report. Georgia 1790–1860. Washington D.C.: United States Printing Office, 1790–1861.

State and Local

Acts of the General Assembly, 1824. Milledgeville, Ga.: Polhill and Fort, 1825.

Anderson, Edward C. Report of Edward C. Anderson, Mayor of the City of Savannah for the Year Ending October 31, 1856. Savannah: George N. Nichols, 1856.

Arnold, Richard D. Report of R. D. Arnold, Mayor of the City of Savannah for the Year Ending September 30, 1860. Savannah: John M. Cooper and Company, 1860.

Bancroft, Joseph. Census of the City of Savannah. Savannah: Edward C. Councell, 1848.

Blair, Rugh, ed. Some Early Tax Digests of Georgia. Atlanta: The Georgia Department of Archives and History, 1926.

Cobb, Howell, ed. A Compilation of the General and Public Statutes of the State of Georgia. New York: E. D. Jenkins, 1859.

Cobb, Thomas R. R., ed. A Digest of the Statutes of the State of Georgia . . . In Force Prior to . . . 1851. Athens, Ga.: Christy, Kelsea, and Burke, 1851.

Georgia Reports. Vol. 25. Columbus, Ga.: Columbus Times Steam Press, 1859.

Lamar, Lucius Q. C., ed. A Compilation of the Laws of the State of Georgia . . . Since the Year 1810 to the Year 1819, Inclusive. Augusta, Ga.: W. S. Hannon, 1821.

Russell, Henry, ed. An Official Register of the Deaths in the City of Savannah, 1820. Savannah: Henry Russell, 1820.

Screven, James P. Report of James P. Screven, Mayor of the City of Savannah for the Year Ending September 30, 1857. Savannah: E. J. Purse, 1857.

Wilson, Edward G., ed. A Digest of All the Ordinances of the City of Savannah . . . Which Were of Force on the 1st, January, 1858. Savannah: John M. Cooper and Company, 1858.

NEWSPAPERS

Atlanta Constitution
Columbian Museum and Savannah Advertiser
Daily Georgian
Gazette of the State of Georgia
Georgia Gazette
Republican and Savannah Evening Ledger
Savannah Daily Republican
Savannah Daily Morning News
Savannah Morning News
Savannah Republican
Savannah Tribune

OTHER PRINTED SOURCES

Adams, Nehemiah. *South-Side View of Slavery; or, Three Months at the South in 1854.* 3rd ed. Richmond, Va.: A. Morris, 1855.

The African Repository. 34 vols. Washington, D.C., 1825-92.

Andrews, Sidney. *The South Since the War: As Shown by Fourteen Weeks of Travel and Observation in Georgia and the Carolinas.* Boston: Ticknor and Fields, 1866.

Ball, Charles. *Slavery in the United States: A Narrative of the Life and Adventures of Charles Ball, a Black Man.* 1837. Reprint, New York: Kraus Reprint Company, 1969.

Benedict, David. *A General History of the Baptist Denomination in America, and Other Parts.* 2 vols. Boston: Manning and Loring, 1813.

Berlin, Ira, Joseph P. Reidy, and Leslie Howard, eds. *The Black Military Experience.* New York: Cambridge University Press, 1982.

Blassingame, John W., ed. *Slave Testimony: Two Centuries of Letters, Speeches, Interviews and Autobiographies.* Baton Rouge: Louisiana State University Press, 1977.

Boney, F. N., ed. *Slave Life in Georgia: A Narrative of the Life, Sufferings, and Escape of John Brown, a Fugitive Slave.* Savannah: Beehive Press, 1972.

Bremer, Fredrika. *The Homes of the New World: Impressions of America.* 2 vols. New York: Harper and Brothers, 1853.

Burke, Emily. *Pleasure and Pain: Reminiscences of Georgia in the 1840s.* Savannah: Beehive Press, 1978.

Charleston Directory and Strangers Guide . . . 1816. Charleston, S.C., 1816.

Coffin, Charles C. *Four Years of Fighting: A Volume of Personal Observation with the Army and Navy from the First Battle of Bull Run to the Fall of Richmond.* Boston: Ticknor and Fields, 1866.

Conrad, Georgia Bryan. *Reminiscences of a Southern Woman.* Hampton, Va.: Hampton Institute Press, n.d.

Dann, John C., ed. "A Northern Traveler in Georgia, 1843." *Georgia Historical Quarterly* 56 (summer 1972): 282–90.

Denison, Frederick. *Shot and Shell: The Third Rhode Island Heavy Artillery Regiment in the Rebellion, 1861–1865.* Providence, R.I.: J. A. and R. A. Reid, 1879.

Directory of the City of Savannah. Savannah: George N. Nicholas, 1858–59.

Emilio, Luis F. A. *Brave Black Regiment: History of the Fifty-Fourth Regiment of Massachusetts Volunteer Infantry, 1863–1865.* 1891. Reprint, Salem, N.H.: Arno Press and the New York Times, 1969.

Fitzpatrick, John C., ed. *The Diaries of George Washington, 1748–1799.* 4 vols. Boston: Houghton Mifflin, Company, 1925.

Foster, Lillian. *Wayside Glimpses: North and South.* New York: Rudd and Carleton, 1860.

Gibson, George H., ed. "The Letters of John Pierpont, Jr. to his Father." part 1. *Georgia Historical Quarterly* 55 (winter 1971): 543–80.

Grimes, William. *Life of William Grimes, the Runaway Slave*. New Haven: William Grimes, 1855.

Hardee, Charles Seton Henry. *Reminiscences and Recollections of Old Savannah*. Savannah, 1926.

Harden, William. *Recollections of a Long and Satisfactory Life*. Savannah: Review Printing Company, 1934.

Holcombe, Henry. *The First Fruits in a Series of Letters*. Philadelphia: Ann Cochran, 1812.

———. *The Georgia Analytical Repository*. 1 (November–December 1802).

Jewett, John P. and Benjamin Drew, eds. *North-Side View of Slavery: The Refugee*. Boston: John P. Jewett and Company, 1856.

Jones, Charles C. *The Religious Instruction the Negroes in the United States*. Savannah: Thomas Purse, 1842.

———. *Suggestions on the Religious Instructions of the Negroes in the Southern States*. Philadelphia: Presbyterian Board of Publication, 1847.

Journal of Proceedings . . . of the Protestant Episcopal Church in the Diocese of Georgia. Savannah, 1854–64.

Kemble, Frances Anne. *Journal of a Residence on a Georgia Plantation in 1838–1839*. New York: Harper and Brothers, 1863.

Killion, Ronald and Charles Waller, eds. *Slavery Time When I Was Chillun Down on Master's Plantation*. Savannah: The Beehive Press, 1973.

Law, J. S. *An Essay on the Religious Oral Instruction of the Colored Race: Prepared in Accordance with a Request of the Georgia Baptist Convention . . . May 18, 1846*. Penfield, Ga.: Benjamin Brantly, 1846.

Lee, F. D. and J. L. Agnew. *Historical Record of the City of Savannah*. Savannah: J. H. Estill, 1869.

"Letters Showing the Rise and Progress of the Early Negro Churches of Georgia and the West Indies." *Journal of Negro History* 1 (January 1916): 69–92.

Lyell, Sir Charles. *A Second Visit to the United States of North America*. 2 vols. New York: Harper and Brothers, 1868.

Melish, John. *Travels in the United States of America in the Years 1806 and 1807*. 2 vols. Philadelphia: T & G Palmer, 1812.

Mohl, Raymond A. "A Scotsman Visits Georgia in 1811." *Georgia Historical Quarterly* 55 (summer 1971): 259–74.

Payne, Daniel A. *Recollections of Seventy Years*. New York: Arno Press, 1967.

Pepper, George W. *Personal Recollections of Sherman's Campaign in Georgia and the Carolinas*. Zanesville, Ohio: Hugh Dunn, 1866.

Roper, Moses. *A Narrative of the Adventures and Escape of Moses Roper From American Slavery*. 1838. Reprint, New York: Negro University Press, 1970.

Shryock, Richard H., ed. *Letters of Richard D. Arnold, M.D., 1808–1876*. Durham, N.C.: Duke University Press, 1929.

Simms, James M. *The First Colored Baptist Church in North America*. Philadelphia: J. B. Lippincott, 1888.

Statistics of the United States (Including Mortality, Property, etc.) in 1860. Washington: Government Printing Office, 1866.

Sterling, Dorothy, ed. *The Trouble They Seen: Black People Tell the Story of Reconstruction*. New York: Doubleday and Company, 1976.

Taylor, Susie King. *Reminiscences of My Life in Camp*. Boston: Susie King Taylor, 1902.

Tustin, J. P. "Andrew C. Marshall. 1786–1856." In *Annals of the American Pulpit*, edited by William Sprague. Charleston, S. C., January 15, 1859.

White, George. *Historical Collections of Georgia*. New York: Pudney and Russell, 1854.

Wightman, William. *Life of William Capers, D.D., One of the Bishops of the Methodist Church, South; Including an Autobiography*. Nashville, Tenn.: Publishing House of the Methodist Episcopal Church, South, Barbee and Smith, Agents, 1902.

Woodson, Carter G., ed. *The Mind of the Negro as Reflected in Letters Written During the Crisis, 1800–1860*. New York: Russell and Russell, 1969.

OTHER SOURCES

Laurel Grove Cemetery, South, Savannah, Georgia.

SECONDARY SOURCES

Books

Alexander, Adele Logan. *Ambiguous Lives: Free Women of Color in Rural Georgia, 1789–1879*. Fayetteville, Ark.: University of Arkansas Press, 1991.

Atwell, Joseph. *A Brief Historical Sketch of St. Stephen's Parish Savannah, Georgia*. New York: Church Book and Job Printing Establishment, 1874.

Avery, Isaac Wheeler. *The History of the State of Georgia from 1850 to 1881*. New York: Brown and Derby, 1881.

Ayers, Edward. *Vengeance and Justice: Crime and Punishment in the Nineteenth-Century American South*. New York: Oxford University Press, 1984.

Berlin, Ira. *Slaves without Masters: The Free Negro in the Antebellum South*. New York: Vintage Books, 1974.

Blassingame, John W. *Black New Orleans, 1860–1880*. Chicago: University of Chicago Press, 1973.

Boles, John B., ed. *Masters and Slaves in the House of the Lord: Race and Religion in the American South, 1740–1870*. Lexington, Ky.: University Press of Kentucky, 1988.

Borchert, James. *Alley Life in Washington: Family, Community, Religion, and Folklore in the City, 1850–1970*. Urbana, Ill.: University of Illinois, 1980.

Bowden, Haygood S. *History of Savannah Methodism: From John Wesley to Silas Johnson*. Macon, Ga.: Press of the J. W. Burke Company, 1929.

Boyd, Jesse L. *A History of Baptists in America Prior to 1845.* New York: American Press, 1957.

Bryan, T. Conn. *Confederate Georgia.* Athens, Ga.: University Press of Georgia, 1953.

Bullock, Henry A. *A History of Negro Education in the South: From 1619 to the Present.* Cambridge, Mass.: Harvard University Press, 1967.

Conway, Alan. *The Reconstruction of Georgia.* Minneapolis: University of Minnesota Press, 1966.

Curry, Leonard P. *The Free Black in Urban America, 1800–1850: The Shadow of the Dream.* Chicago: University of Chicago Press, 1981.

Douglass, Frederick. *Frederick Douglass: The Narrative and Selected Writings.* Edited by Michael Meyer. New York: Random House, 1984.

Du Bois, William E. B. *Black Reconstruction in America, 1860–1880.* New York: Atheneum, 1969.

———. *The Negro Artisan: A Social Study.* Atlanta: Atlanta University Press, 1902.

Dunbar, Paul Laurence. *The Complete Poems of Paul Laurence Dunbar.* Edited by W. D. Howells. New York: Dodd, Mead and Company, 1946.

Eaton, Clement. *The Growth of Southern Civilization, 1790–1860.* New York: Harper and Row, 1961.

Exercises at the Unveiling of the Bronze Tablet Commemorating the One Hundredth Anniversary of the Georgia Infirmary. Savannah, 1933.

Federal Writers Project, Savannah. Savannah: Review Printing Company, 1937.

Flanders, Ralph B. *Plantation Slavery in Georgia.* Chapel Hill: University of North Carolina Press, 1933.

Floan, Howard. *The South in Northern Eyes, 1831 to 1861.* Austin, Tex.: University of Texas Press, 1958.

Franklin, John Hope. *From Slavery to Freedom: A History of Negro Americans.* New York: Alfred A. Knopf, 1967.

Frazier, E. Franklin. *The Free Negro Family: A Study of Family Origin before the Civil War.* Nashville, Tenn.: Fisk University Press, 1932.

Gamble, Thomas. *A History of the City Government of Savannah, Georgia from 1790 to 1901.* Savannah: Review Publishing Company, 1901.

———. *Savannah Duels and Duelists, 1733–1877.* Spartanburg, S. C.: Reprint Company, 1974.

Gay, Evelyn Ward. *The Medical Profession in Georgia, 1733–1983.* Fulton, Mo.: Ovid Bell Press, 1983.

Genovese, Eugene D. *From Rebellion to Revolution: Afro-American Slave Revolts in the Making of the Modern World.* Baton Rouge, La.: Louisiana State University Press, 1979.

Goldin, Claudia Dale. *Urban Slavery in the American South, 1820–1860: A Quantitative History.* Chicago: University of Chicago Press, 1976.

Granger, Mary, ed. *Savannah Writers' Project Savannah River Plantations.* Savannah: The Georgia Historical Society, 1947.

Greene, Lorenzo and Carter G. Woodson. *The Negro Wage Earner*. Washington, D.C.: Association for the Study of Negro Life and History, 1930.

Griffin, Sister M. Julian. *Tomorrow Comes the Song: The Story of Catholicism among the Black Population of South Georgia, 1850–1978*. Savannah: Private Printing, 1978.

Grimshaw, William H. *Official History of Free Masonry among the Colored People in North America*. New York: Negro Universities Press, 1969.

Harden, William. *A History of Savannah and South Georgia*. 2 vols. Chicago: Lewis Publishing Company, 1913.

Harlan, Howard J. *John Jasper: A Case History in Leadership*. Charlottesville, Va.: University of Virginia Press, 1936.

Higginbotham, Evelyn Brooks. *Righteous Discontent: The Women's Movement in the Black Baptist Church, 1880–1920*. Cambridge, Mass.: Harvard University Press, 1993.

Hoskins, Charles L. *Black Episcopalians in Georgia: Strife, Struggle, and Salvation*. Savannah: Private Printing, 1980.

————. *Black Episcopalians in Savannah*. Savannah: Saint Matthews Church, 1983.

Johnson, Michael P. and James L. Roark. *Black Masters: A Free Family of Color in the Old South*. New York: W. W. Norton, 1984.

Jones, Charles C. Jr. *History of Savannah, Georgia*. Syracuse, N.Y.: D. Mason and Company, 1890.

Jordan, Lewis G. *Negro Baptist History, U.S.A.—1750–1930*. Nashville, Tenn.: The Sunday School Publishing Board, 1930.

Joyner, Charles. *Down by the River Side: A South Carolina Slave Community*. Urbana, Ill.: University of Illinois Press, 1984.

Koger, Larry. *Black Slaveowners: Free Black Slave Masters in South Carolina, 1790–1860*. Jefferson, N.C.: McFarland and Company, 1985.

Lebsock, Suzanne. *The Free Women of Petersburg: Status and Culture in a Southern Town, 1784–1860*. New York: W. W. Norton, 1984.

Leslie, Kent Anderson. *Woman of Color, Daughter of Privilege: Amanda America Dickson*. Athens, Ga.: University of Georgia Press, 1995.

Litwack, Leon F. *Been in the Storm So Long: The Aftermath of Slavery*. New York: Vintage Books, 1979.

Love, Emanuel K. *History of the First African Baptist Church from its Organization January 20th, 1788 to July 1st, 1888*. Savannah: Morning News Press, 1888.

Malone, Henry T. *The Episcopal Church in Georgia, 1733–1957*. Atlanta: Protestant Episcopal Church in the Diocese of Atlanta 1960.

Mohr, Clarence L. *On the Threshold of Freedom: Masters and Slaves in Civil War Georgia*. Athens, Ga.: University of Georgia Press, 1986.

Nash, Gary. *Forging Freedom: The Formation of Philadelphia's Black Community, 1720–1840*. Cambridge, Mass.: Harvard University Press, 1988.

Otto, John Solomon. *Cannon's Point Plantation, 1794–1860: Living Conditions and Status Patterns in the Old South*. Orlando, Fla.: Academic Press, 1984.

Patrick, J. Max. *Savannah's Pioneer Theatre: From its Origins to 1810*. Athens, Ga.: University of Georgia Press, 1953.

Perdue, Robert E. *The Negro in Savannah, 1865–1900*. New York: Exposition Press, 1973.

Pessen, Edward. *Jacksonian America: Society, Personality, and Politics*. Homewood, Ill.: Dorsey Press, 1978.

Quarles, Benjamin. *Black Abolitionists*. New York: Oxford University Press, 1969.

———. *The Negro in the Civil War*. Boston: Little, Brown and Co., 1953.

Raboteau, Albert J. *Slave Religion: The "Invisible Institution" in the Antebellum South*. New York: Oxford University Press, 1978.

Range, Williard. *The Rise and Progress of Negro Colleges in Georgia, 1865–1949*. Athens, Ga.: University of Georgia Press, 1951.

Roark, James L. *Masters Without Slaves: Southern Planters in the Civil War and Reconstruction*. New York: W. W. Norton, 1977.

Rogers, George A. and R. Frank Saunders Jr. *Swamp Water and Wiregrass: Historical Sketches of Coastal Georgia*. Macon, Ga.: Mercer University Press, 1984.

Ros, Martin. *Night of Fire: The Black Napoleon and the Battle For Haiti*. Translated by Karin Ford-Treep. New York: Sarpedon, 1994.

Schweninger, Loren. *Black Property Owners in the South, 1790–1915*. Urbana, Ill.: University of Illinois Press, 1990.

Sernett, Milton C., *Black Religion and American Evangelicalism*. Metuchen, N.J.: Scarecrow Press, 1975.

Smith, Julia Floyd. *Slavery and Rice Culture in Low Country Georgia, 1750–1860*. Knoxville, Tenn.: University of Tennessee Press, 1985.

Stampp, Kenneth M. *The Peculiar Institution: Slavery in the Ante-Bellum South*. New York: Vintage Books, 1956.

Sterkx, H. E. *The Free Negro in Ante-Bellum Louisiana*. Rutherford, N.J.: Fairleigh Dickinson University Press, 1972.

Stiles, Margaret Vernon. *Marse George: Memories of Old Savannah*. Savannah: Evans Printing Company, 1959.

Sweat, Edward. *Free Blacks and the Law in Antebellum Georgia*. Atlanta, Ga.: Clark College Southern Center for Studies in Public Policy, 1976.

Thomas, Edgar G. *The First African Baptist Church of North America*. Savannah: Edgar G. Thomas, 1925.

Thomas, Emory M. *The Confederate Nation: 1861–1865*. New York: Harper Torchbooks, 1979.

Wade, Richard C. *Slavery in the Cities: The South, 1820–1860*. New York: Oxford University Press, 1964.

Wagner, Clarence M. *Profiles of Black Georgia Baptists*. Atlanta: Bennett Brothers Printing Company, 1980.

Waring, Joseph F. *Cerveau's Savannah*. Savannah: Georgia Historical Society, 1973.

West, Robert F. *Alexander Campbell and Natural Religion*. New Haven: Yale University Press, 1948.

Wikramamayake, Marina. *A World of Shadow. The Free Blacks in Antebellum South Carolina*. Columbia, S. C.: University of South Carolina Press, 1973.

Wiley, Bell Irvin. *Southern Negroes, 1861–1865*. New York: Rinehart and Company, 1938.

Wilson, Charles Reagan, ed. *Religion in the South*. Jackson, Miss.: University of Mississippi Press, 1985.

Woodson, Carter G. *The Education of the Negro Prior to 1861*, 2nd ed. Washington, D.C.: Association for the Study of Negro Life and History, 1919.

————. *The History of the Negro Church*, 3rd ed. Washington, D.C.: Associated Publishers, 1972.

————. *The Negro in Our History*, 2nd ed. Washington, D.C.: Associated Publishers, 1922.

Articles

Blassingame, John W. "Before the Ghetto: The Making of the Black Community of Savannah, Georgia, 1865–1880." *Journal of Social Science* 6 (summer 1973): 463–88

Brooks, Walter H. "The Evolution of the Negro Baptist Church." *Journal of Negro History* 7 (January 1922): 11–22.

————. "The Priority of the Silver Bluff Church and its Promoters." *Journal of Negro History* 7 (April 1922): 172–96.

Eisterhold, John A. "Savannah: Lumber Center of the South Atlantic." *Georgia Historical Quarterly* 57 (winter 1973): 526–41.

Fitchett, Horace E., "The Traditions of the Free Negro in Antebellum South Carolina." *Journal of Negro History* 21 (April 1940): 139–52.

Flanders, Ralph B. "The Free Negro in Ante-Bellum Georgia." *North Carolina Historical Review* 9 (July 1932): 250–72.

Flanigan, Daniel T. "Criminal Procedure in Slave Trials in the Antebellum South." *Journal of Southern History* 40 (November 1974): 537–64.

Gatewood, Willard. "Aristocrats of Color, South and North: The Black Elite." *Journal of Southern History* 54 (February 1988): 3–20.

Gifford, James M. "Black Hope and Despair in Antebellum Georgia: The William Moss Correspondence." *Prologue* 8 (fall 1976): 153–62.

Haunton, Richard H. "Law and Order in Savannah, 1850–1860." *Georgia Historical Quarterly* 55 (spring 1972): 1–24.

Jackson, Luther P. "Religious Instruction of Negroes, 1830 to 1860, with Special Reference to South Carolina." *Journal of Negro History* 15 (January 1930): 72–114.

Johnson, Whittington B. "Andrew C. Marshall: A Black Religious Leader of Antebellum Savannah." *The Georgia Historical Quarterly* 69 (summer 1985): 173–92.

————. "Free African-American Women in Savannah, 1800–1860: Affluence and Autonomy Amid Adversity." *The Georgia Historical Quarterly* 76 (summer 1992): 160–83.

————. "Free Blacks in Antebellum Savannah: An Economic Profile." *The Georgia Historical Quarterly* 64 (winter 1980): 418–31.

Jones, J. Ralph, and Tom Landers, eds. "Portrait of Georgia Slaves." *The Georgia Review* 21 (spring 1967): 126–32.

Jones, Lawrence N. "They Sought a City: The Black Church and Churchmen in the Nineteenth Century." *Union Seminary Quarterly Reviews* 26 (spring 1971): 253-72.

Lee, Ann S. and Everett S. Lee. "The Health of Slaves and the Health of Freedmen: A Savannah Study." *Phylon* 38 (June 1977); 170–80.

Meeker, Edward. "Mortality Trends of Southern Blacks, 1850–1910: Some Preliminary Findings." *Explorations in Economic History* 13 (January 1976): 13–42.

Miller, Randall M. "Georgia on Their Minds: Free Blacks and the African Colonization Movement in Georgia." *Southern Studies* 17 (winter 1978): 349–62.

Mohr, Clarence L. "Before Sherman: Georgia Blacks and the Union War Effort, 1861–1864." *Journal of Southern History* 45 (August 1979): 331–52.

Parsons, Joseph. "Anthony Odinsells: A Romance of Little Wassaw." *Georgia Historical Quarterly* 55 (summer 1971): 208–21.

Poe, William Allen. "Georgia Influence in the Development of Liberia." *Georgia Historical Quarterly* 57 (spring 1973): 1–16.

Olmstead, Charles. "Savannah in the '40s." *Georgia Historical Quarterly* 1 (September 1917): 236–52.

Rogers, W. McDowell. "Free Negro Legislation in Georgia Before 1865." *Georgia Historical Quarterly* 16 (March 1932): 27–37.

Schweninger, Loren. "Property-Owning Free African-American Women in the South, 1800–1870." *Journal of Women's History* 1 (winter 1990): 13–44.

Strong, Mrs. Paschal N. Sr. "Glimpses of Savannah, 1790–1825." *Georgia Historical Quarterly* 33 (March 1949): 26–35.

Sweat, Edward F. "Social Status of the Free Negro in Antebellum Georgia." *The Negro History Bulletin* 21 (March 1958): 129–31.

Washington, Austin D. "The Dollys: An Antebellum Black Family of Savannah, Georgia." *Savannah State College Bulletin, Faculty Research Edition* 26 (December 1972): 101–3.

————. "Some Aspects of Emancipation in Eighteenth Century Savannah, Georgia." *Savannah State College Bulletin, Faculty Research Edition* 26 (December 1972): 104–6.

Weeks, Sidney. "The History of Negro Suffrage in the South." *The Political Science Quarterly* 9 (December 1894): 671–703.

Williams, David. "Georgia's Forgotten Miners: African-Americans and the Georgia Gold Rush." *The Georgia Historical Quarterly* 75 (spring 1991): 76–89.

Yeates, W. S., S. W. Mc Callie, and Francis P. King. "A Preliminary Report on a Part of the Gold Deposits of Georgia." Geological Survey of Georgia, Bulletin, No. 4-A (1896).

Thesis and Dissertations

Byrne, William A. "The Burden and Heat of the Day: Slavery and Servitude in Savannah, 1733–1865." Ph.D. diss., Florida State University, 1979.

Christler, Ethel M. "Participation of Negroes in the Government of Georgia, 1867–1870." Master's thesis, Atlanta University, 1932.

Gifford, James J. "The African Colonization Movement in Georgia, 1817–1860." Ph.D. diss., University of Georgia, 1977.

Griffin, David James. "Savannah, Georgia, During the Civil War." Ph.D. diss., University of Georgia, 1963.

Haunton, Richard H. "Savannah in the 1850s." Ph.D. diss., Emory University, 1968.

Lines, Stiles B. "Slaves and Churchmen: The Work of the Episcopal Church Among Southern Negroes, 1830–1860." Ph.D. diss., Columbia University, 1960.

Mohr, Clarence Lee. "Georgia Blacks During Secession and Civil War, 1859–1865." Ph.D. diss., University of Georgia, 1975.

Statom, Thomas R. Jr. "Negro Slavery in Eighteenth-Century Georgia." Ph.D. diss., University of Alabama, 1982.

Sweat, Edward F. "Free Negroes in Ante-Bellum Georgia." Ph.D. diss., Indiana University, 1957.

Interview

E. Perry Quarterman, Pastor of Second African Baptist Church. July 15, 1981.

Index